Possession

This illuminating study, addressed both to readers new to Jung and to those already familiar with his work, offers fresh insights into a fundamental concept of analytical psychology.

Anatomizing Jung's concept of possession reinvests Jungian psychotherapy with its positive potential for practice. Analogizing the concept – lining it up comparatively beside the history of religion, anthropology, psychiatry, and even drama and film criticism – offers not a naive syncretism, but enlightening possibilities along the borders of these diverse disciplines.

An original, wide-ranging exploration of phenomena both ancient and modern, this book offers a conceptual bridge between psychology and anthropology, it challenges psychiatry to culturally contextualize its diagnostic manual, and it posits a much more fluid, pluralistic and embodied notion of selfhood.

Craig E. Stephenson is a graduate of the C. G. Jung Institute, Zurich, the Institute for Psychodrama, Zumikon, Switzerland and the Centre for Psychoanalytic Studies, University of Essex. He is a Jungian analyst in private practice in Paris, France.

Possession

Jung's comparative anatomy of the psyche

Craig E. Stephenson

Routledge
Taylor & Francis Group

LONDON AND NEW YORK

First published 2009
by Routledge
27 Church Road, Hove, East Sussex BN3 2FA

Simultaneously published in the USA and Canada
by Routledge
270 Madison Avenue, New York, NY 10016

*Routledge is an imprint of the Taylor & Francis Group,
an Informa business*

Typeset in Times by
RefineCatch Limited, Bungay, Suffolk
Printed and bound in Great Britain by
TJ International Ltd, Padstow, Cornwall
Paperback cover design by Design Deluxe
Paperback cover image: Tantric Art, India, Siglio XVIII, from
the collection of Antonio Tapies, used with permission of
Ediciones Siruela

This publication has been produced with paper manufactured to
strict environmental standards and with pulp derived from
sustainable forests.

British Library Cataloguing in Publication Data
A catalogue record for this book is available from the British Library

Library of Congress Cataloging-in-Publication Data
Stephenson, Craig E., 1955–
  Possession : Jung's comparative anatomy of the psyche / Craig E.
Stephenson.
    p. cm.
  Includes bibliographical references and index.
  1. Jungian psychology. 2. Psychoanalysis. 3. Psyche.
  4. Jung, C. G. (Carl Gustav), 1875–1961   I. Title.
  BF173.S8185 2009
  133.4'26 – dc22

                              2008052121

ISBN: 978-0-415-44651-8 (hbk)
ISBN: 978-0-415-44652-5 (pbk)

This book is for Alberto

Contents

Figures

Acknowledgements

During the writing of this book, many people offered generous advice and encouragement. To Ellynor Barz, Helmut Barz, Janice Boddy, Desmond Clarke, Warren Colman, Doreen Madden Elefthery, Dee Fagin, Leonard Fagin, Leslie Gardner, Alain Godineau, Laurence Kirmayer, Petra von Morstein, Richard Outram, Lucie Pabel, Gottwalt Pankow, Oliver Sacks, Joy Schaverien, Edward Schieffelin, Paul Stoller, and Jean Luc Terradillos, my deepest thanks.

Thanks to my early readers: Josephine Evetts-Secker, Karl Figlio, Susan Rowland, Andrew Samuels, and especially Renos Papadopoulos.

Thanks to Laurel Boone for her invaluable editorial assistance.

Thanks to Kate Hawes, Jane Harris, and Nicola Ravenscroft at Routledge and to everyone else who worked on the production of the book.

Thanks to the following professional associations and journals where early drafts of chapters from this book were presented or published: Chapter 1: International Association for Analytical Psychology and International Association for Jungian Studies (IAAP/IAJS) Congress, ETH (Swiss Federal Institute of Technology), Zurich, July 2008; Chapter 4: IAAP/IAJS Congress, University of Essex, Colchester, July 2002, and *Harvest*, 2004, 50, 1; Chapter 5: the Forty Years Elefthery's Psychodrama Congress, Heeze, The Netherlands, May 2008, and *Psychodrama: Studies and Applications* (2008); Chapter 6: IAAP/IAJS Congress, University of Greenwich, London, July 2006, and *Psyche and the Arts* (Routledge, 2008). Thanks also to the audiences at the Independent Group of Analytical Psychologists, London (IGAP), the International School for Analytical Psychology, Zurich (ISAP), and the Edinburgh Guild of Pastoral Psychology.

Thanks for help with the images: Silvia Meucci and Elena García Aranda, Ediciones Siruela, Madrid; Joan Echtenkamp Klein, Claude Moore Health Sciences Library, University of Virginia; Odile Deslandes, Cabinet du Recteur Chancelier des Universités de Paris; Maria Serrano, Bibliothèque Nationale de France; Sigrid Freisleben, Österreichische Nationalbibliothek; Mott Lin, Clark University Archives; Patricia Jaunet, Conseil Général de la Vienne; Martine Bobin, Médiathèque François-Mitterrand de Poitiers; Cecilia Stoute,

American Psychiatric Association; Carol Greunke, Max Waldman Archives; Cara Gilgenbach, Kent State University Library Special Collections; Yvonne Voegeli and Christian Huber, ETH Bibliothek, Zurich; Elisabeth Paine, Paul and Peter Fritz AG, Literary Agency, Zurich; Meredith Lue, Falkland Road Inc.; Elizabeth Kerr, Camera Press, London. For the images, I am very grateful to Ana Obiols, Suzanne Elefthery, Janice Boddy, Paul Stoller, and Ted Shank. A special thank you to Al Ruban for his generosity and for taking the book to G. R.

Picture Permissions: Figure 1.6 published with permission of Bibliothèque Nationale de France, Paris; Figures 1.7, 1.8, 1.9 published with permission of Österreichische Nationalbibliothek, Collection of Manuscripts and Rare Books, Vienna (Cod. 14.086, fol. lv); Figure 2.1 published with permission of Dr. Janice Boddy; Figure 2.2 published with permission of Clark University Archives; Figure 2.3 published with permission of Dr. Paul Stoller; Figure 3.1 published with permission of the Claude Moore Health Sciences Library, University of Virginia Health System; Figure 3.2 published with permission of Olivier Neuillé, Médiathèque François-Mitterrand de Poitiers; Figure 3.3 published with permission of the American Psychiatric Association; Figures 3.4 and 4.1 published by permission from the Stiftung der Werke von C. G. Jung, Zurich, represented by Paul and Peter Fritz AG, Literary Agency, Zurich; Figures 5.1 and 5.4 published with permission of Doreen Madden Elefthery; Figure 5.2 published with permission of Camera Press, London; Figures 6.1, 6.4, 6.5 published with permission of Al Ruban, Faces Distribution Corporation; Figure 6.2 published with permission of the Max Waldman Archives; Figure 6.3 published with permission of Dr. Ted Shank; Figure 7.1 published with permission of Mary Ellen Mark, Falkland Road Inc.

Thanks to Margaret Atwood for permission to quote from *Negotiating with the Dead*.

My personal thanks to Marion Woodman, who started this ball rolling at London South Secondary School in 1972; to Elaine Bowe Johnson at Huron College, London who showed me how to take my words seriously and also to task, and to John Smallbridge, Althouse College, University of Western Ontario, who embodied his own conviction that good teachers must love their subject and their students; to France Amerongen for fierce inspiration and to Martin Odermatt for sitting on the floor with the images; to Mavis Gallant for advice concerning how to write about possession without sounding like 'the lost Atlantis crowd'; and to Susan Middleton and Kristine Arnet Connidis for comradeship in the educational and academic trenches.

Thanks to Denise Dickin, Mary Lawlis, and Richard Markle, creative cohorts at the Graduate Centre for the Study of Drama, University of Toronto, to Alec Stockwell, who introduced me to the work of the Open Theatre, and to Bonnie Greer, who synchronistically sat beside me when Joseph Chaikin read Beckett's *Texts for Nothing* alone in a chair at the Royal

Court Theatre, London, in August 1996, and who invited me backstage to meet 'Joe'.

Thanks to my professional colleagues in France – Flore Delapalme, Leslie de Galbert, Catherine de Lorgeril, Patrick Michaud, Mariette Mignet, Claire Raguet, Joseph-David Shesko, Brigitte Soubrouillard, Danielle Suarez, and Michel Bénet – for friendship, good meals and good questions.

Thanks to my analysands, whose presence in this book is implicit.

Most important, thanks to Alberto, to whom this book is gratefully and lovingly dedicated.

In memoriam, my *humanitas*: Marguerite Lorraine (Hamilton) Stephenson, Kate Szal, Martin Odermatt, Barbara Howard, Richard Outram, Helmut Barz, Cara Denman, Peer Hultberg, Luigi Aurigemma, Jean Hunkeler.

A portion of the royalties (generously matched by Routledge) from this book has been donated to the IAAP's 2008 Urgent Appeal, to support Chinese students of analytical psychology in their work with victims of the Sichuan earthquake.

Introduction

Jung's concept of possession – an organic approximation

> The experience of understanding something is always the experience of a gestalt – the dawning of an aspect that is simultaneously a perception and a reperception of a whole. One way the facilitation of understanding may proceed, then, is by the judicious selection and arrangement of elements of that whole. Another is by the setting up of objects of comparison.
>
> (Jan Zwicky, *Wisdom and Metaphor*, p. 2)

In an essay completed shortly before his death in 1961, Carl Gustav Jung recommended that psychologists place classical case histories of possession in a parallel and analogous relationship to contemporary secular cases of psychopathology:

> Just as the morphologist needs the science of comparative anatomy, so the psychologist cannot do without a 'comparative anatomy of the psyche'. He must have a sufficient experience of dreams and other products of the unconscious on the one hand, and on the other of mythology in its widest sense. He cannot even see the analogy between a case of compulsion neurosis, schizophrenia, or hysteria and that of a classical demonic possession if he has not sufficient knowledge of both.
>
> (Jung, 1961, para. 522)

This books anatomizes and analogizes Jung's concept of possession: it dissects the concept into its parts for the purpose of analysis, and it sets up a double relation, using the idea of 'as if' to construct correspondences between two things. By anatomizing and analogizing, it lines up fragments of late medieval Catholic history, anthropology, and psychiatric and psychotherapeutic practice side by side. But anatomizing and analogizing do not lead me to a totalizing interpretation; they do not render singular and ordered the diverse phenomena of possession.

Possession is a linchpin of Jung's analytical psychology. Jungian colleagues tell me this is a startling claim, but I hope readers will suspend their disbelief long enough to see where it leads. Possession certainly provides a throughline in Jung's Collected Works, from his 1902 dissertation for his medical degree to the 1961 essay entitled 'Symbols and the Interpretation of Dreams', from which I just quoted, one of the last essays he wrote. 'Possession' is the ubiquitous concept with which he formulates ideas about the dynamic between an ego consciousness and an autonomous unconscious, and it allows him, in turn, to convey phenomenologically the power of neurotic and psychotic symptoms. In a pivotal conversation with Freud about the analogous relationship between modern neurosis and medieval possession, Jung asked Freud a therapeutic question: could one work analytically not so much to eliminate as to discern meaning and value in the suffering of a neurotic possession (Jung, 1939b, para. 72)? Thus he placed his concept of possession even at the centre of how he narrated the history of psychoanalysis.

As Jungian studies gain momentum in the academy and in clinical training programs around the world, both readers relatively new to Jung and readers already familiar with Jungian theory and practice may find it useful to consider critically (as a kind of safety check) this lowly fundamental of analytical psychology. Possession firmly locates Jungian theory and practice in a particular problematic and holds Jungian theorists and practitioners to a particular epistemology. It also highlights how Jungian theorizing can go wrong: Jung himself erred when he essentialized or primitivized possession, and his readers err when they slip from his theory of complexes into esoterics or into a demotic psychologizing stripped of what Jung called 'the religious function'.

Jung's concept of possession can be most clearly anatomized within the context of psychotherapy, but I prefer first to contextualize the concept by analogizing in a number of important ways before getting to the pragmatics of psychotherapeutic practice. This strategy enables the ontological significance of Jung's concept to become more evident, for instance, in the treatment models of what psychiatry is only beginning to acknowledge as the 'cultural syndromes' of contemporary Western psychopathology. However, some readers may want to begin instead with the more anatomical analysis in Chapters 4 and 5 and then work through the contextualizing of the first three chapters, which they should be able to do without, I hope, suffering too much disorientation.

The roots of Jung's concept of possession go back to the Middle Ages, when the words 'possession' and 'obsession' were used synonymously to describe a particular kind of suffering. By the sixteenth century, however, these words were employed to differentiate degrees of the same affliction. Focusing on the seventeenth-century possessions at Loudun, France, shows how the events of this particularly famous case played out at the time and, more significantly, how theorizing about possession changed over almost four centuries of writing about them. Eventually, psychopathology co-opted the word 'obsession', stripped it of its religious connotation, and left the word 'possession' outside medical discourse. Recalling this history situates Jung's concept of possession in a European religious, medical, and intellectual continuum.

The possessions at Loudun occurred just as the study of the mind began to draw away from the context of European Catholicism. With its roots in the Age of Discovery and the Enlightenment, the nineteenth-century science of anthropology prompted the study of the mind in a different way. In Jung's time, anthropology and the new discipline of mind called psychoanalysis parted ways. There were good reasons for this: anthropologists were already discarding notions of primitive versus civilized mentality while Jung was wanting to read anthropological literature in essentialist ways in order to legitimize his psychology as science. Nonetheless, anthropological argument clarifies my own critique of Jung and indeed, in my view, it improves Jung's theorizing. Jung's concept of possession, viewed beside late twentieth-century anthropological research on the phenomena of possession, can facilitate a rapprochement between psychoanalysis, psychology and anthropology, and this is a rapprochement which many anthropologists are currently seeking.

In 1992, the American Psychiatric Association's *Diagnostic and Statistical Manual of Mental Disorders* introduced possession as a defined, carefully described mental disorder. I see this change in two ways: as a negative recuperation of 'possession' into psychiatry's essentializing nosology and as a potential epistemological break, part of psychiatry's attempt to culturally contextualize its discourse and treatment models. Aligning Jung's concept of possession with contemporary critiques of Western psychiatry by medical anthropologist Roland Littlewood and transcultural psychiatrist Laurence Kirmayer exposes the risks inherent in this development. These theorists characterize contemporary Western cultures as impoverished, as lacking vibrant narrative constructions and effective social discourse with which to smooth over the shifting complexities of cognitive functioning. To greater or lesser degrees, these cultures pathologize the ordinary, rendering as psychic rupture suffering that is cognitively normative. As a society and as professionals dealing with the mind, we tend to respond to this impoverishment and these ruptures by overvaluing the coherence which we read in psychiatry's essentializing discourse. Jung's concept of possession helps to break through this pathologizing by critiquing theories of personhood that characterize it as firmly and singularly defined by consciousness; it enables us to posit a much more fluid, pluralistic and embodied notion of the self.

Jung located his concept of possession in an equivocal language which he hoped would do justice to what he called the 'dual nature' of psychological experience. He struggled to remain within a discourse which, though precise in terms of psychiatric knowledge, would be open enough to allow for elements in the experience of suffering and healing that are unconscious, elements that are not directly knowable. I connect Jung's concept of possession explicitly to its etymology, to the forceful image of selfhood sitting in its own seat and of the suffering inherent when selfhood experiences itself as unseated by something Other. For some readers new to Jung, the phrase 'possessed by a complex' may have the ring of esoteric jargon, while in commentaries and theorizing by Jungians and post-Jungians alike, the same phrase can lose much of its conceptual and imagistic impact, diminishing from metaphor to simile to discursive cliché. Metaphors are paradoxical; by saying that two different things are identical, metaphor gives them an impossibly equal onto-logical status. Metaphors metamorphose: both subject and object change; similes assimilate, the subject absorbing the object and making the object resemble itself. Jung's concept of possession is metaphor. He posits, not a discursive 'as if', but an ontological paradox embedded within the psycho-therapeutic frame and the transference–countertransference relationship. By reconnecting the concept with its image, I hope to offer some readers a useful entry point into Jung's theory and others the rediscovery of a concept alive with implications.

Jung applied his concept of possession in his own practice of psycho-therapy; in fact, his theorizing and his practice fed each other. Comparing his theorizing with that of other practitioners who employ complementary con-cepts of possession shows that Jung's concept renders coherent contemporary psychotherapeutic techniques such as temenos/containment, personification/mimesis and integration/synthesis, and it does so without betraying the onto-logical paradox at the centre of these practices, a betrayal of which theorizing is often guilty. Upholding this paradox has laid Jung open to academic and clinical prejudices which denigrate his concept of possession as esoteric. I believe these prejudices to be unfounded, and I differentiate his concept from practices which employ possession within a specific system of belief.

My analysands' hard-won insights inform and colour the thesis of this book; indeed, they motivated me to write it. However, the recently refined ethical standards of my profession prompt me to resist placing their stories in service of a Jungian argument, retelling their experiences as a way to defend Jung's concept. It also seems to me that in this respect, as in so many others, a single work of fiction by a master storyteller can tell a truth more fully than an accumulation of detail from many real-life instances. Rather than employing case material from my practice to elucidate Jung's concept of possession, I have used the case of Myrtle Gordon in John Cassavetes's film *Opening Night* as my example. The 'possession' suffered by this fictional character shows the rich implications of Jung's concept for both theorists and clinicians.

In this book, I address Jung's concept of possession philosophically in terms of his epistemology of paradox, emphasizing its ontological signifi-cance and its implications for the practice of psychotherapy. However, I do not address the moral and legal implications of Jung's concept; these fall outside my frame of reference. I have not written about instances in which psychiatry, law, and religion meet in an attempt to judge a 'possessed' indi-vidual's competence to stand trial, or cases in which parents or religious leaders cite belief in 'possession' as justification for abuse. Psychiatrists, anthropologists, and journalists frequently refer to such instances (for example, Barbano, 2000; Bran, 2005; Ferber and Howe, 2003), and often I have been asked if Jung's concept might throw light on the difficulty of judging possession. Kristine Arnet Connidis, who is both a lawyer and a Jungian analyst, has written about the problems of effective judging in psychiatric review boards (Connidis, personal communication, 25 October 2005; see also Connidis, 2004), but dealing with these legal perspectives is beyond the scope of this book. Even so, Jung's concept of possession at least renders coherent the ontological predicament at the core of such conundrums.

I inscribe Jung's concept of possession most explicitly in the context of the practice of psychotherapy, but only after first using it comparatively, aligning it with anthropological arguments about possession and articulating its epistemological challenge to the assumptions and parameters of the practice of psychiatry. While presenting a fundamental Jungian concept to both general readers and readers already familiar with Jungian theory, from time to time I also address specific readers such as anthropologists, psychiatrists, critical theorists and psychotherapists. These moments have evolved from wonderful conversations and generous exchanges with colleagues in all these fields who appreciate how a Jungian perspective contributes to issues with which they continue to wrestle meaningfully. My argument recommends to all these readers a paradoxical Vichian perspective of looking backwards and forwards at the same time, something akin to what Jung described when he said, 'the peculiar nature of [the psychotherapist's] experience forces upon him a certain mode of thought, and certain interests, which *no longer have* – or perhaps I should say, *do not yet have* – a rightful domicile in the medicine of today' (Jung, 1945b, para. 192, italics mine). By setting chapters on history, anthropology, psychiatry, critical theory, and psychotherapy side by side, by attempting an interdisciplinary synthesis of the diverse material on possession, I hope to generate an organic approximation of Jung's concept of possession and to assess and evaluate his concept with questions such as 'How valid is his formulation?' and, more pragmatically, 'What is it good for?'

I have returned often to an image as a kind of touchstone during the writing of this book: the face of a Canadian girl in her early teens as she speaks to a national television news journalist about an epidemic of gas-sniffing in her hometown and the death of her older brother, who accidentally caught fire. She says she is possessed by her dead brother, who visits her and tells her not to sniff gasoline. She sniffs gasoline, she says, to remain in contact with him, to not lose him, to feel his protective presence, to not feel afraid and alone, to give him her life in the here and now. And it is from within this painful contradiction that she speaks to the questioning journalist.

Figure 1.1 The execution of Urbain Grandier, parish priest of the Church of Saint Pierre du Marché of Loudun, 18 August 1634, attributed to René Allain, Poitiers. Gabriel Legué, *Urbain Grandier et les possédées de Loudun* (Paris: Baschet, 1880).

Chapter 1

The possessions at Loudun

Tracking the discourse of possession

> Although it is, of necessity, finite, . . . historical knowledge is yet superior
> to all other human knowledge, since the comprehension by the actors of
> the parts that, in some sense, their own acting creates, will, if they under-
> stand the regular and recurrent structure of the ends and methods of social
> activity, be superior in kind to the knowledge possessed by spectators,
> however perceptive they may be. In history we are the actors; in the natural
> sciences mere spectators.
>
> (Isaiah Berlin, *Three Critics of the Enlightenment*, p. 88)

One of the best known cases of possession in Western European history
took place in the French town of Loudun, some twenty kilometres west of
Richelieu and sixty kilometres west of La Haye, the birthplace of Descartes.
In 1631, Cardinal Richelieu received royal permission to construct the town
that still bears his name as a monument to his own power. In 1633, in voluntary exile, Descartes suppressed publication of his treatise *Le Monde* after
having learned of the trial of Galileo. From 1632 to 1638, Loudun was the
unlikely epicentre of a collective crisis; it became the stage for a case of
demonic possession that drew crowds from all over Europe. These three
events are related by more than simple location and chronology. Taken
together, they define a Zeitgeist and prefigured the direction in which Western
philosophy and the science of mind would be carried.

Because the documentation of the Loudun possession is extremely copious,
the lines of debate about possession as they shifted over four centuries can
be tracked. Considering the case of Loudun necessarily means rationalizing
and, perhaps, anachronistically psychologizing the data, but I hope to steer a
course that will neither distance and dismiss the documented human suffering nor remystify a series of events that culminated in an appalling injustice
and a collective act of great cruelty. Situating Jung's concept of possession
within this historical continuum shows how a Jungian perspective contributes
a useful new approach to the debate.

Figure 1.2 'Next exit: Richelieu, Loudun, Descartes'. The 1630s Zeitgeist is geographically defined by an A10 autoroute sign, France, 2008.

Possession and the religious wars

After about 1520, Lutheranism began to gain a foothold in France, and by the 1550s, many had converted to the new religion from Catholicism, including a significant group of nobles. In 1562, the Edict of Saint-Germain granted the Protestant Huguenots some freedom of worship, but over the next thirty-six years it was withdrawn, restricted, or reinstated in no fewer than eight religious wars. Finally, in 1598, the Edict of Nantes granted permission for Protestants to worship as they chose. During these Wars of Religion, Catholic and Huguenot forces alternately pillaged and burned Loudun. The precarious equilibrium set by the Edict of Nantes allowed the town's mostly Protestant population a period of consolidation, but in 1628, the fall of La Rochelle, a rebellious Huguenot port to the southwest, marked an ominous shift. Louis XIII made explicit his antipathy toward his subjects who had adopted the 'so-called Reformed Religion', and he began to demolish the outer walls and towers of towns to safeguard his kingdom from any opposition that might arise in Huguenot strongholds.

Loudun's fate was both typical and exceptional. Typically, in 1617, its Protestant governor was replaced by a Catholic. Exceptionally, as a personal favour to the new governor and in contradiction to his command, Louis XIII granted the donjon, or great tower of Loudun, a reprieve from his wrecking crews; it still stands today. The people of Loudun responded to the fate of their donjon like secular citizens: for the most part, civic pride outweighed religion, with Catholics and Protestants alike rejoicing in the decision to safeguard the symbol of their city's autonomy when neighbouring towns such as Mirebeau were losing theirs. This civil society did not last, however; the case of demonic possession that began in 1632 would drag the people back into irreconcilable fundamentalism.

The case of possession at Loudun did not appear out of the blue; in fact, four important cases can be seen as precedents. The first occurred in 1566 near Laon, in northern France. A sixteen-year-old girl, Nicole Obry, was said to be possessed by as many as thirty devils, primarily by one identified as Beelzebub. For two months, she was exorcised almost daily in front of large crowds on public stages constructed first within the church at Vervins and then at the cathedral of Laon. The principal tool employed by the exorcists was the Eucharist, a technique uncharacteristic of the contemporary procedures of exorcism defined in the *Malleus Maleficarum* (Sprenger and Kramer, 1486/1968); the exorcists apparently intended to convert the Huguenots, or at least confute them, by demonstrating the Real Presence in the consecrated Host. Certainly, the public dialogues between the exorcists and the demon Beelzebub residing within Nicole Obry vindicated several Catholic practices and beliefs that the Protestants attacked as superstitions: transubstantiation, the veneration of relics, the use of holy water, the signing of the cross, and the power of names (Walker, 1981, p. 23).

The second precedent took place in 1582 at Soissons, also in northern France. Among the group of four possessed persons, the most notable was a fifty-year-old married man, Nicolas Facquier. His devil, named Cramoisy, claimed he was possessing Facquier to force three of his cousins, who were Huguenots, to convert to the true Church. Following the eventual and somewhat coerced conversion of all three, Facquier was successfully dispossessed. In this case, the propagandizing function of exorcism was explicit.

The third case involved propaganda even more clearly. In 1598, twenty-six-year-old Marthe Brossier, having apparently studied a book on the Miracle of Laon, travelled with her father to Paris just as the Paris Parliament was registering the Edict of Nantes, in which Henri IV granted all Huguenots freedom of worship. A year earlier, at Angers, a bishop had already tested Brossier's symptoms of possession: by alternating holy water with ordinary water and words from his book of exorcisms with the first lines of the *Aeneid*, he had established that she was a fraud. Still, Brossier insisted that her possession was authentic, and during her public exorcisms in Paris, she 'said marvellous things against the Huguenots'. Fearing that the fragile spirit of religious tolerance codified in the edict might be undermined with catastrophic results, the king ordered her detained, examined, and eventually escorted home and monitored by a resident judge. Dr. Michel Marescot's report, published by royal command in 1599, argued that, in the opinion of the best physicians in France, nothing done by Brossier was preternatural; their diagnosis was '*nihil a Spiritu, multa ficta, pauca a morbo*': 'nothing from the Spirit, many things simulated, a few things from disease' (Walker, 1981, p. 15). This report registered two significant official acknowledgements: that exorcism had become an important tool in the service of religious propaganda, and that physicians (and even bishops) had begun to identify fraud and naturally occurring sickness as possible causes for a demoniac's behaviour.

The most important precedent to the events in Loudun occurred in 1611 at Aix-en-Provence. Here, for the first time, a connection was made between possession and witchcraft; though the demoniac was still perceived as suffering the traditional torments of the occupying demon, the demon was now deemed to be acting at the behest of a sorcerer. This shift from a dyad consisting of demoniacs and exorcists to a triad including a sorcerer is significant: legally, spiritually, psychologically, the demoniacs who gave voice to 'evil spirits' were freed from personal responsibility for their behaviour. They still had to undergo exorcism, but now the exorcists worked not only to expel the invading spiritual agent but also to identify and exterminate a guilty third party. In the case at Aix, based on evidence provided by Madeleine Demandolx and other nuns of her Ursuline order, a priest named Louis Gaufridy was convicted of sorcery and burned at the stake.

Polarization in Loudun

According to ecclesiastical records, the events at Loudun began on 22 September 1632, when Jeanne des Anges, the prioress of the Ursuline convent, Sister de Colombiers, the sub-prioress, and Sister Marthe de Saint-Monique, a junior nun, were each visited separately during the same night by an apparition of 'a man of the cloth' asking for help. On the evening of 24 September, in the refectory, another spectre in the form of a black sphere knocked Sister Marthe to the ground and Jeanne des Anges into a chair. Strange disturbances continued: the nuns heard mysterious voices, experienced physical blows from unseen sources, and found themselves gripped by fits of uncontrollable laughter. Finally, physical evidence of possession appeared: three hawthorns were seemingly passed from a ghostly hand into the palm of the prioress. After this, most of the nuns were stricken with bouts of uncontrollable convulsions and irrational behaviour. The first exorcisms were conducted on 5 October 1632, and many more followed, eventually expanding into huge public events which attracted thousands of curious onlookers from all over Europe. On 18 August 1634, Urbain Grandier, parish priest of Saint-Pierre-du-Marché in Loudun, was found guilty of the crimes of sorcery and casting evil spells; above all, he was declared responsible for the possession visited upon the Ursulines. He was burned at the stake the same day. Even though the sorcerer had been executed, the exorcisms continued, though no longer as public spectacles, until 1638.

The hundreds of books and essays about the possession at Loudun and the trial and execution of Urbain Grandier show how abruptly the brief period of tolerance and civic cooperation between Catholics and Protestants ended. The first account, *Véritable relation des justes procédures observées au fait de*

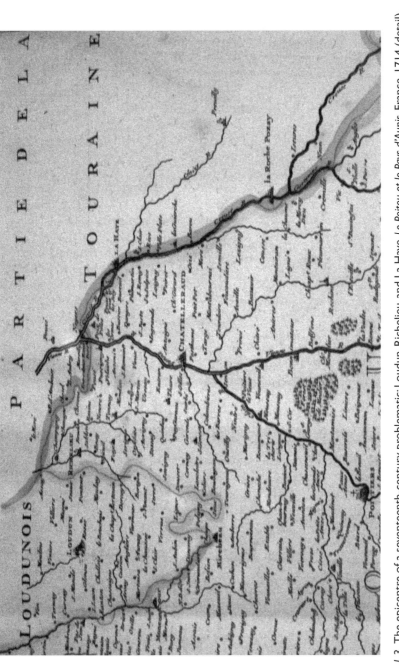

Figure 1.3 The epicentre of a seventeenth-century problematic: Loudun, Richelieu, and La Haye. *Le Poitou et le Pays d'Aunis*, France, 1714 (detail).

la possession des Ursulines de Loudun, et au procès de Grandier, by Reverend Father Tranquille (1634), a member of one of the earliest teams of exorcists, is a polemic on behalf of the exorcists and the rites of the Church. Tranquille's rhetoric demonstrates his purpose: to defend his own actions and to condemn the considerable public scepticism about the nuns' possession and disapproval of Grandier's judges. Tranquille's argument emphasized that a possession is either genuinely demonic or it is voluntary and wilful. But Tranquille did not acknowledge the skewed political situation in the town. The dissenting audience to whom he addressed his arguments had no voice during Grandier's trial. A court order announced from the pulpits of Loudun and posted in public places forbade debate or disagreement about the possessions or the legal proceedings, on pain of death.

As early as 1637, in 'Relation de M. Hédelin, abbé d'Aubignac, touchant les possédées de Loudun', a visitor to Loudun voiced scepticism about what he witnessed (Hédelin, 1637). It could be argued that the possessions at Loudun unfolded like a textbook case, that details right down to the hawthorns in the prioress's hand occurred in accordance with books such as *Histoire admirable de la possession et conversion d'une pénitente*, which the exorcist Father Sébastien Michaëlis of Aix-en-Provence had written in 1613. Indeed, just a week after the first exorcisms on 5 October 1632, Father Mignon, the nuns' confessor, was already citing the case of Aix and the possessed Ursulines, with its unprecedented outcome, the execution of a priest as a sorcerer. Although d'Aubignac was a Catholic witness, he remained unconvinced that the criteria for possession had been adequately established, nor did the manner in which the exorcisms were performed please him.

Grandier's trial had legitimized the evidence of the demoniacs and the exorcists, and the court order rendered all objections illegal. As a result, the opposing Protestant position was not available in print, and in 1685, the Edict of Nantes, which had granted the Huguenots a grudging tolerance, was revoked. Not until 1693 did Nicolas Aubin, a Huguenot from Loudun who had lived in exile in Amsterdam for seven years, publish his *Histoire des diables de Loudun*. Aubin argued that the Huguenots of Loudun had been maliciously undermined by 'the long and deadly intrigues of a convent of nuns and a great number of ecclesiastics, supported by a body of magistrates, of habitants of the town, and favourites of the court'. Aubin even identified a culprit at the centre of the affair: Father Mignon, the nuns' confessor at the time of the first events. Aubin dramatized Father Mignon's instructions to the nuns about how best to perform during the public exorcisms so they would both incriminate Grandier, who was reputedly a libertine and an embarrassment to the Catholic cause, and, more importantly, demonstrate the power of Catholic ritual over the devil and thereby undermine the all-too-powerful Huguenot position in Loudun. Circumstantial evidence to support Aubin's argument is not difficult to find: following the execution of Grandier, the court confiscated what had been, until that moment, a reputable Huguenot college and rehoused the Ursulines there, to their great advantage.

The language of possession

The language of possession has been fluid during the history of European religion, and the 'set texts' on which d'Aubignac relied for a clear statement of diagnostic criteria were orthodox only to his particular time and place.

In early medieval medical terminology, 'possession' probably referred more to the intermittency of manic attacks than to any notion of causation (Demaitre, 1982). Differences in emphasis can be attributed to different conceptions of 'devil', a word that, in the medieval imagination, synthesized to varying degrees the biblical Satan, the mythic fallen angels, and the *daimones* of Hellenistic paganism (Pagels, 1995; Boureau, 2004). In the early Middle Ages, the devil's field of action was the imagination, not the body or corporeal reality. Between the third and fifth centuries, Tertullian, Augustine, and John Cassion portrayed the devil as, most importantly, a deceiver who employs *fantasmata* to lead the soul astray, and one falls prey to the devil particularly in dreams. True dreams come from God; the devil fills dreams with false and tempting images. The *Canon Episcopi* (916) described 'certain wicked women, instruments of Satan who were themselves deceived by diabolical apparitions', believing that they rode by night on herds of animals following the sorceress Holda (or, as William of Auvergne, Bishop of Paris, more tolerantly called her, Abundia or Satia). The Church denounced these alleged nocturnal voyages associated with pagan fertility rites. It argued that the participants mistakenly believed that these phantasms actually occurred in time and space rather than in their imaginations, and it took upon itself the duty to heal people whose sick imaginations were leading them away from God.

In the thirteenth and fourteenth centuries, however, the church reversed this position and attributed corporeal reality to the devil's *fantasmata* (Schmitt, 1982). The pontifical constitution *Vox in Rama* (1233) described paying homage to Satan as a feudal *osculum* in reverse – kissing the devil's anus – and it rendered nocturnal dream voyages into quasi-religious meetings marked by physical (not imaginary) acts of incest, sodomy, infanticide and cannibalism. Jean Vineti, a theologian and inquisitor, circumvented the argument in the *Canon Episcopi* that witches' sabbaths were only diabolical illusions and sorcerers deceived souls; in his *Tractatus contra daemonum invocatores*, he identified devil worship as a new phenomenon, distinct from traditional rustic sorcery. Jacobus Sprenger and Heinrich Kramer, two inquisitors of the Rhineland, specified in their *Malleus Maleficarum* (1486) that this change took place around the year 1400. The devil, whose influence was formerly limited to the imagination, now acted in corporeal reality. It is tempting to see a connection between this change and the collective trauma of the bubonic plague epidemic that had decimated Europe during the fourteenth century (see Odermatt, 1991). Certainly, by 1484, according to the Papal Bull *Summis desiderantes affectibus* promulgated by Innocent VIII, witches and sorcerers abjured their Christian faith by fornicating with devils, and this abjuration was depicted as the unfaithful inviting the devils to enter their bodies.

As the body became the target of diabolical attack, the terms 'possession' and 'obsession', which had been used almost synonymously, diverged in meaning. Etymologically, *obsidere* denotes 'to sit at or opposite to', 'to sit down before', or 'to beseige', as when an enemy force sits down before a fortress. Hence an obsessive spirit was thought to assail, haunt, harass a person from outside, while a possessing spirit was considered to have taken up residence inside the body (see Chapter 4). In 1616, in *An English Expositor*, John Bullokar wrote, 'A man is said to be obsest when an euill spirit followeth him, troubling him at diuers times and seeking opportunity to enter into him', and in 1871, the anthropologist Edward Tylor noted, 'These cases belong rather to obsession than possession, the spirits not actually inhabiting the bodies, but hanging or hovering about them' (see Walker, 1981). The distinction is not so very far away from current psychopathological diagnostic criteria, which differentiate, for example, between paranoid feelings of being persecuted from without and delusional preoccupation with thoughts which are not one's own but which one believes have been inserted into one's mind. At Loudun, on 1 October 1632, three nuns were declared 'possessed'; by December 1634, nine were declared 'possessed' and eight others 'obsessed' or 'maleficiated'.

Still, in 1637, when d'Aubignac expressed his dissatisfaction with these declarations of possession, his reason was that the exorcists had not sufficiently matched the behaviour of the nuns to the criteria for possession established in the *Malleus Maleficarum*. In his view, the language of the exorcists should have corresponded to that of the canonical texts on demonology. Certainly, the first task of an exorcist was probative and diagnostic: to identify by name the devil to whom the demoniac gave voice and to discover – because devils did not possess the whole of a demoniac's body but only a small part – where in the body it resided. For example, during the public exorcisms in Laon, the devil who identified himself as Beelzebub, chief of demons, and who was supposed to have been temporarily expelled from Nicole Obry when shown the Host, simply retired into her left arm. Similarly, at Loudun, the body of Jeanne des Anges housed seven possessing demons, among them one lodged in the middle of her forehead, one below the last rib of her right side, and another in the second rib of her right side; Behemoth, in her stomach, was the last to leave.

A map of the correspondences between the diabolical and bodily hierarchies in Jeanne des Anges's case (see Certeau, 1970, p. 38) demonstrates how the demons took up their physiological residences in an orderly fashion according to rank: Seraphim in the head, Powers in the upper body, Thrones further down. The exorcists alone constructed this far-from-haphazard map, since the demoniac herself was expected to emerge from each attack with no memory of what the devil inside her had said or done. The public mapping of Jeanne des Anges's demons functioned as authentication, but d'Aubignac based his doubts about the possessions on Catholic dogma. Devils must be heard to converse with the exorcist in foreign languages unfamiliar to the demoniac, and they must perform remarkable acts of clairvoyance or prevision, as well as acts of supernatural strength such as levitation. According to d'Aubignac, the nuns of Loudun had not demonstrated any of these criteria sufficiently to merit a declaration of possession.

Supernatural or natural

Diagnostically, seventeenth-century French exorcists were primarily pre-occupied with recognizing 'who' (that is, which spiritual agent and which sorcerer) was responsible for the suffering of the possessed, while physicians were identifying 'what' in the body and the mind was the cause. Yet to imagine priests and physicians as polarized would be oversimplification. Published discourses of authentication and counter-challenge show the political divisions among the Catholic clergy and also among the medical experts, both Catholic and Protestant.

The divisions in the medical world came to the fore in the 1598–1599 case of the demoniac Marthe Brossier. In 1599, Brossier was examined four times in Paris. A first group of theologians and physicians noted two morbid symptoms, an inflamed tongue and a heart murmur, but they reported no evidence of the supernatural (though possibly much of counterfeiting) in her behaviour. But the next day, two of these doctors conducted an additional examination and, finding an insensitive spot between her thumb and index finger, asked for a postponement. A new group of doctors and theologians were gathered, but this time, apparently under the auspices of the Capucins who had been exorcising her, they tabled a report that favoured a declaration of possession. Finally, after the forty days of detainment commanded by the king, Brossier was again examined by many doctors, who attested that they found no evidence of the supernatural.

Discours veritable sur le faict de Marthe Brossier de Romorantin pretendue demoniaque (1599), the report commissioned by Henri IV and published by Michel Marescot and his medical colleagues after the fourth and final examination, sets out a well-argued differential diagnosis, including the report of the second team of doctors with a refutation of each of its points. Epilepsy was unanimously eliminated because a distinct diagnostic feature of epileptic seizures was 'loss of sense and judgement', whereas Brossier remained conscious during her convulsions. The second team had argued for the traditional criteria for possession – understanding foreign languages and clairvoyance – but Marescot easily demonstrated the ambiguity and weakness of that evidence. The second team had defended Brossier against charges of fraud by citing medical evidence: during her fits, 'deepe prickings of long pinnes' produced no blood or pain, and her pulse and rate of inhalation remained steady. Marescot's team countered that, because pushing a needle vertically into a fleshy part of the body does not always produce blood or pain, such evidence must not be employed to identify demoniacs and sentence sorcerers to the stake. To the second team's observations about pulse and breath rate, Marescot responded with a hypothetical diagnosis of melancholia: he had seen cases of 'sundrie Melancholicke persons, not onley many daies and moneths, but also many yeeres, to have runne up and downe crying very strangely, and howling like dogs, without any change, either in pulse, or in breathing, or in colour' (Marescot, translated by Abraham Hartwel, 1599, in Walker, 1981). Marescot also observed that, if Brossier were suffering from melancholia, she might sincerely believe herself to be possessed, even though, at the same time, she might cunningly employ symptoms based on her reading about the Miracle of Laon to persuade others.

Thirty-five years later, the physicians at Loudun were equally divided about what is natural and what is supernatural. On the one hand, Hippolite Pilet de la Ménardière, a doctor of the faculty of medicine at Nantes, argued in his *Traité de la mélancholie* (1635) that melancholy is unable to produce the effects he witnessed (see Certeau, 1970, pp. 117, 129). On the other hand, Doctor Pierre Yvelin said in his *Apologie pour l'autheur de l'examen de la possession des Religieuses de Louviers* (1643) that physicians must emphasize to the ecclesiastics how stagnating melancholic humours can produce uncanny and extraordinary effects.

The experiences of Marc Duncan, a doctor living at the time in nearby Saumur, illustrate the degree to which the situation at Loudun deteriorated. Duncan was a Scottish Calvinist, a philosopher interested in mathematics and theology, an amateur poet who had written an homage to Henri IV, and the principal of a renowned Huguenot college. Summoned to Loudun to conduct tests for preternatural strength, he had testified that, on the contrary, it was not at all difficult to hold the wrist of one of the demoniacs and to prevent her from striking him or breaking out of his control. He was asked to return to witness an exorcism of Jeanne des Anges in which the devil Asmodée had announced that he and two others would depart. It seems that Duncan attended under duress, because he did so only after invoking Article Six of the Edict of Nantes, which granted liberty of conscience and the free exercise of religion. Still, by the end of the day's proceedings, he hurriedly returned to Saumur to seek the protection of his patron, the Marquis de Brézé, from an order for his arrest. In 1634, the Protestant doctor jeopardized his relationship with de Brézé by the hypothesis he elucidated in his *Discours de la possession des religieuses de Loudun* (Duncan, 1634).

The concern of Duncan's *Discours*, much like that of Marescot's report on Marthe Brossier, was that neither the priests nor the physicians attended to the obvious suffering of the young nuns. Duncan argued against chicanery and accounted for the facts by theorizing along the same lines as earlier thinkers: the imagination is the mental faculty that is most susceptible to infection and interference, to *fantasmata*. He attributed neither trickery nor fabrication to the possessed women but error of the imagination, reinforced by fasting, vigils and solitary religious life; these errors had perhaps been instilled by the confessor and the Mother Superior who attributed 'certain evil desires' (such as the wish to leave the convent to marry) to demonic possession and who incited the young girls to take their dreams for visions and their fears for visits by devils.

A century after the Loudun possessions, François Gayot de Petaval published *Histoire d'Urbain Grandier, condamné comme magicien et comme auteur de la possession des religieuses Ursulines de Loudun* (1735). In it, he added the 'medico-scientific' possibility of nymphomania and hysteria to the differential diagnosis of demon possession or willed chicanery on the part of the nuns. In 1860, Louis Figuier argued in a similar vein: the nuns were neither possessed nor faking their convulsions but suffered from a 'convulsive hysteria with diverse complications'. And in 1880, the anti-Catholic Doctor Gabriel Legué supported a similar hypothesis by citing the works of his contemporary, the neurologist Jean Martin Charcot.

Descartes's demon

When René Descartes recorded his famous dreams of 11 November 1619, which marked the turning point of his life and defined the agenda for that life's work, he was billeted in a military post at Neuburg (Germany), at the border between the opposing forces of the Roman Holy Empire and the Protestant claimants to the throne. Descartes had studied in the vibrant late scholastic tradition of the Jesuit college at La Flèche, and he always remained nominally a Catholic, but he was also intellectually more attuned to the Protestant doctrine of private judgement. Following the course outlined in his dreams led him in the direction of neither Catholicism nor Protestantism but to an epistemology that enthroned reason.

Descartes was born sixty kilometres east of Loudun at La Haye in 1596; the town now bears his name. By the time of the possessions of Loudun, he was living in permanent and peripatetic exile in the Netherlands, hoping to evade the hostilities of both Catholic and Calvinist theologians. In 1633, in a manuscript entitled *Le Monde*, he argued that sensation and imagination are ontologically distinct functions of body and, therefore, subject to falsehood. (In this sense, he would have agreed with Huguenot Marc Duncan's assessment of the Ursulines' suffering at Loudun.) For Descartes, thinking is the function of soul or mind and therefore capable of generating methodological certitude. However, when he learned of Galileo's condemnation by the Inquisition, Descartes suppressed and did not publish his argument about the thinking soul. He continued to develop his dualistic distinction between

RENATVS DESCARTES.

NOBILIS GALLVS, PERRONI DOMINVS, SVMMVS MATHEMATICVS ET PHILOSOPHVS.
NATVS HAGÆ. TVRONVM PRIDIE CALENDAS APRILES *1596*. DENATVS HOLMIÆ.
CALENDIS FEBRVARIIS. *1650*.

C. V. Dalen sculp.   Corn. Banheenung excudit.

Figure 1.4 René Descartes, philosopher-in-exile of the new sciences of the seventeenth century. Engraving by Cornelis van Dalen.

res extensa (physical, extended substance that can be measured and divided, including the human body, the brain and the nervous system) and *res cogitans* (the unextended and indivisible mind, including thoughts and volition). However, he defended this distinction only in private letters: 'The soul is a substance which is distinct from the body . . . its nature is merely to think' (March 1637, AT I, 348–351, Descartes, 1999, pp. 58–60).

Descartes theorized about both domains. He waited in vain for his work on modes of extension, which constituted a new mechanical and corpuscular physics, to be discussed approvingly, and likewise he waited for his philosophical system based on modes of thought to be understood as fundamental to the new sciences. In 1641, to justify this dualism and his defence of reason, he introduced into his *Meditations* the notion of a *malin génie*, an omnipotent deceiver. He used the hypothesis of a possessing demon to clarify his epistemological and metaphysical claim about how to attain certainty. If such a demon existed, he said, it could cause him to doubt the existence of all physical objects, the vast realm of *res extensa*, including his own body with its emotions and sense perceptions, but it could not lead him to doubt his existence as a thinking being. Certitude could be anchored in *res cogitans*.

Descartes was charting the same territory that the exorcists were mapping on the bodies of the Ursulines at Loudun and that the physicians and theologians were debating with regard to the natural versus the supernatural. Descartes with his *cogito ergo sum* was seeking by virtue of an indivisible reasoning mind a universal science that would counter the internecine splitting of the Wars of Religion. That his system achieved this goal by splitting reality into two distinct irreconcilable realms, *extensa* and *cogitans*, is its major weakness. And although his metaphysical system ostensibly depended on the existence of an omniscient, non-deceiving deity, critics of his proof for the existence of God considered it so unsuccessful that they claimed it deviously supported the opposite conclusion (Clarke, 2006, p. 212). In 1643, he had to defend himself against charges that dangerously compared him to Lucilio Vanini, a 'lying, irreligious homosexual atheist' (in other words, a freethinker) burned at the stake in Toulouse. In 1663, thirteen years after his death further afield in Sweden, the Vatican condemned Descartes's works of scientific rationalism.

Cui bono?

In 1920, an orthodox Catholic writer addressed the effect of the public staging of the exorcism rituals at Loudun. In his *Histoire littéraire du sentiment religieux en France, depuis la fin des guerres de religion jusqu'à nos jours*, Henri Brémond (1967) argued that performing the exorcisms in public perverted the rites; it was the public performance that rendered Duncan's refusal to attribute supernatural causes to the suffering of the nuns an indictable offence and Grandier's trial and execution as sorcerer an absolute necessity.

Figure 1.5 Louis XIII and Cardinal Richelieu at the victory over the Protestant stronghold of La Rochelle, 1628. La Sorbonne, Paris.

In order to better evaluate the outcome of the public exorcisms and Grandier's trial, it may be useful to consider the following etymological detail. The verb 'exorcize' comes from the Greek *exorkizein*, meaning 'swear an oath', and is translated into Latin as *adjuro* or *conjuro*. Etymologically, *exorkizo*, 'to exorcise', combines the prefix *ex*, meaning 'out', to the root *[h]orkos* or Horkos, the daemon-son of Eris, goddess of Discord or Strife, who punishes oath breakers. But the name Horkos also denotes 'fence' or 'bulwark', suggesting that taking an oath functions as a protective enclosure. The etymological image behind exorcising is not only of 'casting out a devil' but also of 'invoking and putting on oath' (Renos Papadopoulous, personal communication, 19 December 2005). By naming God, the exorcist solemnly invokes a devil in an attempt to establish a truth.

The irony of using a devil to discern truth had not escaped a committee of learned theologians at the Sorbonne. They had discussed the admissibility of diabolic evidence in legal proceedings, and in 1610 they had issued their decision: one must never admit the accusation of demons or exploit exorcisms to determine whether a man is a sorcerer, even if the exorcisms were applied in the presence of the Holy Sacrament and the devil forced to swear an oath, since the devil is always a liar and the 'Father of Lies'. Clearly, the trial and execution of Grandier in 1634 defied this ruling.

According to Michel Carmona in *Les Diables de Loudun: Sorcellerie et politique sous Richelieu* (1988), the decision to proceed against Grandier was made by Cardinal Richelieu and approved by Louis XIII. Carmona argues that Grandier's fate was sealed for three reasons: he was a well-known anti-cardinalist who had vehemently defended the walls and donjon of Loudun against the demolition ordered by the king, he had publicly humiliated Richelieu in an incident in 1618, before he was appointed cardinal, and he opposed the construction of the new city twenty kilometres east of Loudun granted to Richelieu by royal proclamation in 1631. According to Carmona, Richelieu co-opted and took advantage of the polarized conflicts between religion and medicine and between the Catholic and Huguenot citizens of Loudun for his own purposes. Carmona's insight is supported by Gabriel Legué's observation in *Documents pour servir à l'histoire médicale des possédées de Loudun* (1874): throughout all the transcriptions of the exorcisms which he examined, the nuns blasphemed God, Christ, and the Virgin Mary, but never Louis XIII and never Richelieu.

A feminist perspective: demonizing the feminine/ absolving the feminine

The orthodox criteria for determining a case of demonic possession – speaking in foreign languages, clairvoyance, preternatural physical strength, levitation – were, frustratingly, also the criteria for determining a case of possession by the Holy Spirit. The lives of the saints are replete with incidents of speaking in tongues, prophesying, and levitating. Keeping in mind this supernatural symmetry between the infernal and the celestial, a feminist reading of the possession at Loudun charts the process by which the non-rational experiences of the Ursuline nuns were rendered demoniacal.

There was nothing new in demonizing manifestations at first deemed supernatural. In 1578, Jean Boulaese published an account of the Miracle of Laon. In this version of the story, sixteen-year-old Nicole Obry, while alone at church, was confronted by a spirit who claimed to be the soul of her recently deceased maternal grandfather, Joachim Willot. The spirit entered her body and spoke to her, explaining that because he had died unexpectedly and unconfessed, he was confined to Purgatory, and he asked Obry to have Masses said, alms given, and a pilgrimage made on his behalf. The family addressed the first two requests but, presumably because of the exorbitant expense, attempted to overlook the third. Obry had suffered two head injuries that caused her almost permanent headaches, and she had recently begun to menstruate; following her possession, the headaches stopped, but she began to experience convulsive fits, accompanied by rigidity and insensibility, all of which she attributed to the fact that the pilgrimage hadn't been made. The parents even attempted a fake departure, but Nicole was not deceived. A local priest, a schoolmaster, and a Dominican from a nearby monastery intervened on the parents' behalf and conjured the spirit under oath to identify itself. The dialogue in Boulaese's account tracked the transposition of the young woman's experience of speaking with the dead into the orthodox discourse of the priests, whose manuals included Menghi's *Compendio dell'arte Essorcisticia* (1586) and *Sacerdotale ad consuetudinem S. Romanae Ecclesiae* (1579). Such manuals identified as heretical the ideas that either the souls of the dead or good angels could enter people's bodies (Walker, 1981, p. 22). The spirit that originally identified itself as the suffering soul of the grandfather, then describing itself as his good angel, admitted later, under duress, that it was demonic. Thereafter, the voice inside Nicole Obry renamed itself Beelzebub. The exorcist Sébastien Michaëlis explains in *Histoire admirable de possession et conversion d'une penitente* (1613) that the miracle was the paradox: a devil housed within a virgin repeatedly speaking on a stage in the cathedral of Laon in a manner which confirmed the Catholic faith and converted many heretics.

Michaëlis makes the ambiguous nature of possessing spirits even more explicit in his account of the 1611 possessions at Aix-en-Provence. In that case, an Ursuline called Louise Capeau, possessed by a devil identified by the name Verrine, preached sermons in the grotto at Sainte-Baume. Contradicting the 1610 Sorbonne ruling that, by nature, demons were liars, Verrine insisted that his homilies were truthful because he spoke them under oath. These speeches became increasingly extemporaneous rather than responses to the exorcists' questioning. While setting them down in his account, Michaëlis apologized if anyone should misconstrue them as positive examples of preaching by a woman, forbidden in 1 Corinthians 14:34–35. This apology states the case precisely: Louise Capeau's sermons were spoken and received as paradoxically inspired, as 'good possession'. This seems to have been a traceable pattern in seventeenth-century France: 'one of the only routes for women to achieve public, influential, vocal sanctity was by means of a good possession disguised as, or sometimes combined with, a diabolic one' (Walker, 1981, p. 77).

Jeanne des Anges, the Mother Superior of the Ursulines and the main demoniac at Loudun, published an autobiographical account in 1644, only a few years after her possession. She told the story of her supernatural experiences as an absolving and mystic transformation of a negative into a

Figure 1.6 The mystic transformation of demons lodged in the body into four signatures on the sacred hand of Jeanne des Anges, Mother Superior of the Ursulines at Loudun. This transformation changed a negative into a positive possession. Published with permission of Bibliothèque Nationale de France, Paris.

positive possession rather than as a deliverance through exorcism from demonic invasion instigated by the sorcerer Grandier. Although the seven named devils who took up residence inside her and afflicted her were apparently expunged, her cure was marked, not by absence, but by even more preternatural presence. Miraculously, four names – Jesus, Maria, Joseph, and Francis de Sales, the eventually canonized bishop of Geneva – were found indelibly traced on the surface of her left hand. In 1638, she embarked on a triumphant five-month 'pilgrimage' in which she displayed her left hand like a living reliquary to the royal family, to Richelieu, to members of parliament, and to crowds of up to five thousand people per day. Most interestingly, her memoir describes a subsequent series of communications with her 'good angel', which she published and circulated as divine revelations.

Robert Rapley (1998) traced the supernatural experiences of Jeanne des Anges and the Ursulines of Loudun back to a few initial images and emotions. Based on his reading of a manuscript attributed to the Ursulines themselves, Rapley argued for a sequence of events in October 1632 that differs slightly from the sequence recorded by the priests. According to this manuscript, not Jeanne des Anges but Sister Marthe, the junior nun, was the first sufferer. One night, she was troubled by dreams of Father Moussaut, the convent's recently deceased confessor. The next day, Sister Marthe found herself preoccupied with difficult and improper thoughts, which she described to Father Mignon, the replacement confessor and her new spiritual director. Among other things, she confessed desiring that Mignon should 'fall into a great sin' and then felt chagrin for having confessed this. Three nights later, while not dreaming but lying awake in bed, Sister Marthe saw the phantom of an unidentifiable man of the cloth, which she took to be the spirit of the late Father Moussaut; it approached her and asked for prayers to be said on his behalf. Only after Sister Marthe reported her nocturnal vision to her superiors were they also visited by the image of a phantom.

This supernatural figure underwent several intriguing permutations. Certainly, as in the case at Laon, during the first exorcisms of Jeanne des Anges on 5 October, the obsessing spirit changed from something unknown into a frightening, pitiful, recently mourned masculine figure begging for help, then into a handsome seducer, and still later into a menacing devil. By 11 October, the figure, now demonized and internalized in the Mother Superior, had named itself Astaroth, a Canaanite horned goddess of love and fertility mentioned in the Old Testament, a goddess whom the Philistines also associated with war (Lurker, 1987, p. 42). Two days later, seven devils claimed to reside within Jeanne des Anges. Only then did one of the devils refer to Urbain Grandier, the reputedly licentious priest of the nearby church of Saint-Pierre, as the sorcerer who had appeared to her at night in an attempt to seduce her. Because she had resisted him, she said, he had sent seven demons to take possession of her body.

Few feminist scholars are inclined to claim or recuperate Jeanne des Anges. Her memoir remains in print but with the subtitle *Autobiographie d'une hystérique possédée* (1886). This edition was annotated by Doctor Gabriel Legué and Georges Gilles de La Tourette, the neurologist whose name now identifies Tourette's Syndrome and who was born near Loudun in the village of Saint-Gervais-les-Trois-Clochers. It includes a dedication to the nineteenth-century neurologist Jean Martin Charcot and an appendix of facsimiles, including a letter from Jeanne des Anges to the king's commissioner Laubardemont, who presided over Grandier's trial, and a letter in her handwriting but signed by the demon *Asmodée* announcing the date of its retreat from her body. As this autobiography makes clear, the metaphors of warfare and battlefield common in the orthodox discourse about exorcism momentarily liberated the Ursulines to provoke and attack their male overseers. Although the women were led in chains onto the stage constructed in the cathedral, as soon as the devils were invoked, they were freed physically and verbally to mock, manoeuvre and even wrestle with their male exorcists. But as the rites of exorcism and the public spectacle drew to a close, the patriarchal authority of the Church and the power of the court of Loudun reasserted themselves, often horribly:

> Father Lactance threw the body of the possessed woman roughly to the
> ground, trampled it violently beneath his bare feet, then with one foot on

her throat repeated several times: '*Super aspiden et basilicum ambulabis et conculcabis leonem et draconem* (Thou shalt tread upon the asp and the basilisk / Thou shalt trample underfoot the lion and the dragon)'.

(Certeau, 1970, p. 106)

Rapley's research disturbingly implies that the original image appearing to Sister Marthe was altered and diabolized, not only by the language of exorcism, but possibly beforehand by the 'personal equation' of the Mother Superior herself. For Jeanne des Anges, the encounter with the unknown phantom gave form to a frightening erotic problem. The grieving Sister Marthe interpreted the visitation of the fantastic figure as a haunting by the soul of the recently deceased Father Moussaut; Jeanne des Anges experienced it as a terrifying seduction. After Moussaut had died in September 1632, Grandier's name had been put forward to her as a potential replacement confessor for the convent, but Grandier had declined the position. A month later, during the first week of Jeanne des Anges's exorcisms, the devil Astaroth declared under oath that Grandier, a sorcerer, had gained entry into the convent and into the bodies of the nuns through a bouquet of musk roses left on a dormitory step. These white flowers with their heavy, sensual perfume were associated with an aphrodisiac produced from the gland of the male musk deer, the word deriving from the Sanskrit *muska* meaning 'scrotum'. Their image introduced a foreign and forbidden erotic element into the convent, a parallel realm of sexual love existing on par with but separate from Christian *agape*. For Jeanne des Anges, Grandier was quite literally foreign. Only recently arrived in Loudun, he was reputedly an eloquent preacher and a ladies' man; by 1632, rumours circulated that he had seduced a young parishioner and written an anonymous tract questioning the requirement of celibacy for priests. He was without doubt an inviting hook for erotic projections. Four years after Grandier's execution, Jeanne des Anges described in her memoir her visions of her spiritual bridegroom or '*saint Ange*'; his physical details corresponded to another seductive beau, the blond, handsome eighteen-year-old duc du Beaufort, who had come to watch her being exorcised. Perhaps inadvertently, in her descriptions of possession and exorcism she recounted a horrific battle with Eros.

Aldous Huxley argued in *The Devils of Loudun* (1952) that only the arrival of Father Jean-Joseph Surin in December 1634, four months after the execution of Grandier, shifted the outcome for Jeanne des Anges towards something less destructive, towards images of absolution. Surin was thirty-four years old at the time and had already acquired a reputation as an honest but oddly credulous man, an excessively pious eccentric who suffered from melancholia. He introduced Jeanne des Anges to the works of Teresa of Avila and to the vocabulary of mysticism, proposing that she rely less on her passive role in the public spectacles of exorcism and more on an active but private compensation, through prayer and penitence, for the continued presence within her of possessing demons. This discourse of hagiography (Ferber, 2004, p. 146) allowed Jeanne des Anges to speak an erotic vocabulary of 'ravishment' and '*jouissance*' within a positive spiritual context. At the same time, in his role as exorcist, Surin took the utterly unorthodox strategy of praying for her devils to possess him instead, in order to take the suffering of his charge upon himself.

Surin's memoir, written in 1640 and published in 1828 as *Histoire abrégée de la possession des Ursulines de Loudun, et des peines du Père Surin*, described how the Mother Superior's devil came to obsess him, first somatically, with headaches, breathing difficulties, fits of trembling, and physical hallucinations, such as the sensation of animal paws walking and pressing down on his reclined body or of a snake crawling over his skin; finally it entered him, manifesting frequently as terrible pain at the base of his stomach (not unlike her Behemoth). His account of his psychic symptoms combined an erudite use of the literature of mysticism with a keen articulation of his own pathological feeling-states, for, unlike the nuns, Surin remained self-aware and oriented during his experiences of possession:

> I cannot explain to you what happens in me during this time and how that spirit unites itself with mine without depriving me either of my senses or of my freedom of soul, and becoming nevertheless as another myself, and as if I had two souls, one of which is dispossessed of its body and the use of its organs, and stands aside. . . . These two spirits do battle with each other in the same field that is the body; and the soul itself is as if divided.
>
> (Surin, 1828/1966)

Taken together, the autobiographies of Jean-Joseph Surin and Jeanne des Anges attest to the power exercised by the vocabulary of mysticism, which provided her with new strategies for manoeuvring towards what she regarded as absolution. Strikingly, too, the autobiographies record the extent to which Surin's state deteriorated as the Mother Superior's improved; as his patient got better, he felt worse.

Huxley, too, employed the term 'possessed' to describe Grandier as sufferer, identifying the first instance of possession, not in the Ursulines, but in the so-called sorcerer himself. To account for Grandier's seduction of his parishioner, Philippe Trincant, Huxley employs two languages, the archaic religious simile 'as though he were possessed' and the twentieth-century scientific 'fact' of psychological mechanism:

> Every now and then sensible and fundamentally decent people will embark, all of a sudden, on courses of which they themselves are the first to disapprove. In these cases the evil-doer acts as though he were

possessed by some entity different from and malignantly hostile to his ordinary self. In fact, he is the victim of a neutral mechanism, which (as not uncommonly happens with machines) has got out of hand and, from being the servant of its possessor, has become his master. Philippe Trincant was exceedingly attractive and 'the strongest oaths are straw to the fire in the blood'. Trincant's father was the parson's best friend. The very act of recognizing that such a thing was monstrous created in Grandier's mind a perverse desire to betray him.

(Huxley, 1952, p. 34)

Huxley identifies Grandier's problem as a psychological mechanism or reflex that no longer functions in service of the self, that unseats the self and leads the subject into destructively one-sided behaviour.

But Huxley's reading situates the experiences of Surin, rather than those of Jeanne des Anges or Grandier, at the boundary between good and bad possession. Jeanne des Anges portrayed herself in her memoir as not only wholly absolved and liberated but also henceforth engaged in a positive mystic dialogue with a 'good angel'; Huxley read Surin's autobiographical texts as the records of a fool-saint who saw himself as the sacrificial victim in a continual battle, in his mind and his body, between the Word Incarnate and radical Evil. Because he experienced reality as singular, in which he and his charge were parts of a whole, in which mind and body were also one, and because of the resulting alienating profundity of his melancholia, hypochondria and despair, Surin suffered virtual ostracism within his Jesuit community.

Fascinated by Surin's effectiveness as a kind of wounded healer, Huxley went so far as to contrast Surin's end with the fates of the more orthodox exorcists at Loudun. Lactance died in 1634, after the execution of Grandier, and Tranquille died in 1638, after the last exorcisms in Loudun; both suffered severe mental disturbances, horrible convulsions, and loss of faith. Surin underwent a similar ordeal, but, Huxley argued, his conflict was self-inflicted, consciously endured, and carefully articulated in his devotional writings. Although he despaired at times and even attempted suicide, he survived, continuing to study and write, until 1665.

Freud and Jung: psychodynamic interpretations

Freud never mentioned Loudun in his writings, but he did write a psychoanalytical interpretation of a case of exorcism in his essay 'A Seventeenth-Century Demonological Neurosis' (1923a). A Bavarian artist, Christoph Haitzmann, came to Mariazell, near Vienna, in 1677 to ask for deliverance from visions and convulsions caused by two pacts with the devil that, after nine years, were coming to term. Like the French cases in Laon and Loudun, this Bavarian case began with a death – the death of Haitzmann's father – and with the metamorphosis of the image of a loved one into something demonic.

Figures 1.7, 1.8, 1.9 Painting by Bavarian artist Christoph Haitzmann (1677–1678). In Freud's interpretation, this votive painting shows how grief for his dead father tipped Haitzmann into subjection to a tyrannizing devil-surrogate. In the detail on the left, his human father speaks to him. The detail on the right shows his father transformed into a winged devil with breasts. Published with permission of Österreichische National-bibliothek, Collection of Manuscripts and Rare Books, Vienna (Cod. 14.086, fol. 1).

In a series of paintings, Haitzmann depicted his dead father gradually transformed into a devil with breasts holding an open book in his hand. Through the rites of exorcism, Haitzmann felt himself released from the two pacts he said he had signed with his devil. In the end, however, he chose not to return to his work as a painter but to enter a monastery.

Freud read the case as a neurotic evasion of the ambivalent image of God the Father in which Haitzmann unconsciously defended himself against feelings of abandonment and deprivation. He portrayed Haitzmann as having avoided the necessary mourning of the natural father and interpreted his having sold his soul to the devil as an attempt to recast himself as son and obedient subject to a nurturing father-figure, to remain within the classic Oedipal complex rather than live his adult life bereft. By submitting himself through the two pacts to the father-as-devil, Freud argued, Haitzmann employed a 'feminine attitude' by which he neurotically preserved his threatened status as 'son' for a period of nine years. (This argument resembles Freud's well-known 1911 reading of a feminine strategy adopted by Schreber, although in that case the psychological result was not demonological neurosis but paranoia.) In Freud's view, Haitzmann's demonological neurosis permitted him to continue to feel contained within the inferior status of vassal-like 'subject' and 'son', even though at great psychological cost and with much suffering from the convulsions, visions, and creative blocks that, after nine years, culminated in a crisis and eventually the shift into another form of containment, holy orders.

Freud's psychoanalytic argument hangs on his theory that the repression of difficult feelings and thoughts renders them even more negative because they are unavailable to but nevertheless impinge on consciousness. Freud knew the *Malleus Maleficarium* well and wrote to his colleague Wilhelm Fliess about the correspondences he could see between a possessed woman and a hysterical patient, between an inquisitor/exorcist and an analyst, between demons and repressed affects (see Freud, 'On the History of the Psychoanalytic Movement', 1923b, pp. 41–43; letters to Fliess, 17 and 24 January 1897). In terms of psychological economies, he theorized, maintaining neurotic solutions such as Haitzmann's takes a terrible toll, repression stealing libido that would normally be accessible to the ego.

In 'Mourning and Melancholia' (1917), Freud described how a bereaved ego 'cannibalizes' and 'incorporates' a lost object in order to deny its death. In healthy mourning, he said, the ego needs to both internalize and eventually expel this incorporated object. In melancholia, the ego finds itself destructively supplanted and ruled by the object with no possibility for change. Thus Haitzmann incorporated and thereby resurrected the lost father, and his ego suffered under the consequent demonic tyranny for nine years, until he sought deliverance from his symptoms through exorcism. For these reasons, Freud considered Haitzmann's manoeuvre out of his subjugation to the devil and into the monastic order as perhaps progressive but still evasive, neurotic, and, by implication, diabolical; Haitzmann's decision not to return to his vocation of painting but to enter a cloistered order perpetuated the neurotic splitting. His ego remained in some sense possessed when he abdicated a third time to a superordinate unconscious father-image rather than claiming his own space and sitting in his own seat.

Extrapolating from the psychoanalytic interpretation of Haitzmann's case, I conjecture that Freud would also have identified 'demonologically neurotic' strategies in the possession at Loudun. The death of the father confessor Moussaut was concurrent with the first appearances of the mournful phantom figure to Sister Marthe, and I think Freud would attribute the 'uncanny' quality of her psychological experiences of grieving to the reviving of repressed infantile complexes, to their furtive power, and to a conflict of judgement about what was real or not real, about what was good or evil (Freud, 1919). Furthermore, as in the case of Nicole Obry at Laon, what Freud would regard as the necessary and healthy incorporation or internalization of images of a mourned loved one (in this case, a father substitute) was transposed by the discourse of the Church into possession by a demon. At the same time, Sister Marthe's possession by the image of the phantom father-turned-devil neces-sitated the increased ministering and protective presence of the replacement father confessor Mignon, providing what Freud called a secondary gain to her illness.

Unlike Freud, who never referred to the possessions at Loudun, Jung did mention them – but only once, in a definition of demonism that he prepared upon request in 1945 for the publishers of the *Schweizer Lexikon*:

> Demonism (synonymous with daemonomania = possession) denotes a peculiar state of mind characterized by the fact that certain psychic contents, the so-called complexes, take over the control of the total personality in place of the ego, at least temporarily, to such a degree that the free will of the ego is suspended. In certain of these states ego-consciousness is present, in others it is eclipsed. Demonism is a primordial psychic phenomenon and frequently occurs under primitive conditions (Good descriptions in the New Testament, Luke 4:34, Mark 1:23, 5:2, etc.). The phenomenon of demonism is not always spon-taneous, but can also be deliberately induced as a 'trance', for instance in shamanism, spiritualism, etc. . . . Medically, demonism belongs partly to the sphere of the psychogenic neuroses, partly to that of schizophrenia.
>
> Demonism can also be epidemic. One of the most celebrated epi-demics of the Middle Ages was the possession of the Ursulines of London [*sic*], 1632. The epidemic form includes the induced collective psychoses of a religious or political nature, such as those of the twen-tieth century.
>
> (Jung, 1945c, para. 1473–1474)

Jung used his theory of complexes to account for the phenomena of possession. For Jung, a feeling-toned complex is an image to which a highly charged affect is attached and which is incompatible with the habitual attitude of the ego. Often attributable to a trauma that splits off a bit of the psyche or to a moral conflict in which a subject finds it impossible to affirm the whole of his or her being, a complex is a splinter psyche that behaves with a remarkable degree of autonomy and coherence, like an animated foreign body in the sphere of consciousness, and it can override will or volition and block memory. In a conflict with an unconscious complex, the individual ego is relatively powerless. In his essay 'A Review of the Complex Theory', Jung explicitly described possession as 'a momentary and unconscious alteration of personality known as identification with the complex', although the opposing phrase 'assimilation of the ego by the complex' could just as appropriately convey the action (Jung, 1934a, para. 204).

Jung (1939b) credited Freud with the first illustrative case to support a theory that 'coincided with the medieval view once we substitute a psychological formula for the "demon" of priestly fantasy.' Jung acknowledged Freud's debt to Charcot, who described hysterical symptoms as ideas 'taking possession of the brain', and to Janet, who elaborated Charcot's theory of possession and obsession in his *Névroses et idées fixes*. But, unlike the 'rationalistic Janet', Jung argues:

> Freud and Breuer did not gloss over the significant analogy with possession, but rather, following the medieval theory, hunted up the factor causing the possession in order, as it were, to exorcise the evil spirit, they being the first to discover that the pathogenic 'ideas' were memories of certain events which they called 'traumatic'.
>
> (Jung, 1939b, para. 62)

Freud realized that the symptom-producing ideas were rooted in unconscious affects which had to be brought to consciousness and re-experienced so the symptoms could be relieved.

At the same time, Jung argued that psychoanalytic theory does not adequately convey the power and the positive potential of these symptom-producing ideas. In Jung's view, Freud wanted to unmake as illusion

> what the 'absurd superstition' of the past took to be a devilish incubus, to whip away the disguises worn by the evil spirit and turn him back into a harmless poodle – in a word, reduce him to a 'psychological formula'.
>
> (Jung, 1939b, para. 71)

Referring to his own favourite myth of Faust and the black poodle, an incarnation of Mephistopheles, Jung (1920) claimed that psychoanalytic theory is reductionist, and, he argued, his own theory contributes to and corrects psychoanalytic theory by emphasizing the inherent ambiguity of complexes that the ego experiences as negative:

> Spirits are not under all circumstances dangerous and harmful. They can, when translated into ideas, also have beneficial effects. A well-known example of this transformation of a content of the collective unconscious into communicable language is the miracle of Pentecost.
>
> (Jung, 1920, para. 596)

How might Jung have added to Freud's commentary on the case of Haitzmann's possession? Freud interpreted the breasts on the devil as signifying either the nurturing aspect of the lost father or the projection of the feminine attitude adopted by the submissive son, and he portrayed the neurotic strategy adopted by Haitzmann as rendering him vulnerable to the negative characteristic of the feminine, to the lack of a penis, that is to say, to castration. Freud considered this interpretation supported by two facts: Haitzmann travelled some distance for his exorcisms because he was convinced that only the power of the Holy Mother of God of Mariazell could help him, and he delivered himself from his pact with the devil on the day of her nativity. Jung might have argued that the gender ambiguity of the devil suggests a mercurial rather than castrating role for the hermaphroditic father figure, and that the nine-year gestation period and the regression during the crisis towards the Mother held the potential for a creative synthesis of the neurotic split. Still, I suspect Jung would agree with Freud that Haitzmann's decision to abandon his vocation as a painter and subjugate himself to holy orders suggests that he did not find sufficient strength or coherence within himself, not because taking orders was necessarily an evasion, but because, as Freud himself notes, shortly after entering the monastery, Haitzmann apparently took to drink.

Although Freud wrote about group psychology, he did not include any hypothesis about collective factors in the case of Haitzmann's demonological neurosis. Significantly, on the other hand, Jung's definition of demonism does include a collective component. For Jung, the possession at Loudun was an epidemic comparable to what he called the 'induced collective psychoses' of the twentieth century, and as a result, an interpretation of possession in an individual such as Jeanne des Anges should take into account not only the possibility of trauma and the activation of repressed contents in the personal unconscious but also the effects of the collective unconscious. In other words, Jung would argue, Jeanne des Anges's demonological neurosis psychically infected the other Ursulines, polarized Loudun, and drew crowds from across Europe because her possession articulated both a personal repressed conflict and a collective dilemma in which the collective unconscious was active. The tensions between Catholic and Huguenot factions in the town and the container for these effected by the Edict of Nantes; the practice of chastity in Catholic religious orders and the parallel cult of Eros in secular society; the destruction of the walls of Loudun and the decree by Louis XIII to build a city called Richelieu twenty kilometres away; Descartes's decision not to publish his epistemology for fear of the Inquisition – all these social and political phenomena can be reread psychodynamically as 'surface' events concurrent with an eruption from the collective unconscious of contents experienced as a 'collective psychosis'.

Curiously, in his definition of demonism, Jung referred neither to evil nor to his theory of the shadow, an inferior part of the individual personality and of society that can be integrated only to the extent that it can be realized and suffered. Elsewhere, in connection with evil, Jung said that, while conscious constructs tend towards groups of three, natural totalities form fours, the implication being that any teleological movement towards wholeness would require the inclusion of a fourth element which consciousness is inclined to abhor or reject. Thus, he observed, 'In the case of the religious triad the Fourth is obviously the devil, a metaphysical figure missing in the Trinity' (Jung, 1973, Vol. 1, p. 412). Certainly, with regard to the devils at Loudun, Jung's shadow theory would support Huxley's distinction between the orthodox exorcists who sought to repress and expel evil from the bodies of the Ursulines, with catastrophic results for both the collective and themselves, and Surin, who attempted a confrontation with that evil from inside himself, wrestling with the Mother Superior's Behemoth at the base of his own belly.

Jung's short definition of demonism does not mention 'good possession', but this idea may be implied in his references to trance, shamanism, and spiritualism. Jung would not have been surprised by the observation that almost the only means for a seventeenth-century French woman to achieve a public voice was through a good possession disguised as, or combined with, a demonic one; at the core of his medical dissertation on spiritualism is the argument that the medium Fräulein SW's trance states provided opportunities in which a healthy future personality could gain momentary expression (Jung, 1902). Consequently, because these aspects of Jung's theory parallel, to some extent, anthropological reports about possession cults that differentiate between spirits that must be exorcised and those with which one must enter a contractual relationship or even a marriage (see Chapter 2), Jung might well have looked for a teleological or prospective component in the fantasies of Jeanne des Anges.

Of course, Freud and Jung were addressing, not seventeenth-century, but twentieth-century problems in which psychological disturbances usually manifested in organic terms rather than in terms of gods and demons. Nevertheless, Jung defined demonism in the present tense and set the possession at Loudun in parallel with contemporary events. In a 1945 essay, he made this comparison even more explicit:

> Psychology has discovered where those demons, which in earlier ages dominated nature and man's destiny, are actually domiciled, and, what is

more, that they are none the worse for enlightenment. On the contrary, they are as sprightly as ever, and their activity has even extended its scope so much that they can now get their own back on all the achievements of the human mind. We know today that in the unconscious of every individual there are instinctive propensities or psychic systems charged with considerable tension. When they are helped in one way or another to break through into consciousness, and the latter has no opportunity to intercept them in higher forms, they sweep everything before them like a torrent and turn men into creatures for whom the word 'beast' is still too good a name. They can then only be called 'devils'. To evoke such phenomena in the masses all that is needed is a few possessed persons, or only one. Possession, though old-fashioned, has by no means become obsolete; only the name has changed. Formerly they spoke of 'evil spirits', now we call them 'neuroses' or 'unconscious complexes'. Here as everywhere the name makes no difference. The fact remains that a small unconscious cause is enough to wreck a man's fate, to shatter a family, and to continue working down the generations like the curse of the Atrides. If this unconscious disposition should happen to be one which is common to the great majority of the nation, then a single one of these complex-ridden individuals, who at the same time sets himself up as a megaphone, is enough to precipitate a catastrophe.

(Jung, 1945a, para. 1374)

Jung thus argued against historical distancing from the horrific events at Loudun. His use of the words 'primitive' and 'primordial' to account for the phenomena of demons often leaves him vulnerable to charges of primitivism when he discusses other cultures, but here he applied the words to twentieth-century Western European culture in order to contradict its rational bias, as he had explained eleven years earlier:

I use the term 'primitive' in the sense of 'primordial' and . . . I do not imply any kind of value judgement. Also when I speak of a 'vestige' of a primitive state, I do not necessarily mean that this state will sooner or later come to an end. On the contrary, I see no reason why it should not endure as long as humanity lasts. So far, at any rate, it has not changed very much, and with the World War and its aftermath there has even been a considerable increase in its strength. I am therefore inclined to think that autonomous complexes are among the normal phenomena of life and that they make up the structure of the unconscious psyche.

(Jung, 1934a, para. 218)

Implicit in Jung's definition of demonism is his argument that, contradictory as it may seem, in order to address contemporary mental disorders cast in the secularized, demotic language of 'mind', the practice of psychotherapy needs to take into account a religious function in the experience of healing (see Chapter 5). Indeed, and perhaps not surprisingly, the Zurich editors of the *Schweizer Lexikon* used only the first sentence of his definition of demonism and the citations and cut the rest.

Foucault and Certeau: structuralist and Lacanian commentaries

In the early 1960s, Michel Foucault noted that the shift from the two-sided structure of earlier witchcraft and sorcery trials to the three-sided public exorcisms of the Ursulines at Loudun, with the implicit presence of the sorcerer as a third element, significantly coincided with the impulse to present the conflict differently, to stage it (Foucault, 1961/1965). In fact, public exorcisms were not typical in the Middle Ages; not until the late sixteenth and early seventeenth centuries did exorcism combine public spectacle and ritual action in response to demonic possession (Koopmans, 1997). For Foucault, theatre is synonymous with a problematic which is publicly performed. Seventeenth-century French society, he said, could no longer endure the splitting of God the Father by the Wars of Religion; they evaded or abdicated this conflict by shifting their projection of paternal power from the Godhead onto the head of state, Louis XIII, and Cardinal Richelieu co-opted this power for his own purposes. The exorcisms at Loudun repeatedly dramatized to audiences from across Europe, over a period of six years, the contemporary collective conflicts in religion, medicine, and politics.

In 1970, Michel de Certeau concurred with Foucault's structuralist hypothesis. He supported Foucault's view of the exorcisms as the enactment of a problematic which was then edited and re-enacted repeatedly, the drama eventually prefiguring or anticipating the direction in which French society as a whole would move, including the movement towards a Cartesian epistemology with its pre-Enlightenment demotion of sensation and imagination. However, in 'Language Altered: The Sorcerer's Speech', an important essay published in 1975, Certeau revised this position by describing the staged exorcisms as a theatricalized collective encounter with the 'Other'. The place from which Jeanne des Anges and the Ursulines spoke, he said, is indeterminate, not only feminine, not only somatic, but also a 'somewhere else' that revels in its power to elude and evade. The exorcists and the physicians responded with a patriarchal power play: naming and confining the women and this Other to a discourse circumscribed by their theological and medical knowledge.

Certeau's argument portrayed the priests and doctors as analysts opposing a patient's escape into the signified because that escape represented not only a frightening exile for the nuns from shared language but also a betrayal by all concerned of the linguistic map upon which the social order was organized. Earlier, Certeau presented Jeanne des Anges's symptoms as a demoniacal textbook case; five years later, he emphasized the gap between what the Mother Superior may have said and what the priests recorded in the trial documents in accordance with the demonological treatises. Arguing against a feminist assumption that the possessed nun's discourse exists beneath an overlay of patriarchal interpretations, Certeau claimed that what she said during the exorcisms cannot be established as a discourse of the Other, opposed to and buried under the discourses of religious or medical knowledge. Rather, what she said is 'a transgression that is not a discourse' (Certeau, 1975, p. 249).

For Certeau, regardless of the layers of commentary which frame it – the trial records, the autobiography in which she objectified her own experiences in language that accorded with both orthodox demoniacal treatises and hagiographical understandings of possession, the eye-witness accounts of her grand tour – the Other that Jeanne des Anges embodied can never cease to be *diabolically* Other. To defend this interpretation, he referred to Freud's notion of the 'uncanny', with its emphasis on the furtive power of repressed contents, and to the pressure of instinct (*Drang*), described in *Psychopathology of Everyday Life*, that distorts or effaces names. Even more useful for his argument was Lacan's notion of the *réel*: 'that before which the imaginary falters, that over which the symbolic stumbles, that which is refractory, resistant' (Lacan, 1966, pp. ix–x).

Ferber (2004) opposed Certeau's Lacanian interpretation, arguing that Jeanne des Anges did not situate herself as outside and 'other' but endorsed, amplified and partook of the power of the exorcists. Like Huxley, Ferber characterized Jeanne des Anges as eventually employing Surin's discourse of hagiography in order to position herself inside an approved system of meaning. But by concluding that demonic power is paradoxically both central and peripheral to Christian discourse, in that the purpose of Christian discourse is to expel the very element which defines its moral universe, Ferber (2004, p. 146) seemed to align herself, perhaps unwittingly, with Certeau's Lacanian argument.

Certeau compared the exorcisms at Loudun to psychiatric assessments which can fragment a 'mad' person's discourse according to diagnostic classifications. He described how an interned 'mad' patient's discourse levels off, how the idiosyncrasies dwindle as speech conforms increasingly to the code which the hospital provides, but also how the spaces or silences which mark or signify what has been eliminated are inherent in the medical discourse and the therapeutic process. Certeau's career culminated in the publication of *The Mystic Fable* (1982), in which he argued for an unspoken dimension in seventeenth-century mysticism, a '*je ne sais quoi*' that alters the discourse of theology with a space rather than with a different hagiographic, medical or legal discourse. In the spaces between the established languages of the exorcists, physicians and lawyers at Loudun, Certeau found evidence for his hypothesis of a '*je ne sais quoi*' as furtive as Freud's 'uncanny' and as powerfully raw as Lacan's *réel*. Employing another Lacanian term, Certeau said that the demons 'slipped' about within the bodies of the Ursulines as if to avoid classification, mocking their interlocutors, changing names. He agreed with Foucault: the questions evoked by the presence of this Other in the voices and bodies of the nuns were intolerable, they undermined social discourse, and they precipitated and provoked a collective splitting in which the negative power of God as patriarchal progenitor was projected onto the libertine Grandier as scapegoat while Louis XIII and Cardinal Richelieu recuperated the positive power. Surin, Certeau's hero, wrestled with these questions for the rest of his melancholic life. The Enlightenment let these questions drop altogether, but Freud's concept of the 'uncanny' and Lacan's concept of *réel* picked them up again for twentieth-century psychology and philosophy, and Certeau, with his fascination for seventeenth-century mysticism, resurrected them for postmodernism.

Otherness and the irreducible

For nearly four centuries, the possession at Loudun has provoked numerous political, religious, and social interpretations, all of which can be useful from a psychological perspective. For example, they show how a psychological problem can be distorted or appropriated. The debate was first seen as religious, between Catholics and Huguenots. The exorcisms affirmed the efficacy of Catholic ritual and refuted the claims of the reformed religions, but they failed to address the individual psychological suffering of the Ursulines – the grief of Sister Marthe, the erotic problem of Jeanne des Anges – to say nothing of the anguish of Grandier, the scapegoat.

Even in its own time, in contradiction to the set texts and the criteria of religious dogma, the language of possession was fluid. Theological language divided possession into 'genuine' (i.e., demonic) and 'counterfeit' (i.e., deliberate, willed, with a purpose). Medical arguments had played a pivotal role in the earlier case of Marthe Brossier, introducing a third possibility, a clinical diagnosis of melancholia, but they did not alter the increasingly polarized positions at Loudun. In the eighteenth century, the diagnosis of hysteria entered the literature, although by that time the diagnostic criteria had changed and shortness of breath, for instance, was no longer mandatory. Neither the accepted demonological language of the exorcists nor the official medical language of the doctors allowed for the elusive medieval notion of *fantasmata*. Marc Duncan attempted to introduce the diagnostic idea of possession by an infected or sick imagination into the Loudun debate, but the court rejected his argument for extraneous political reasons.

Possession enacts radical differences in social position created by unconscious power. The possessed demonstrate supernatural physical strength, knowledge of foreign languages, and foresight or telepathy, but in order to have access to these powers, they must be unconscious. Both opponents – the exorcists and the physicians – remain conscious, and central to their powers is the diagnostic act. The identification, the naming of the possessing spirit or the disease, begins a process that is supposed to liberate possessed individuals from a state of isolation and unconsciousness and integrate them back into a culturally accepted network of signs or signifiers. This did not happen at Loudun. Even the legal discourse failed, perhaps, as Foucault and others have argued, because the religious and legal rituals were co-opted for the purposes of the state. The exorcisms continued for another four years after the conviction and execution of the alleged sorcerer.

In psychosocial terms, possession is a collective phenomenon. The public staging of the exorcisms at Loudun functioned as repeated enactments of a problematic. Certeau argued:

> one of the definitions of possession is to be that unstable moment, to symbolize that moment in a language that gives it an expression *at once archaic and new,* and in the chemical sense of the term, thus to 'precipitate' a process in which positions are staked out.
>
> (Certeau, 1970, p. 27, italics mine)

In this sense, a Vichian argument would define the possession at Loudun as a collective enactment of a *ricorsi* (see Chapter 4) which may prove to be either destructively regressive or positively providential, or of a process which Gaston Bachelard would identify as an epistemological break *in potentia* (see Chapter 3). Sadly, at Loudun, the outcome of the performances symbolically prefigured an approaching crisis and schism in France: the revocation of the Edict of Nantes, the subsequent sanctioned persecution of the Huguenots, the splitting of a projection of an ambivalent Godhead which could no longer be collectively maintained, and the political co-opting of that projection. In other words, within the 'theatre' of Loudun and Richelieu is presaged what, in his definition of demonism, Jung called an 'induced collective psychosis'.

A psychological reading of possession identifies a personal and a collective component in the individual's experience of being paradoxically disempowered and yet 'filled with spirit'. Jeanne des Anges's experiences of possession expressed both an individual and a collective dilemma. Her body was a battlefield upon which, for seven years, war was waged, not only between her ego identity as prioress and an unconscious erotic Other, but also between her celibate life and the profane cult of Eros. Jeanne des Anges's public exorcisms exacerbated this conflict, bringing it into the open without healing it. Surin introduced two elements that radically altered her suffering. He offered a vocabulary of mysticism and hagiography which included a permissible discourse of eroticism, and he enacted 'taking on himself' the possession. Like a shamanistic wounded healer, Surin attempted to identify with Jeanne des Anges's suffering while paradoxically maintaining his identity as exorcist. He did not seek to cast out or psychologically repress the demon inside her but confronted it from within himself.

An etymological reading of possession locates an occupying entity exercising power over the sufferer as if it were tyrannically sitting in the sufferer's seat, claiming his or her chair. Freud's notion of demonological neurosis emphasized the idea of evasion, of possession as the ego's abdication of its seat: the individual employs a defensive strategy against difficult experiences such as grief or thwarted sexual desire and subsequently lives a diabolic parody of responsible adult life. Likewise, Jung's discourse emphasized the power of complexes which assimilate the ego and render a life 'provisional'. But Jung also recommended psychological discernment when he argued that the archetype at the core of the complex carries negative and positive qualities for psychic equilibrium. Therefore, psychodynamically, the exorcists and doctors only opposed the negating tyranny of the symptoms of possession, whereas Surin shifted the opposition both by confronting the negative aspect of the archetype of Eros in Jeanne des Anges and by buttressing her embattled ego, allowing her to adopt a potentially positive teleological point of view in her suffering.

Possession as a psychological phenomenon can be mapped by various discourses but, paradoxically, is best evoked in discursive 'spaces'. The debate about Loudun continues, perhaps because the signifier has no natural connection to the signified (Saussure, 1916/2006). Even when the possessed speak the language which is imposed upon them by the exorcists and doctors, their discourse bears the trace – the 'wound' – of the Other from which they seek distance. This is similar to the argument that the innumerable changes in the criteria for identifying 'hysteria' reflect not only the shifting nature of signifiers but, more importantly, the furtive quality of the image of hysteria itself, of the 'womb that walks' in both women and men (Micklem, 1996). This may be why Jung praised Freud's analogical argument about medieval demons and repressed ideas but criticized his psychoanalytic signifiers as reductionist. Similarly, addressing the dilemma of how to speak about a so-called ineffable experience, Certeau found Freud's notion of the 'uncanny' and Lacan's *réel* useful but rejected Jung's 'collective unconscious' as too *réductible* (Dosse, 2002).

To evaluate the effectiveness of any discourse about possession, including Jung's concept of possession (and even, for that matter, the attempt to write about Jung's concept) – and this is surely Certeau's most important and unorthodox contribution to our postmodern notion of 'otherness' – one criterion is to ask to what extent it allows for, rather than contradicts, these irreducible irrational spaces. Until the Reformation and beyond, the Catholic Church associated the suffering attributed to possession with demonism; it demonized the experience of possession and addressed the suffering with the rituals of exorcism. Since the mid twentieth century, Jung's psychological definition of demonism has thrown a different light on the subject in two ways: by differentiating between the individual and social components of a 'demoniacal neurosis' or an 'induced collective psychosis', and by acknowledging a potential prospective function inherent in the suffering of 'being unseated' psychologically by 'otherness'. If it can be understood as counter-rational, Jung's concept of possession, secular as it is, contributes an irreducible new view to the religious historical case of the possessions at Loudun.

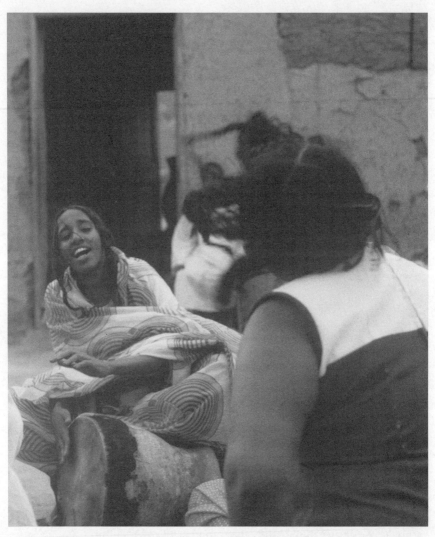

Figure 2.1 The incarnation of a *zar* spirit, invoked by drumming and the singing of its musical thread, Hofriyat, northern Sudan, 1976. Published with permission of Dr. Janice Boddy.

Chapter 2

The anthropology of possession
Studying the other

> Modern thought and experience have taught us to be sensitive to what is involved in representation, in studying the Other, in racial thinking, in unthinking and uncritical acceptance of authority and authoritative ideas, in the socio-political role of intellectuals, in the great value of a skeptical critical consciousness. Perhaps if we remember that the study of human experience usually has an ethical, to say nothing of a political, consequence in either the best or worst sense, we will not be indifferent to what we do as scholars.
>
> (Edward Said, *Orientalism*, p. 327)

> Anthropology is a science of mutual surprise.
> (Anne Carson, 'The Anthropology of Water', p. 117)

Jung's psychological concept of possession is located in the religious context and the historical continuum of the Loudun literature. An equally important source of his concept was his interest in anthropology. Examining this interest poses difficulties, however, because Jung uses anthropological research in modernist ways that are unacceptable when judged according to today's ethical standards and relativism. Nevertheless, fortunately, Jung (and Jungians, let us hope) can demonstrate ethically nuanced responses to the problems of how a Westerner might study the resources of other cultures.

Anthropologists investigate and interpret a conglomerate of phenomena to which they apply the word 'possession'. How best to benefit from this vast literature in order to refine an understanding of Jung's concept? It seems useful to look at examples of what ethnographers report as 'possessions' from other cultures and examine some of the strategies these cultures employ when they perceive their possessed members as suffering. My intention is to respect anthropology's hard-won relativism; rather than misusing these examples to formulate comparatively a universalist theory about 'possession', I have collected images from contemporary anthropological research about other cultures to evaluate and enrich the Jungian concept of possession.

Can Jungian theorizing possibly enrich anthropology? At least since the publication of Irving Hallowell's seminal *Culture and Experience* (1955), anthropologists have expressed interest in a rapprochement with psychology. However, many have deliberated about how to describe possession in non-Western settings without resorting to psychological description; they argue (quite rightly) that inherent within psychological language is a tendency to objectify and pathologize. They attempt to report without pathologizing what the cultures they are studying do not themselves pathologize. Jung also attempted to describe the psyche and, specifically, the experience of possession in terms of consciousness, identity, and the experience of an Other without pathologizing these experiences, and I believe that Jung can offer anthropologists a surprisingly useful conceptual bridge.

Jung's selective reading of anthropology

Anthropology was conceived as a formal study of human beings in the eighteenth century, and early on, it set out a generalizing theory that proposed a psychic unity of humankind. The argument of most nineteenth-century anthropologists was evolutionary and unilinear (Stocking, 1974). The German ethnologist Adolf Bastian proposed to compare 'ethnic thoughts' (*Völkergedanken*) shaped by local geography and history in order to arrive at underlying psychological kernels or 'elementary thoughts' (*Elementargedanken*) which were universal and intrapsychic in origin. His contemporary, the English anthropologist Edward Tylor, also emphasized the physical and psychological unity of all human beings and a progressive evolutionary relationship between primitive and modern cultures. He identified the earliest form of religious belief in all cultures as 'animism', a belief in spiritual beings that animate or possess animals, plants, and objects. This belief, he thought, was arrived at by primitive attempts to explain the difference between a living body and a corpse, as well as the separation of soul and body in dreams. Tylor was praised for tracing animism 'from the lower races up to the religious beliefs of the highest races ... [thus demonstrating] the survival of rudiments of old customs'. Jung found both Bastian's theory of elementary thoughts and Tylor's evolutionary argument appealing, and he quoted both as precursors of his own theory of archetypes and the collective unconscious (Jung, 1938, para. 89; 1948, para. 119).

A generation later, the German-born American anthropologist Franz Boas criticized attempts to organize anthropology's cultural investigations around comparisons in order to advance a theory of orthogenesis. He objected, not to the Darwinian theory of evolution itself, but to orthogenetic misreadings of Charles Darwin's works. These misreadings characterized all societies as progressing through the same stages in the same sequence, from lower to higher; they resemble the popular misconception that Darwin said human beings are descended from chimpanzees, when in fact Darwin argued that chimpanzees and humans are equally evolved. Boas first investigated the sense perception of the Inuit on Baffin Island – for example, how the Inuit (as Other) perceived the colour of ice and seawater – but he was less inclined than most to place his investigations in the service of an argument that depicted the Inuit as living in a stage of development through which the primitive ancestors of Europeans had already progressed. Instead, Boas increasingly emphasized the value of describing individual cultures as integrated isolates, without using comparison to develop hierarchies.

Boas's paper 'Psychological Problems in Anthropology', read at the Clark University Conference in 1909, challenged orthogenetic evolutionism by differentiating between mental characteristics based on race and cultural characteristics attributable to 'the habitual reactions of the society to which the individual in question belongs' (Boas, 1910). In this address, Boas perhaps uncomfortably straddled his mentor Bastian's 'elementary thoughts' and his own cultural relativism. On the one hand, in this paper Boas can be seen as a physical anthropologist, acknowledging his interest in the evolutionary changes in mental capacities such as sense perception; on the other hand, he can be seen as a cultural anthropologist, forging a crucial set of distinctions between race and ethnicity, 'between mental endowment and mental characteristics attributable to the habitual reactions of a society' (Shore, 1996, p. 21). But did Boas merely disengage culture from mind in an intellectual sleight of hand, with the result that he could conceive of culture as the 'contents of mind' rather than as a defining 'attribute of mind'? If the study of culture could be dissociated from the study of mind, Boas seems to say, then anthropology could declare its independence from psychology.

Boas's 1909 Clark University address was a moment of parting between psychoanalysis and anthropology. By critiquing the comparative method which Freud and Jung, both participants at the same Clark University Conference, applied to their readings of ethnographical research, Boas undermined the strategy of employing anthropological observations as proof that psychoanalytic principles are transhistorical and universal (Shamdasani, 2003, p. 277). His argument effectively subverted Freud and Jung's efforts to enlist anthropology to legitimize psychoanalysis as a positivist science.

In this light, it is perhaps not surprising to note how often Jung emphasized the rich parallelism between the phenomenology of the unconscious investigated by psychologists, psychiatrists and psychotherapists and the findings of anthropology (Jung, 1941a, para. 318), and yet how seldom he referred to Boas himself. In a series of lectures given at Fordham University in 1912, Jung mentioned in passing Boas's early work on North American Indian sagas, published in 1895. In two articles (Jung, 1930, 1931d), writing about the effects of environment on physical features as well as psychology, Jung referred to Boas's physical anthropological research concerning the average

Figure 2.2 Franz Boas, Sigmund Freud, and Carl Gustav Jung at the 1909 Psychology far left; Freud is fourth from the right, and Jung is third from the right. Published

cranial size of American immigrants; Boas's data showed, for instance, that children born within ten years of their mothers' arrival in the United States differed significantly in average cranial size from children born more than ten years after their mothers' arrival. But Jung never referred to *The Mind of Primitive Man* (1911), arguably Boas's most important book, in which he definitively divorced anthropology from the notion of unilinear evolution from simple to complex cultural forms.

Conference Group at Clark University, the parting of the ways. Boas is in the front row, with permission of Clark University Archives.

A cross-cultural psychology of inner experience

Although Jung travelled extensively, observed rites and ceremonies, and studiously compared mythologies and dreams of 'primitives', he over-relied on a few early anthropological writers, including Bastian and Tylor, and his arguments resembled theirs. He posited that primitive peoples function like primordial peoples or like children; civilized adults develop out of a primitive psychology of collective projection into individuated beings, but primitive peoples do not. Even though Jung was well aware of the ideas Franz Boas articulated in his 1909 Clark lecture, he clung to his position. In 1913, he wrote: 'Primitive people and animals have nothing like that capacity for reviving memories of unique impressions which we find among civilized people' (Jung, 1913, para. 403), and in 1916, still a primitivist, he maintained that 'primitive people, especially, are very much bound to their infantility' (Jung, 1916a, para. 564).

However, Jung began to change his mind. Freud's method, articulated in his 1913 book *Totem and Taboo*, came to seem to Jung like appropriation of ethnographical research in the service of an already existing theory. 'My method was a comparative one', he said later.

> I have reason to believe the latter [i.e., a comparative method rather than the application to an existing theory] yields better results. The main reason is that our new psychology is in no way advanced enough to present a theory of the mind that would have universal application.
>
> (Jung, 1931b, para. 1298)

Freud seems to have been a shadow or scapegoat onto which Jung could project his own misuse of anthropology and thus recognize its negative result. By portraying Freud as over-identified with positivist science, Jung differentiated himself from it; he showed both his desire for such a science and his resignation to a more relativist and subjective position (Ellenberger, 1970). In 1921, he argued in *Psychological Types* that Freud and Adler were necessarily constructing subjective psychologies that could contribute to the cumulative possibility of an objective psychology. This argument implies that, although Jung's own research was inherently subjective, he thought it nevertheless deserved the status that modern science granted to objectivity (Samuels et al., 1986, p. 112).

In 1929, Jung articulated the problem inherent in his own universalist argument in terms of a dichotomy between the psychologies of West and East: 'Western consciousness is by no means consciousness in general', he said. 'It is rather a historically conditioned and geographically confined dimension, which represents only a part of mankind' (Jung, 1929, para. 84). This awareness led him to qualify and sometimes cautiously contextualize his psychological commentaries on texts from India, China, Tibet, and Japan. In a 1932 seminar and a 1936 essay on the psychology of Kundalini yoga, he acknowledged the limitations of his European perspective. His essay, published in the journal *Prabuddha Bharata*, declared that a contextualized consciousness is fundamental to his position in this difficult matter:

> I will remain silent on the subject of what yoga means for India, because I cannot presume to judge something I do not know from personal experience. I can, however, say something about what it means for the West.
>
> (Jung, 1936, para. 866)

Through his reading about and inquiry into the 'precivilized' and 'prelogical' behaviour of 'primitive' peoples, Jung was investigating subjectively his own unconscious and the cultural unconscious of the Western European:

> In travelling to Africa to find a psychic observation post outside the sphere of the European, I unconsciously wanted to find that part of my personality which had become invisible under the influence and pressure of being European. This part stands in unconscious opposition to myself, and indeed I attempt to repress it. In keeping with its nature, it wishes to make me unconscious (force me under water) so as to kill me; but my aim is, through insight, to make it more conscious, so that we can find a common *modus vivendi*.
>
> (Jung, 1962, p. 244)

Jung's attempts in Africa to dislocate himself from the European sphere of influence were unsuccessful (Burleson, 2005), but describing these travels later in his life, Jung explained that his fear of 'going black' was not a fear of the peoples he met in Africa so much as of the possibility of succumbing to the primordial power of his own autonomous complexes. His idea that mass movements and totalitarianism are peculiarly Western phenomena seems to reinforce this interpretation of his fear. Even more important, his early studies about collective projection in so-called primitive psychology led to his more scholarly and sophisticated interpretation of alchemy. This had not been a pseudo-science, he concluded, but a way for the individual to conceptualize and map the emergence of consciousness by projecting intra-psychic processes onto matter (Samuels et al., 1986, p. 112).

Jung's life and work have been perceptively summed up as 'a progression of reformulations of the problematic of the Other' (Papadopoulos, 1991, p. 88). Some of his best theorizing about the Other arose from his psychotherapeutic role, rather than the other way round (see Chapter 5). In a 1932 seminar and in an essay published in 1937, he presented case material concerning a twenty-five-year-old patient born in the Dutch East Indies of European parents and raised by an Indonesian nurse, with whom she spoke Malay. As a Swiss analyst working with fantasies and dreams steeped in Indonesian motifs, Jung described his work with this woman as 'a saga of blunders, hesitations, doubts, gropings in the dark, and false clues which in the end took a favourable turn' (Jung, 1937, para. 564). He took advantage of his predicament by noting potentially meaningful correlations between the progressive localization of her symptoms and his 1919 readings about the chakra system of Kundalini yoga. Jung was convinced that a little shared information about the Tantric map eventually helped his patient to integrate the Indonesian-based aspect of herself which she first experienced as a child with her Malay nurse and which conflicted with her adult European consciousness.

Jung hypothesized that a discipline such as Kundalini yoga initiates inner processes that change the personality. These might be universal and archetypal, he thought, even though the map of the psyche offered by that discipline is culturally specific, and he wondered to what extent the experiences of psychoanalytic psychotherapy sparked a similar psychological process in his client. I myself wonder whether introducing the images of the chakras as a third language, utterly foreign and Other to both sides of the patient's European–Malay inner conflict, provided a space within which she could manoeuvre, within which she could bridge the opposing elements of her personality. Although Jung's theory of archetypes seems to proffer a naive patriarchal universalism supported by a primitivist argument, the notes of his 1932 seminar on Kundalini yoga demonstrate that he was also asking how to develop 'a cross-cultural comparative psychology of inner experience' (Shamdasani, 1996, p. xxix).

Anthropological reporting about possession in non-Western settings

Possession: Demonical and Other, T. K. Oesterreich's survey of anthropological literature on possession, was first published in 1921 and republished most recently in 2002. Encyclopaedic in the breadth of its coverage, it was an attempt to generate anthropological theories about the universality of possession. Oesterreich collected and ordered reports of all the methods he could find for identifying and redressing possession through medicine, autosuggestion, psychological treatment and exorcism in ancient Egypt and Greece, in the early Christian period, through the Middle Ages and into modern times, and in contexts other than those fundamental to the Western European tradition. Although he tried to construct a theory out of this massive compilation, in the end, the collector overwhelmed the theorist, and he managed only to categorize the phenomena of possession into pairs such as 'spontaneous' and 'voluntary', 'somnambulistic' and 'lucid'. He theorized about possession mainly in terms of suggestion and of multiple personalities in the self.

Oesterreich's book is obviously of its time and place, and to appreciate its value, it is as necessary to read beyond attitudes such as anti-Semitism as it is to see beyond Jung's leanings toward evolutionary primitivism. The very richness of Oesterreich's anecdotal material led him into many objectivist pitfalls. Like other social scientists at the time, including psychologists and psychoanalysts, he indiscriminately lumped together material from shamanism, trance and spiritualism, employing all these to render the irrational and parapsychological ordered and rational. While he admitted that 'civilized' people show a high degree of autosuggestibility under certain circumstances, he portrayed the 'primitive' mind as more vulnerable to possession by means of autosuggestion (Oesterreich, 2002, p. 237). But a few pages later, he contradicted his own supposition by noting that primitive susceptibility to possession is more 'studied', that it entails a kind of deliberate play-acting or theatricality within a frame fixed by custom (ibid., p. 241). In other words, cultures deemed primitive actually know a good deal more about the mechanisms and the expressiveness inherent in the experience of possession than do most Western cultures. Indeed, hinting at Western ignorance and vulnerability (and hubris), Oesterreich said:

> The Christians made their appearance throughout the whole world as exorcists of demons, and exorcism was a very powerful missionary and propagandist weapon. . . . It is interesting that Christianity, engaged in combat with possession, should have professed to have a greater power of overcoming it than exorcists of any other persuasion.
>
> (Oesterreich, 2002, p. 164)

Much of the ensuing debate about possession among anthropologists exists *in potentia* in Oesterreich's survey.

In the 1970s and 1980s, I. M. Lewis, a social anthropologist, and Gananath Obeyesekere, a psychoanalytical anthropologist, developed complementary theories about possession. Lewis's goal was essentialist and objectivist; in 1971, he said that he intended 'to reach conclusions which will be independent of cultural particularities' (Lewis, 1971/1989, p. 135). Out of his comparative approach to ethnographic particulars, he sought to construct an anthropological theory about human nature. He argued that possession and shamanism are two components of ecstatic religion that can best be interpreted from within a structural functionalist framework of delineating power and social status. From this perspective, in oppressive, predominantly patriarchal cultures, possession works as an obliquely aggressive strategy within which disempowered or marginalized individuals, especially women, seek to redress their political subordination. The suffering caused by possession is linked to status deprivation, and possession cults operate as socially motivated manoeuvres which heal, at least in part, by enhancing the social status of sufferers, recasting them in fantasy or belief as humans 'seized by divinity'. As a structural functionalist, Lewis portrayed the compensatory impulse as devious and deliberate, the victims as conferring responsibility on 'forces outside society', and the cults and their members as remaining socially peripheral to the dominant culture (Lewis, 1971, p. 106).

By 1986, however, Lewis had opened his argument to the possibility that possession cults may carry more social status and participants may function less peripherally than he initially supposed. In his conclusions about the compensatory social functioning of possession in a number of cultures, he acknowledged an additional component outside the frame of traditional functionalism. 'I do not believe that social phenomena such as spirit-possession can be explained in terms of psychiatric illness or the malfunctioning of the individual psyche', he said.

> [Still] my approach to the topic . . . assumes that all significant behaviour has an affective (i.e., 'psychological') dimension. It is not possible to seek to understand spirit-possession in particular, any more than religion in general, without recognizing and acknowledging this.
>
> (Lewis, 1986, p. 74)

As much as he preferred to explain the social component of possession in a structural functionalist framework, he regretted that his own discourse relegated other components, such as individual affect, which he associated with a psychological discourse, to the shadows; they lay outside his frame of reference and the boundaries of his discussion.

Gananath Obeyesekere (1981, 1990) added to Lewis's argument an affective dimension with which to explain possession in terms of the malfunctioning of an individual psyche. Obeyesekere set Sri Lankan possession cults in the framework of Freudian theory, establishing connections between culture and individual motivation. His psychoanalytic arguments present a kind of corollary to Lewis's inclusion of social status as a factor in possession:

> On the basis of the psychological problems arising from the status-role situation of Sinhalese women we could draw certain inferences regarding demonic possession. The existence of hysterical predispositions in the personality make-up of women could lead to a general propensity towards expressing conflict in terms of possession and towards accepting possession as a culturally constituted projective system.
>
> (Obeyesekere, 1970, p. 102)

For both Lewis and Obeyesekere, possession functioned as a cathartic abreaction in response to social inequity, Lewis generalizing the suffering as an extraverted, willed, and oblique power-manoeuvre within a collective setting, Obeyesekere generalizing it as an introverted, hysterical regression within the individual psyche. Both characterized possession as an inferior and feminine strategy; neither validated women in their experiences of possession, nor did either account satisfactorily for men's experience of possession, except by giving men the supposedly feminine attributes of inferiority and hysteria. Freud's discourse was consonant with his goal to establish a positivist science, and this psychoanalytic discourse led Obeyesekere towards Lewis's goal of reviving generalization and positivism in anthropology. However, Obeyesekere did not take the next step: opposing the social functionalist viewpoint that could theorize independent of cultural particularities.

Four recent anthropologists, Bruce Kapferer, Paul Stoller, Edward Schieffelin, and Janice Boddy, are remarkable for their ethnographic descriptions of field encounters with the Other and their critical attitudes towards the theoretical tensions within which they write. Again and again they strengthen and reshape these frameworks to make more space for Otherness.

In the 1980s and 1990s, Bruce Kapferer formulated a theory of possession that rejected Lewis's social functionalism and Obeyesekere's reduction of Sinhalese beliefs and practices to Western psychoanalytic or psychotherapeutic terms. Kapferer focused on Sinhalese demon possession as expressed in the Karava caste community of Galle, Sri Lanka, looking at the aesthetics of healing made real in components of exorcism such as music, dance and comic drama. 'These design/logics and their aesthetization in performance', he said, 'are more than mere expressive cultural frames or idioms for universal psychological processes and resist an unproblematic reduction to such psychology' (Kapferer, 1983/1991, p. xiv). To avoid the reductionist tendency that he found inherent in the analytical categories of ordinary social science, such as those employed by Lewis and Obeyesekere, Kapferer recommended a phenomenological approach 'which aims to account for aspects of demonic attack and its treatment without reducing them to individual psychological explanation, and without depending on possibly unwarranted assumptions about human personality in a cultural situation which is not my own' (Kapferer, 1983/1991, p. 14).

Kapferer identified less with the structuralist approach of Claude Lévi-Strauss, who analysed culture as a 'text' independent of its situated production in practice, and more with Victor Turner. Turner (1969) analysed meaning as it emerges through the concrete articulation of symbols in the performance of ritual; he thought the symbolic action of a ritual affirms a given cosmology and, at the same time, provides creative moments which generate new ways of interpreting reality. Kapferer characterized the possessed Sinhalese person as fragmented, reduced, and alienated (suffering from *tanikama*, meaning 'aloneness') and the demonic realm as 'a false oppressive totalitarian world which refuses possibility'. Within the Sinhalese cosmology, he noted, demons occupy a less powerful place in the vertical hierarchy of being than deities and humans, but demons cause illness by creating the illusion that they can tyrannize and thus disorder human beings. Through the ritual of exorcism, the Sinhalese differentiate between demons and deities, who also have the power of generating illusions but do so only for some ultimately edifying purpose. Kapferer saw ritual as holistic and its liminal space as paradoxical in order to argue that Sinhalese exorcism publicly affirms the given cosmological structure and at the same time presents the suffering individual with an opening into the possible:

> The demon basket is taken by the exorcist and passed three times over the patient's head. The patient is then expected to touch the basket and to wipe his or her face three times, and to place flowers, betel leaves and rice

in the basket. This action . . . is an offering by the patient to the demon but is also an invocation to the gods. It transfers the demonic illness of the patient to the offering basket. As an offering to the demon it signifies the patient's subordination to the demonic will, but it also indicates the freeing of the patient from demonic control and the subordination of the demons to the deities.

(Kapferer, 1991, p. 200)

On the one hand, *yaksabhuta cidyava* as 'exorcism' literally denotes taking the demon out of the possessed patient and transferring it to the basket, from there to the exorcist, and finally to a cock, which is sacrificed. On the other hand, *yaksabhuta vidyava*, 'the science of spirits', enacts the diagnostic problem of differentiating demons from deities and addresses the suffering of the possessed individual by reordering what the demons have disordered:

In the *vilakku pade* the dancers place torches at the demon palace, lighting it up and opening it to view. The demon palace is revealed in its full completed objective meaning as not just the place of demonic disorder, but also as the place in which the deity resides.

(Kapferer, 1991, p. 281)

By 1997, partly in acknowledgement of criticism in a postmodernist argument by Michael Taussig (1987), Kapferer changed his mind somewhat; he had come to see his descriptions of the dynamic of exorcism as 'overordered' and 'totalizing'. He now argued that Sinhalese sorcery does not privilege a hierarchical logic and ordering but celebrates instead an unresolvable dynamic between structure and antistructure in which neither ultimately dominates. He also redirected his phenomenological approach away from the aesthetics of performance and towards a more egalitarian notion of practice (Bourdieu, 1972). Kapferer feared that focusing on exorcism as ritual performance rendered the humanity of the practice exotic and mystical. He also hoped to emphasize how 'sorcery reveals aspects vital to the way human beings constitute themselves and their realities, whether this be in Sri Lanka or elsewhere':

I consider the practices I discuss to have relevance and authority for an understanding of the dynamics of human action beyond Sri Lanka's shores. Through Sinhalese sorcery I address some issues at the heart of the contemporary discipline of anthropology and moreover attempt to demonstrate the significance of sorcery practices in the exploration of larger questions relating to the nature of human consciousness, the embodied character of human mental activities, the constitutive force of the human imaginary, the power of the passions, the dynamics of violence, and so forth.

(Kapferer, 1997, p. xii)

While his analysis remained phenomenological and ethnographic in its approach and its particularity, Kapferer extended his argument beyond his cultural relativist position as anthropologist and addressed 'human nature' in general.

Paul Stoller (1989), too, viewed possession through the frame of its theatricality when he investigated the phenomena among the Songhay of Tillaberi, Niger. Inspired by French scholars such as André Schaeffner, Michel Leiris, Gilbert Rouget (1980), and especially the ethnographic filmmaker Jean Rouch (1954), Stoller focused on possession as a form of cultural theatre. The possession troupe, he thought, functions like a repertory company, the *zima* as stage director and dramaturge, the mediums as actors. The ceremonies are theatrical events in which music induces a fusion between human and spirit, and this fusion is expressed through dance. The theatrical metaphor reinforces the extent to which Songhay possession troupes set into motion compensatory existential reenactments of an ancestral world, replete with historical, sociological and cultural themes. He also noted that, unlike the Songhay ceremonies, Hauka possession theatrics lampoon and critique current political dilemmas, and Sasale possession rituals flauntingly celebrate violation of the Islamic hegemony's moral code. At the same time, Stoller took care to keep the metaphor of theatre from causing the ethnographer to lose sight of the mental and physical suffering of the patient and the mediums; by 1997, he had come to emphasize the importance of understanding the Songhay's 'sensuous epistemology', in which textual interpretation has little importance.

For Stoller, the central concept of Songhay possession was a fusion of the human and the spirit, and the sorcerer must induce and then liberate the mediums from this fused state:

> On the morning of the third day, Adamu Jenitongo organized the *hannandi* (to make clean). . . . First he collected five millet stalks and broke them into numerous small segments. He gave to the mediums the number of millet pieces that corresponded to the number of spirits they each carried. The novice, again dressed in a white robe and shawl, received two millet pieces for the two spirits she was carrying. . . . They followed Adamu Jenitongo out of the compound and walked until they reached a large ant hill at a crossroads outside the village where one road ends and two new ones begin. Adamu Jenitongo ordered everyone to stop. The crossroads, where one road ends and two new ones begin, represents the point where the social and spirit worlds are fused. Adamu Jenitongo positioned the violinist to the east of the ant hill and told the mediums to place themselves behind the musician. The old *zima* moved the novice who was flanked by her initiator and her protector, north of the ant hill. The *zima* placed himself to the west, between the ant hill and the village. [He] recited instructions to the mediums. 'Throw your millet pieces into the ant hill, count to three, and run back to the village. Don't look back.'

All the mediums . . . threw their millet into the ant hill and raced back to [the] compound.

(Stoller, 1989, pp. 67–68)

Fusion of the human and the spirit, Stoller thought, signifies a white-heat meshing of elements foreign to each other, an active seizing, a loss of identity for each of the elements, a loss of soul, an interpenetration. The Songhay sorcerer leads the mediums to the crossroad, to the place where one road becomes two roads, to perform a ritual of separation and cleansing. The mediums fling the millet pieces (which correspond in number to the spirits

Figure 2.3 Adamu Jenitongo, Sohanci sorcerer and Songhay possession priest, in his Tillaberi compound, Niger, 1987. Published with permission of Dr. Paul Stoller.

with whom they have been fused) onto the ant hill at the crossroads and flee from their state of fusion and oneness to the separated and enclosed compound. More recently, stimulated by Paul Connerton's ideas of memory, Stoller has added a more introverted corollary, the fusion of an individual human mind/body with the symbols of the collective imaginary, to his concept of the fusion of the spirit and the social (Stoller, personal communication, 31 October 2007).

Edward Schieffelin warned against confusing such symbols with similes. Symbols do not just 'stand for' something else; they are not 'like' something else. Instead, they constantly and actively 'bring things into meaning'. In the introduction to his seminal 1976 study of the Kaluli people of Mount Bosavi, Papua New Guinea, he said, 'Rendering into meaning is the symbolic process by which human consciousness continually works reality into intelligible forms' (Schieffelin, 1976, p. 2). Twenty years later, he described a diagnostic moment in a Kaluli séance in which a symbolic language sung by a spirit renders a child's illness socially meaningful:

> The focus returned to illness when a woman asked for one of Walia's most effective healing spirits to come so she could ask about another person who was sick. Amid shouts of ribald jokes and men declaring they were going to go to sleep, the new spirit came up and started to sing. In a short time, the jokers fell silent. It became clear, as people deciphered the song's poetic images of birds, waterfalls, and journeying, that it contained an underlying message. Directed at members of the sick child's family, the song suggested that they had recently had a dispute in which one antagonist had come off the loser and had angrily left the community to live for a while in another place. The implication was that the dispute was responsible for the child's illness because the anger among the antagonists drew witches to the family.
>
> (Schieffelin, 1996a, p. 74)

Schieffelin questioned the validity of viewing rituals through the frame of performance theory; to view a Kaluli spirit seance as a genre of performance distorts certain realities which ethnographic analysis must convey as clearly as possible. For example, Western performance theory would characterize the Kaluli mediums as theatrical performers creating an imaginative reality for an audience by *impersonating* spirits, whereas the Kaluli would view the spirits themselves as the performers. The analogy between Western theatre performance and rituals in non-Western contexts, Schieffelin feared, misrepresents the reality of the ritual and misconstrues the phenomenology of the experience for the participants. Instead he proposed a series of determinative 'issues' with which to translate annotatively any performative moment for the purpose of ethnographic understanding. By designating 'form', 'authority', 'embodiment', 'historicity' and 'emergence' as issues rather than

as categories of anthropological analysis, he could discuss with his inform-
ants the degree of relevance these issues had to *their* construction of what was
happening (Schieffelin, personal communication, 21 February 2008).

Schieffelin's cautious objection seems to express a concern that theatricality denotes a Western ontological differentiation between two realities
that assigns less power to the imaginary. As a result, building an interpretation on analogies between the phenomena of possession and Western
theatre performance skews the ethnographic description. In another context,
Schieffelin (1996b) also criticized a description that characterized 'wild
man behaviour' in the Bosavi people as a form of 'theatrical amusement'.
Deploying the notion of 'mimesis', he describes the behaviour instead as a
'mimetic cultural creation'. Adeline Masquelier forcefully stated a similar
objection: interpreting possession, even in all its cultural particularities,
sacrifices the reality of the experience in favour of meaning:

> Such an approach has the distinct disadvantage of allowing one to
> ignore just how important possession 'really' is to those who experience
> it. The symptoms of possession are not free-floating signifiers; they are
> anchored in an 'organic' medium that partly controls their generation,
> emergence, and proliferation. . . . The challenge, then, is to explain the
> 'real' of possession without explaining it away through a singular focus
> on the 'meaningfulness' of the phenomenon.
>
> (Masquelier, 2001, p. 14)

Janice Boddy (1989) delineated in terms of cultural symbolism and morality
several levels at which *zar* possession, in the northern Sudanese village of
Hofriyat, performs a therapeutic function. For instance, in a case in which
a *zar* usurps a woman's fertility, the husband must enter into an exchange
relationship with her spirit(s), thus implicitly renegotiating his relationship
with his wife. Both human beings are equally powerless before a transcendent
third, the *zar*. Neither sex sees itself capitulating to the other; the balance of
power is preserved and the marriage renewed.

For Boddy, the central concept of the Hofriyati *zar* cult was the possession
ceremony as marriage. A *zar* of three to nine days, she observed, requires the
purchase of incense and cologne for the ceremony, along with tea, cigarettes,
liquor, a sacrificial animal, and other specific material demands of the spirit
to be appeased. Regardless of sex, the patient is referred to as the 'bride' of
the *zar*, has abstained from sexual relations and physical work before the rite,
and is kept in virginal seclusion throughout the event. At the chosen time,
the participants and musicians assemble in the bride/patient's (or the *shay-
khalzar* practitioner's) courtyard. The patient faces the front door, the musicians sit to her left, and the *shaykha* on her right, and the other attendants
form the shape of a U or arena for the ritual; all are oriented toward the
principal opening of the walled enclosure. The drumming begins. Blessings

are requested from Allah and the Muslim saints. Next, the *zayran* as a group are invoked by a chant. Then the musicians begin to play a series of 'threads', musical numbers appropriate to each *zar*, generally in order of its social standing, for the *zar* world invisibly parallels the human: Holy Ones, Ethiopians, Westerners and Europeans, desert nomads, West Africans, southern Sudanese and black Africans, and finally, at the bottom, witches and crocodiles. One by one, the *zar* descend into the bodies of one or a number of the women. A well-behaved spirit releases its hosts' bodies when its chant is over, but should it prove reluctant to leave, the *shaykha* must bargain with it. At least once in these proceedings, the 'bride' is expected to become entranced, thereby confirming or challenging the original diagnosis of her affliction. The responsible spirit becomes accessible, open to dialogue with the *shaykha* and, through her mediation, with the patient herself. On the last evening, a sheep or goat draped in the red and gold veil-cloth of a traditional bride is sacrificed as a covenant between the *zar* and its host. The *shaykha* anoints the patient's forehead and any painful areas of her body with its blood, and, similar to the orthodox practice of thanking Allah for good fortune, a sacramental meal is prepared for all. The following morning, the cooked head of the sacrificial animal is torn open, the headmeats are eaten, and in a final closing ceremony, the bones are carried to the Nile and the blood-caked bowl washed in river water. The *zar* concludes with the patient remaining in semi-seclusion for seven days. The Hofriyati enact the collaboration between spirit and human as a sacrifice in deference to the spirit who rides the host/bride, integration as an act of incorporation. This version of 'marriage', the quintessential ceremony of integration, is so central to Hofriyati culture that even a boy entering a circumcision rite is called a 'bride'.

The social functionalist analysis of *zar* possession is inadequate because it glosses over the issue of belief. In the above example, *zar* practitioners, though not with conscious intent, open the potentially destructive ambiguities in a marriage to a symbolic performance and subsequently to interpretations which might lead the marriage in a positive direction. The performance does not necessarily resolve the conflict or its ambiguities, despite the adoption of a spirit idiom. Part of its therapeutic potential resides in the fact that, as Kapferer, too, noted, the ceremony articulates a possible world and a possible way of orienting oneself within it. In the case of the marriage troubled by infertility, if the husband chooses to believe (i.e., receive) this other language elucidated by the adepts, the marriage relationship may be enriched by new meanings and by new ways of communicating.

According to Boddy, the *zar* is a cultural resource used only by specific individuals within the culture. A spirit must make sense to those whom it encounters; the sense it makes is a product of human and spirit collaboration. Consequently, possession by a *zar* requires control on the part of the possessed. The hosts must have the ability to enter a trance, at the same time remaining alert to their surroundings. Even when the spirits descend, they are expected to be sensitive to cues from other spirits and the audience of human observers. Seriously disturbed people would focus on their own intentions and neglect those of the spirits; thus they would be classed as misdiagnosed and seen as engaging in idiosyncratic fantasy, which the *zar* patently are not, or accused of playing with the spirits and provoking their wrath. Individuals who can successfully enact such dramas become increasingly familiar with the 'roles' they may – as spirits – be required to play. Boddy preserved in her commentary the ontological paradox that she perceived at the core of the Hofriyati experience of the *zar*: 'Possession by *zayran*, however social they may be, creates a paradox in and for those involved, as the possessed are simultaneously themselves and alien beings' (Boddy, 1989, p. 9). Even more paradoxically, the possessed are able to subordinate their own substantial concerns in deference to those of the *zar*.

Boddy's use of ritual performance theory privileged neither order nor structure over antistructure. Rather, she interpreted the villagers' experiences of spirits as affirming their conscious moral universe and, at the same time, critiquing it. She argued that, in Turner's (1982) terms, the ceremonies are as much 'liminoid' as 'liminal'. They evoke moments of release from normal constraints and make possible the deconstruction of commonsense notions, dividing them into cultural units which may then be reconstructed in new ways. In their liminal function, such rituals are socially required rites of passage that one enters in order to emerge as an altered person in society. In their liminoid function, they are not socially obligatory; they involve both choice and play. As symbols affirming cultural notions of outsiders, *zar* spirits are 'ultimately eufunctional even when seemingly inversive', and thus they are liminal. But they are also liminoid when they criticize society, express revolutionary thoughts, or expose social injustices or immoralities. Thus, she said, the *zar* is paradoxically supportive and subversive: supportive when it reflects a commitment to mainstream cultural values, and subversive when it critiques cultural constraints.

The anthropological offer: bringing closer intellectual labour and life

Anthropologists reporting on the phenomena of possession manoeuvre between two opposing approaches: the ethnographic impulse to gain access through interpretation to a conceptual world which is Other, and the explanatory impulse to build theories about human beings. Those in the first camp say that anthropology is an interpretative science in search of meaning, not an explanatory science that establishes pseudo-scientific laws, and that through 'thick description' it seeks to gain access to a conceptual world that initially appears opaquely foreign (Geertz, 1973, 1988, 2000). But even a brief survey of anthropological writing about possession demonstrates that, regardless of intention, anthropology has been and is both interpretative and explanatory.

Lewis and Obeyesekere tried to move beyond cultural particularities to universals, while Schieffelin articulated the relativist's cautions about distortions in applying an ontologically loaded Western vocabulary to a foreign culture, positing the extent to which a theorizing analogy to 'performance' – even the use of the word 'possession' – distorts the meaning of a Kaluli practice. Kapferer proposed a phenomenological approach to avoid the dangers of ethnographic description versus essentialist theorizing; later, however, he extrapolated implications from his observations about Sinhalese sorcery practices to theorize about human consciousness in general. And although large-scale comparisons continue to be out of fashion in postmodernist-influenced anthropology, Boddy defended a limited comparative approach to concepts such as embodiment and personhood: she allowed for the possibility that a distinction between body and mind is 'not just universal in thought but perhaps imperative for health' (Boddy, 1999, p. 261).

Boddy is not alone in this view. Karen McCarthy Brown (1991) had acknowledged many of these theoretical concerns, as well as the risks of either confining oneself within an ethnographer's descriptive frame or attempting to work without one. In her introduction to an ethnographic study of *Vodou* spirit possession in a Haitian community in Brooklyn, she mentioned in passing important 'archetypal dimensions' that link New York Haitian spirits to those in other cultures. She nevertheless confessed that she had specifically 'avoided drawing these parallels' and, at the same time, rejected a strictly relativist position:

> I have thought many times that academics have overemphasized those things that separate individuals and cultures from one another. . . . I do not want to throw away the hard-won insights of anthropologists into the limits of intelligibility and the reality of diversity. But I do want to balance them with my own experiences. . . . And I want to avoid substituting a theoretical picture of Haitian culture, one with firm boundaries, for the experiences I have had . . . that attest to a constant overlapping of cultures and a good deal of routine culture mixing. . . . When the lines long drawn in anthropology between participant-observer and informant break down, then the only truth is the one in between; and anthropology becomes something close to a social art form, open to both aesthetic and moral judgment. This situation is riskier, but it does bring intellectual labor and life into closer relation.
>
> (Brown, 1991, pp. 13–15)

In 2004, attempting precisely what Brown recommended, Paul Stoller brought his life and his intellectual labour together. In a memoir about his personal experiences with cancer, Stoller (2004) risked using his ethnographic knowledge of Songhay sorcery to judge his diagnosis and treatment for lymphoma. Arguing against a Western biomedical attitude towards illness, which he characterized as one-sidedly combative and militaristic, Stoller juxtaposed the account of his diagnosis, treatment and subsequent liminality as a cancer patient with compensatory memories of the 'wise old sorcerer' Adamu Jenitongo. Finally, he accepted Western medicine, but in the juxtaposition he discovered that the words of the Songhay rites he memorized as an ethnographer carried new embodied meanings that addressed his predicament of suffering and illness:

> Faced with a disease that can be 'managed' but not 'cured', I began to wonder about my obligations as an anthropologist. Should I continue to try to refine social theory? Should I continue to write 'thickly' described stories? Cancer has shifted my sense of priorities. I now believe that the anthropologist's fundamental obligation is to use her or his repertoire of skills to bear witness. ... In the end this turn may take us to that elusive and oft forgotten end of scholarship: wisdom, the knowledge that enables us to live well in the world.
>
> (Stoller, 2004, p. 200)

Opposition between objectivist explanation and subjectivist interpretation in anthropology has parallels in most social sciences and in Western philosophy in general. In psychoanalysis, Henri Ellenberger (1970) characterized Freudian theory as heir to nineteenth-century positivism and scientism (which is why Obeyesekere's application of Freudian theory to Sri Lankan possession cults produced a universalist argument), while Jung's psychology appears in this context more subjectivist. And yet Jungian psychology itself denotes not only a cross-cultural description of inner experience and a psychotherapeutic practice but also a psychological theory with nominally universalist concepts such as 'archetypes'. In practice, therapists do not explain images from the unconscious to their clients; they interpret them. But outside the analytic frame, Jungians do theorize, not only about consciousness, but also about the nature of that opaquely foreign Other, the unconscious, as it manifests intrapsychically in case histories, transferentially in the analytical field, and intersubjectively in the collective. Attempting to work responsibly in this contradictory place, within Jung's epistemology of paradox, creates dilemmas about integrity and ethics (Beebe, 1992; Solomon, 2004).

The dilemmas between the conscious subjective experience of the ego and the world of objects, both outer and inner, may be surpassed by the autonomous image-creating capacity of the psyche itself, which, according to Jung, functions as a mediating agency – *esse in anima*:

> Psychic images point beyond themselves to both the 'historical particulars' of the world around us and the 'essences' and 'universals' of the mind and metaphysics. ... Perhaps the most important function psychic images perform is to aid the individual in transcending conscious

knowledge. Psychic images provide a bridge to the sublime, pointing toward something unknown, beyond subjectivity.

(Kugler, 1997, p. 84)

Jungian psychology's approach to psychic imaging can be a useful alternative to the current opposing positions of relativism and universalism, deconstruction and essentialism. The moment when Paul Stoller reconnected with the Songhay rituals, not with their enactment but with the images embedded in the incantations, advances this Jungian idea. Stoller was not afraid to locate 'wisdom' in the bridging capacity of the images which Adamu Jenitongo passed on to him. As a Western ethnographer, he once reported how these images connect Songhay past to Songhay present, and now, as Western sufferer, he could describe how these same images meaningfully bridge cultures. But then Stoller the ethnographer was not utterly surprised by this discovery: after all, the Songhay *genji how* celebrates this bridge-making capacity itself with words that invoke the image of *N'debbi*, the Songhay bridge-maker between gods and human beings, between worlds.

Enriching the Jungian concept of possession: three anthropological images

Images from this brief survey of anthropological literature on possession offer possibilities for Jungians to meet on common ground because they carry analogical implications that can enrich and refine Jung's concept of possession. Among these images are the Kaluli image of a spirit singing a diagnosis, the Hofriyati image of marrying the *zar*, and the Galle Sinhalese image of lighting the demon palace.

Schieffelin described the diagnostic moment in a Kaluli séance as poetic and imagistic. The spirit sings the answer to the diagnostic question using symbols of 'birds, waterfalls, and journeying'. The listeners interpret the diagnosis, transposing its meaning into the human, rendering it specific until it rings true for them. Interestingly, in the specific séance which Schieffelin described, two spirit-singers participated, but one failed. Schieffelin honoured the ontological weight the Kaluli give to the spirits by reporting the failure in two ways: first, he described one singer failing in his performance to engage his audience convincingly, and second, he described two spirits offering two diagnoses and, through the interplay of the two singers, demonstrating the inadequacy of the differential diagnosis. Schieffelin's ethical approach to Kaluli ontology reminds me of Jung's reading of the delusions of the patient at the Burghölzli Clinic who said that she lived on the moon, where she was possessed by a vampirish male spirit. Jung discovered how crucial therapeutically (and, indeed, how sound ethically) it was to give the unconscious image – that she lived on the moon – the same ontological weight as the objective reality – that she resided in the Swiss sanatorium (Jung, 1962, pp. 128–130).

Extrapolating from Jung's autobiographical anecdote to contemporary Jungian writing, I find myself asking how many case histories convey the integrity that Schieffelin demonstrated in his anthropological report? Meeting the challenge of his example, for instance, Jungian editorial policy would advise contributors who include case material to address the ethical issue of writing more inclusively. They might be asked to write up, in addition to the patient's anamnesis and the analyst's countertransferences, the narrative of the complex from the point of view of the archetype at its core. Schieffelin's work with Kaluli images casts a critical question on anthropological writing about possession; by analogy, its ethical stance also implicates writing about analytical psychology with Jung's concept of possession as its throughline. To what extent is a good deal of Jungian writing ontologically skewed?

Boddy observed that the Hofriyati differentiate between *zar* spirits, which the culture believes can be integrated through ceremonial marriage, and others, such as black *jinn*, which must be exorcised if possible. This observation stimulates thought about diagnosis in response to suffering attributed to possession. The diagnostic act of giving the spirit its right and proper name, of differentiating between *zar* and black *jinn*, is positive in itself, and it seems to me to align with Jung's description of a similar effect in analysis: 'The true symbol, the true expression of the psychological fact, has that peculiar effect on the unconscious factor, that is somehow brought about by giving it the right name' (Jung, 1984, p. 581). Boddy's observation and Jung's description contrast with the accounts in Chapter 1 of diagnostics gone wrong, of names that distorted psychological facts such as the grieving for a grandparent or the sparking of an erotic fantasy so badly that the facts had to be expunged. (The implications for the American Psychiatric Association's *Diagnostic and Statistical Manual of Mental Disorders* are addressed in Chapter 3.) Boddy carefully delineated how, once specific *zar* spirits have been named, the image of marriage to the *zar* grants to the sufferers a paradoxically positive change of status. After the image is embodied through the rites, the spirits will not simply seize the sufferers; rather, they will allow themselves to be invoked, and the interplay will potentially be productive. In this interplay Boddy discerned liminal moments that partake of and reinforce culturally shared values as well as liminoid moments that subvert the collective; she described the Hofriyati image of marriage both reinforcing and subverting itself.

Kapferer explained that the Galle Sinhalese differentiate between demons and deities who both create illusion but for different ends. Demons cannot be transformed or reconstituted at a higher level in the cosmic hierarchy; they can only intensify the chaos of lower-level orders of the cosmic whole. Sinhalese exorcists, as 'scientists of spirits', light up the demon palace and thereby alter the sufferers' perceptions of their suffering, emphasizing not so much the exorcising of the tyrannical spirit as the placing of the demonic in context with the divine, illness in relationship with health, disorder with order. Kapferer saw significance in this Sinhalese image for Western theorizing:

When I wrote this book I was conscious of the fascination non-Western ritual forms and healing practices had for the West. They held out alternative solutions to human anguish and avenues for personal liberation. Moreover, they challenged the canons of a Western scientific rationalism which many held to be not only at the root of individual suffering but also the source of much destruction emanating from the West. Some of the post-modern developments in current anthropology are an extension of such critiques. There is no doubt that the kind of anthropology which Victor Turner inspired, and which continues to influence me, gathered impetus in its attack on scientific rationalism and its demand that other approaches, like those of Freud and especially Jung who drew so much from civilizational sources outside the West, should be addressed.

(Kapferer, 1991, p. xx)

Like Kapferer, Jung characterized Western fascination with non-Western ritual as partly an essential confrontation with the external 'not us'. At the same time, he wondered when it could mark an evasion of the difficult work of coming to terms with the 'not us' within, as this manifests in the paradox of Western consciousness. Freud and Jung attempted to bolster psychology as a positivist science by aligning themselves with anthropological research, but Kapferer points out how anthropology also inspired them to see how their psychologies could function therapeutically in a compensatory capacity within Western culture. They identified anthropology's imaginative response to cross-cultural experience as collectively therapeutic, with what psychoanalysis might call the anthropologists' articulation of their countertransferences functioning as a healing response to the destructive one-sidedness of Western societies.

With this cultural one-sidedness in mind, Claude Lévi-Strauss observed:

It would be tempting to distinguish two contrasting types [of societies]: those which practise cannibalism – that is, which regard the absorption of certain individuals possessing dangerous powers as the only means of neutralizing those powers and even of turning them to advantage – and those which, like our own society, adopt what might be called the practice of anthropemy (from the Greek *émein*, to vomit); faced with the same problem, the latter type of society has chosen the opposite solution, which consists in ejecting dangerous individuals from the social body and keeping them temporarily or permanently in isolation, away from all contact with their fellows, in establishments specially intended for this purpose.

(Lévi-Strauss, 1955, p. 388)

Michel de Certeau (1970, 1975) applied Lévi-Strauss's structuralist distinction between ingurgitating and vomiting to his Lacanian argument about the

possession at Loudun (see Chapter 1). Certeau suggested two opposing responses to the suffering caused by spirit possession: to vomit out and exorcise
the spirit as Other, or to absorb, to literally incorporate and integrate the spirit
in an attempt to neutralize and even turn to one's advantage its dangerous
power. Most of the iconography of the Christian West confirms its one-sided
identification with anthropemy. In the case of the possession at Loudun,
Surin very uncharacteristically cast himself as an intermediary, taking on
(ingurgitating) the possessing spirit and, at the same time, introducing a
vocabulary of mysticism with which Jeanne des Anges could eventually
rewrite (and incorporate) her experience of possession.

Lévi-Strauss's distinction and Certeau's suggestion stimulate the thought
that, on the one hand, Lacan, as the great reader of Freud, rescued psychoanalysis from the positivist medical interpretation that rendered Freud
anthropemic in his approach to the unconscious, that read him as characterizing all untoward psychological symptoms as foreign elements which ought
to be expelled. On the other hand, Jung gave the name 'individuation' to the
goal of the psychological life-process of differentiating and, as much as possible, integrating otherwise dangerous and possessing complexes from the
unconscious into consciousness. Jung argued that this goal is best symbolized
by the alchemical image of a 'marriage of opposites'. By the time he wrote
Aion in 1952, Jung was struggling to open up and refine that notion. Instead
of using marriage as a symbol of ordered wholeness, he had come to see
marriage as representing an intricate and never-ending interplay of opposites
(Henderson, 2003).

The admirable and inspiring anthropological work of Bruce Kapferer, Paul
Stoller, Edward Schieffelin, and Janice Boddy has much to teach those in
other disciplines about possession. Their encounters with the Other in their
field work and their scepticism about the theoretical tensions of their discipline enabled them to remake the usual frameworks to create room for both
liminal and liminoid, order and chaos, meaning and meaninglessness, interpretation and embodiment. Jungian practitioners and theorists can learn a
great deal from their work on possession, especially about the difficult ethical
work of countering one-sidedness and continually opening more spaces for
mutual surprise.

Following up the Clark Conference: possibilities of rapprochement

At the Clark Conference in 1909, Franz Boas carefully manoeuvred anthropology away from the essentialist tendencies of psychology and psychoanalysis. A century later, in a similar manner, many Western anthropologists
attempt in their writings to describe possession in non-Western settings without lending it a psychological description, because they find a tendency to
pathologize inherent in psychological language. Schieffelin remarked that,

in his extensive field experience, the trances of mediums 'are not considered pathological. Indeed they are voluntarily entered and used for healing consultations with spirits' (Schieffelin, personal communication, 2 June 2004). For this reason, he is careful to report his observations without pathologizing what the specific culture itself does not pathologize. Ironically, the oft-times essentializing Jung also placed a non-pathologizing concept of possession at the very centre of his theorizing (Jung, 1973, Vol. 2, p. 104). When they are investigating the variety of altered states, behaviours and illnesses to which they attach the word 'possession', anthropologists such as Kapferer and Schieffelin find Jungian psychology interesting because Jung described the psychological experience of possession by using archetypal images to express consciousness, identity, and the experience of an intrapyschic unconscious as Other without necessarily pathologizing these experiences.

Rapprochement between disciplines does not signify a melding. Rather, as with building bridges between nations, the difficulties of approach provoke the refining of connections and differences. Kapferer rejected Obeyesekere's application of Freudian theory to Sinhalese possession because it produced a universalist argument; at the same time, he moved from performance theory to practice theory to avoid the connotation of exoticism and mysticism which he perceived in the application of performance theory. Schieffelin, too, rejected Freudian theory and performance theory because the notions of the unconscious and of theatricality skewed his reporting, giving more ontological weight to the performer than to the spirit. Granting equal ontological weight to both realms – to body and spirit, to the corporeal and the imaginary – exposed Jung to charges of mysticism, but he worked to refine his psychology precisely here, to address the problem of Western consciousness and the suffering caused in cases of possession by autonomous complexes. Like Certeau, Jung investigated the dynamic meaning of the unconscious as 'Other' in Western cultures, and like contemporary anthropologists, he considered the uncritical appropriation of the practices of the cultural Other as an evasive manoeuvre, an avoidance of the 'horns of the dilemma' of divided consciousness which characterizes many Western societies. As contemporary Jungian theorists and practitioners continue to locate themselves in this dilemma, they can compare notes with anthropologists who wrestle to establish an ethical stance as they gather their ethnographic 'thick descriptions' of the Other, articulate their 'countertransferences' in their fieldwork, and improve their generalizing theories.

Boas's strategic argument that personalistic and essentialist perspectives were mutually exclusive prompted the parting of anthropology, psychology and psychoanalysis at the 1909 Clark Conference. Revisiting Boas's lecture, anthropologist Bradd Shore attempted an interpretive approach to culture based on both humanistic rhetoric and a more generalizing approach to mind drawn from positivistic science. For him, 'the choice between characterizing humankind in terms of psychic unity or psychic diversity is based on a false dichotomy and an overly essentialistic biology', and he attributed both local differences in cognition and universals of human cognition to 'the common architecture of the human nervous system' (Shore, 1996, p. 312). For instance, employing Lakoff and Johnson's (1980/2003) theory of metaphor, developed within the cognitive sciences, Shore formulated the existence of 'foundational image schemas', and he used them to construct a theory of cultural difference as a constituting dimension of mind. According to Shore, different cultural models share a family resemblance 'because they are organized in relation to [these] common foundational schemas' (Shore, 1996, p. 312).

Jungians have employed the same cognitive research to clarify ambiguities concerning the potentially universalist concept of 'archetype', differentiating between definitions which suppose pre-experiential innate structures and those which suggest implicit but post-experiential internal working models (Knox, 2001, p. 629; 2004a, 2004b). Post-Jungians have argued with clarity the degree to which Jung viewed archetypes, not as 'hard-wired', genetically inherited structures, but as innate predispositions with an organizing function. So, by and large, both Jungians and post-Jungians would find useful Shore's cognitive-research-based anthropological notion of 'foundational image schemas'. At the same time, the Jungian use of the word 'archetype' connotes more precisely than 'schemas' the numinous or affective aspects of these general organizations of experience, since, as Shore himself observed, these numinous or affective aspects 'are not explicitly cognized by members of a community', 'are not easily accessible to verbal articulation by the people who know them most intimately', and 'are commonly found in myth and ritual models of religious traditions' (Shore, 1996, p. 366). Jungians and anthropologists who meet at this place will find grounds for fruitful discussion of how their words work (see Chapter 4).

Cognitive research also inspired anthropology to reclaim the concept of *participation mystique*, which had been proposed early in the twentieth century by French philosopher and ethnologist Lucien Lévy-Bruhl. *Participation* denotes a direct relationship between subject and object to the extent of an identification (or what Stoller would describe as a 'fusion'). British anthropologists (with the notable exceptions of Edward Evans-Pritchard and Rodney Needham) attacked the evolutionism inherent in Lévy-Bruhl's description of *participation* as both 'primitive' and 'prelogical' with such vehemence that he eventually rejected much of his own concept. However, as early as 1955, Jung defended Lévy-Bruhl's anthropological notion of *participation mystique* as psychologically valid. For Jung, *participation* was less 'prelogical' or 'illogical' than psychologically 'irrational' in the sense of 'counterrational', that is, outside the Aristotelean law of non-contradiction. In addition, Jung regretted that Lévy-Bruhl conceded to his critics and dropped the word *mystique* when it aptly characterized the affective quality associated with such identifications between subject and object:

Participation mystique has been repudiated by ethnologists for the reason that primitives know very well how to differentiate things. There is no doubt about that; but it cannot be denied, either, that incommensurable things can have, for them, an equally incommensurable *tertium comparationis*. . . . Furthermore, 'unconscious identity' is a psychic phenomenon which the psychotherapist has to deal with every day. Certain ethnologists have also rejected Lévy-Bruhl's concept of the *état prelogique*, which is closely connected to *participation*. The term is not a very happy one, for in his own way the primitive thinks just as logically as we do. Lévy-Bruhl is aware of this, as I know from personal conversation with him. By 'prelogical' he meant that primitive suppositions are often exceedingly strange, and though they may not deserve to be called 'prelogical' they certainly merit the term 'irrational'.

(Jung, 1955, para. 336, n. 662)

In Jungian circles, a good deal of controversy surrounds Jung's appropriation of this rejected anthropological concept (see Shamdasani, 2003; Segal, 2007; Bishop, 2008). Some Jungians still borrow *participation mystique*, while others adopt Melanie Klein's concept of projective identification as a synonym. According to Steven Flower (2006), Klein's term superseded Jung's in developmental Jungian writing partly because Jungians were seeking to legitimize their concepts by rewriting them in a more scientifically rigorous discourse. Referring to his clinical experience, Flower hypothesized that the Kleinian and Jungian terms may describe two different kinds of interpenetration. The defensive experience of projective identification evasively projects unbearable unconscious contents onto objective others, where with good attunement, they may be modified and reflected back; participation describes a fusion of subject and object amounting to a partial identity which may be either evasive or positively numinous (Jung described this at great length in his imagistic approach to the quandaries of the transference–countertransference relationship). When an object relations theorist such as Wilfred Bion (1961) introduced an interpersonal or intersubjective component into Klein's intrapsychic concept of projective identification, noting that often the projection uncannily or fatefully falls upon not just any object but a most fitting object, he may have acknowledged these two different kinds of interpenetration.

Reclaiming Lévy-Bruhl for anthropology required correcting the notion that *participation* is a kind of mental functioning that can be exclusively associated with any single human group (i.e., primitives), as well as that it is a 'lower' form of human cognition than so-called rationality. *Participation*, Shore said, approximates the process of analogical schematization that underlies meaning construction for all humans. Phenomenologist Maurice Merleau-Ponty (1945/2002, p. 162) and ecologist and philosopher David Abram affirmed this position, taking up Lévy-Bruhl's concept of *participation* and its positive potential as a defining attribute of perception itself: 'perception always involves, at its most intimate level, the experience of an active interplay or coupling between the perceiving body and that which it perceives' (Abram, 1996, p. 75). At the same time, anthropology demonstrated that certain cultures collectively value this cognitive process far more than others (Shore, 1996, pp. 28, 314). Anthropology can now pose to Jungians the question: why do Western cultures pathologize certain kinds of cognitive functioning that they do not value, and what is the psychological effect of this pathologizing (see Chapter 3)?

The study of eating disorders has marked out another mutually beneficial meeting place between the disciplines of anthropology and analytical psychology. Janice Boddy noted that, as a teacher, she found it useful to compare her anthropological investigations of problems of embodiment addressed in Hofriyati *zar* rituals with an analysis of anorexia nervosa in Western societies. She observed that in anorectics, embodiment of the body's alienness is especially pronounced: they experience not only hunger but also other physical sensations – pain, cold, heat – as invasive, originating from outside the self, and she likened this phenomenon to the way in which the *zar* initiates experience the spirits. 'One difference between possession and anorexia may be that the West has no curing rites adequate to the cultural complexities of the condition', she said, lamenting that such curing rites could offset conventional embodiment through counter-mimesis and 'cultivate a healthier distance between "body" and "mind" ' (Boddy, 1999, pp. 262–263).

If Boddy were to cast an anthropological gaze on analytical psychology's psychotherapeutic triad of temenos, mimesis, and synthesis (see Chapter 5), would she identify analytic psychotherapy as a Western equivalent to a 'curing rite'? After all, Jung's theoretical concept of possession is grounded in his practice of creating a safe, ritualized, intersubjective space within which to work through 'active imagination' and analytic transference towards a healing differentiation and resynthesis of 'body', 'mind', 'soul', and 'spirit'. Jungians writing about anorexia nervosa have described their work in similar terms (see Woodman, 1980, 1982; Schaverien, 1995), and medical anthropologist Roland Littlewood insists on the idiom of possession as the most effective way for Western psychopathology to describe the culturally specific suffering caused by eating disorders (see Chapter 3).

From a Jungian perspective, anthropology functions in a perpetual compensatory integrating role for society: anthropologists study the cultural Other in their ethnographic descriptions and their personal responses and interpretations, in much the same way that analysts write down their patients' dreams and their own countertransferences as manifestations of the unconscious as Other. Both are working towards wholeness. Anthropology has a great deal to teach Jungians about the cultural context of the 'curing rites' they are attempting to enact and about establishing an ethical stance towards something unknown. The challenge for Jungians is not to misuse anthropology; in this sense, Jung often showed what not to do. At a time when the control of psychotherapy is increasingly handed over to psychiatrists, clinical psychologists and insurance companies, it is the anthropologists who could best tell psychotherapeutic practitioners what constitutes good practice.

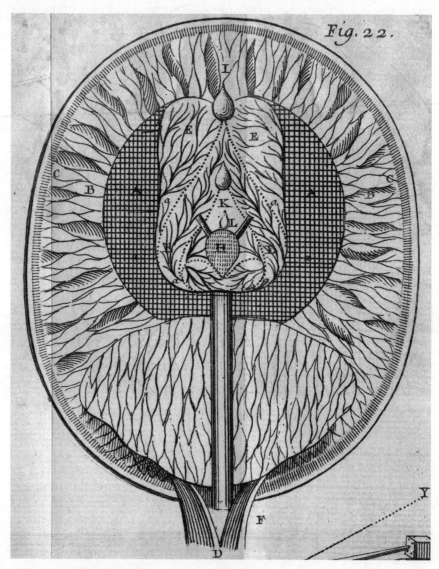

Figure 3.1 Descartes's diagram of the human brain, Figure 22 in *L'Homme de René Descartes, et la formation du foetus.* Paris: Compagnie des Libraires, 1729. Published with permission of Historical Collections, Claude Moore Health Sciences Library, Universiy of Virginia.

Chapter 3

Possession enters the discourse of psychiatry

Recuperation or epistemological break?

> The scientific spirit is essentially a rectification of knowledge, a widening of the frameworks of knowledge. It judges its past history by condemning it. . . . Scientifically one thinks of the truth as historical rectification of a longstanding error, one thinks of experience as rectification of an initial common illusion. The whole of the intellectual life of science plays dialectically on this differential of knowledge, at the frontier of the unknown. The very essence of reflection is to understand what one has not understood.
>
> (Gaston Bachelard, *Le Nouvel Esprit scientifique*, trans. Mary Tiles, 1984, pp. 177–178)

> A clinic is not always the best place for observing disease. . . . The clinic, the laboratory, the ward are all designed to restrain and focus behaviour, if not indeed to exclude it altogether. They are for a systematic and scientific neurology, reduced to fixed tests and tasks, not for an open, naturalistic neurology. . . . James Parkinson delineated the disease that bears his name not in his office but in the teeming streets of London. Parkinsonism has to be seen in the world to be fully comprehended, and if this is true of Parkinsonism, how much truer must it be of Tourette's, especially in its most extravagant form in which the individual is virtually possessed by compulsive imitations and impersonations.
>
> (Oliver Sacks, 'Possessed', pp. 18–19)

Bruce Kapferer, an anthropologist, revealed that the Galle Sinhalese scientific practice of diagnostics lights up the demon palace, thereby altering the possessed ones' perceptions of their suffering; rather than banishing the demonic, it places the demonic in context with the divine, illness with health, disorder with order. Michel de Certeau, a historian, emphasized how, in making their diagnosis, the exorcists at Loudun framed the suffering they were seeking to alleviate; the language of the *Malleus Maleficarum*, their main diagnostic tool, condemned certain experiences of the possessed and powerfully endorsed – yet distorted – others. Does the contemporary Western psychiatric assessment also work like this? How effectively does psychiatry's discourse illuminate the disordering effects of mental diseases? To what extent does its vocabulary approve yet distort certain kinds of suffering at the same time that it disallows others? Could possession provide an idiom through which psychiatry might reflect upon and rectify its diagnostics?

The *Diagnostic and Statistical Manual of Mental Disorders* (*DSM*), published by the American Psychiatric Association (APA), is a model by means of which problems inherent in cataloguing and classifying mental disease can be addressed. The discourse of the *DSM* reflects the inherently dialogic or contradictory nature of its stated mandate to demonstrate both 'nosological completeness' and 'inclusiveness'; nonetheless, psychiatry employs this dialogic discourse in a one-sided, positivistic manner by identifying what it considers to be universal mental disease entities, stripped of their cultural context. The introduction of 'possession' as a mental disorder among the dissociative disorders listed in the *DSM-IV* (APA, 2000) may provide the potential for an epistemological break, a means by which psychiatry could better understand and evaluate the assumptions inherent in its discourse as well as its limits as a cultural practice. Jung's concept of possession contributes constructively to this process of scientific rectification and epistemological change.

Possession enters the *DSM*

In 1992, the editorial committee of the *DSM-IV* proposed to introduce a new category of dissociative disorder called 'Dissociative Trance Disorder' into Appendix B: Criteria Sets and Axes for Further Study. It would parallel a similar diagnostic category in the *ICD-10 Classification of Mental and Behavioural Disorders*, which the World Health Organization (1992) had published in the same year.

The essential feature of the proposed Dissociative Trance Disorder, as it manifests in either trance or possession states, is its involuntariness. The editorial committee emphasized, first, that the disorder is an unintentional, spontaneous state that is not accepted 'as a normal part of a collective cultural or religious practice and that causes clinically significant distress or functional impairment'. However, the committee added, 'some individuals undergoing culturally normative trance or possession trance states may develop symptoms that cause distress or impairment and thus could [also] be considered for this proposed disorder'. They identified the associated features of 'pathological possession trance' as typically 'a limited number of agents (one to five) in a sequential, not simultaneous, fashion'; these agents would most often be described as spiritual in nature, originating external to the sufferer's body, and experienced as antagonistic to the individual (APA, 2000, pp. 783–785).

Etzel Cardeña (1992), who participated in the *DSM-IV* Dissociative Disorders Task Force and in the phrasing of the diagnostic criteria for Dissociative Trance Disorder, noted that the criteria address both trance disorder (which involves alteration but not replacement of embodied identity) and possession disorder (which involves partial or full replacement of embodied identity and also amnesia). The criteria appear to distinguish sharply between culturally sanctioned alterations of consciousness, which are a form of religious transcendence and/or a therapeutic technique, and peripheral pathological alterations of consciousness, which cause maladjustment and distress because they occur outside of ritual containment and are spontaneous, beyond the conscious control of the person. The criteria also differentiate between the chronic course of Multiple Personality Disorder or Dissociative Identity Disorder, associated with reports of early physical and sexual abuse, and the typically acute course of pathological possession. The criteria differentiate as well between the delusions of possession experienced by psychotic patients and the delusions of possession disorder; accordingly, Schizophrenia, Mood Disorder with Psychotic Features, and Brief Psychotic Disorder are listed as differential diagnoses, although no help is offered for making such differentiation. Cardeña's primary argument in favour of including Dissociative Trance Disorder in future editions of the *DSM* focused on the need to

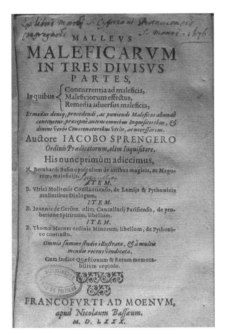

Figures 3.2, 3.3 Title page of the 1486 diagnostic manual of demonological disorders, the *Malleus Maleficarum*, as published in Frankfurt am Main in 1580. Published with permission of Olivier Neuillé, Médiathèque François-Mitterrand de Poitiers. Cover of *Diagnostic and Statistical Manual of Mental Disorders*, Fourth Edition, Text Revision, 2000. Published with permission of the American Psychiatric Association.

differentiate among all these psychopathologies; if such differentiation is possible, the proposed criteria would describe a unique disorder.

Roberto Lewis-Fernández (1992), who also participated in the *DSM-IV* Dissociative Disorders Task Force, said that psychiatric diagnosis necessarily privileges a formal descriptive definition of pathology, but that the criteria for Dissociative Trance Disorder go further. He contrasts Western psychiatry with other 'indigenous' classifications that use contextual evidence and formal, descriptive characteristics equally to distinguish pathology from normality. Lewis-Fernández portrays this contrast in terms of etic versus emic perspectives, a distinction originally named by linguistic anthropologist Kenneth L. Pike (1954; later elaborated by Pike and Janowsky, 1996). In order to fulfil its etic mandate as a global practice, Western psychiatry needs to portray clinically and evaluate the psychiatric features of every possible condition; to be complete, its nosology needs the diagnostic niche of possession disorder. But Pike paired etic perspectives with an opposing need: the emic complexity of intrinsic cultural distinctions and specificity. The contextual work of the ethnographic analyst articulates the emic perspective that complements the perspective of the formal nosologist. Without the complementarity provided by 'indigenous particularities', Lewis-Fernández pointed out, clinicians risk employing nosologies that totalize. He recommends retaining a conceptual separation of etic and emic perspectives, of formal/descriptive nosologies and indigenous/contextual nosologies. However, the criteria for Dissociative Trance Disorder in the *DSM-IV*, which Lewis-Fernández supports, do not separate these nosologies, nor do they alert the reader to the privileging of the formal over the culturally specific.

Lewis-Fernández's argument draws attention to questions about the *DSM*'s mandate; among the many critiques, some of the most telling are the documentation collected by Christopher Lane (2007) and Allen Horwitz and Jerome Wakefield (2008) showing that psychiatry's discourse turns normal shyness and sorrow into disorders. However, a point argued by Michael Kenny (1992) indicates the complexity of the issue. In 1980, Robert Spitzer observed that his editorial board for the *DSM-III* tried to classify conditions based, not on objective criteria universally considered valid, but on how psychiatrists in North America actually practise; that is to say, the criteria are explicitly American in their context. Twelve years later, the editorial policy of *DSM-IV* clearly favoured phenomenological over etiological or theory-based classification. Kenny pointed to a contradiction still inherent in psychiatry's use of the *DSM*: although the theoretical framework for the writing of the *DSM* may be explicitly American and phenomenological, the underlying assumptions of the American Psychiatric Association are positivistic. In other words, the practitioners for whom the *DSM* is intended regard the described mental disorders as natural, disease-like entities that have causes and, in some cases, cures. Reading the criteria positivistically means generalizing universal disorders from the particularities of American practice.

Since Arthur Kleinman (1980) published his seminal work on the cultural context of healing, American psychiatry has had to confront, at the very least in actual practice, the increasingly multicultural nature of its client base, to say nothing of the uses made of the *DSM* around the world. Kleinman argued:

> Clinicians tend to be simplistic about clinical practice. Their tendency toward positivistic scientism and atheoretical pragmatism discourages attempts to understand illness and care as embedded in the social and cultural world. Their reliance on 'common sense' often masks ignorance of relevant behavioural and social science concepts that should be part of the foundation of clinical science and practice. This is the reason social science needs to be brought into medicine and psychiatry as a clinically applied science that systematically analyses the clinically relevant effects of sociocultural determinants on sickness and care.
>
> (Kleinman, 1980, pp. xii–xiii)

By 1992, the editorial board of the *DSM-IV* had redefined its mandate so the new edition would be more inclusive than previous editions. It stated its intent to incorporate, not only elements of Spitzer's focus on American practice and Lewis-Fernández's etic globalism, but also Kleinman's 'explanatory' contextualizing, and it would attempt a rapprochement with the *ICD-10*. On the surface, introducing Dissociative Trance Disorder into the *DSM-IV* looks like evidence of this inclusiveness and cultural sensitivity.

Unfortunately, many critics argue that the criteria for Dissociative Trance Disorder fail particularly in these respects. In a special issue of the McGill University journal *Transcultural Psychiatry*, for example, Michael Lambek (1992) argued that naturalized disease entities (of which the *DSM* is a catalogue) and cultural complexes (such as spirit possession) are fundamentally incommensurable. To characterize the nature of this contradiction, Lambek cited Kleinman's distinction between 'disease' and 'illness', between 'curing' and 'healing'. Kleinman defined 'disease' as the 'malfunctioning of biological and/or psychological processes', whereas illness 'refers to the psychosocial experience and the meaning of perceived disease', with disease and illness 'expressing different interpretations of a single clinical reality' (Kleinman, 1980, pp. 72–73). Lambek emphasized just how important it is for naturalizing/etic and cultural/emic perspectives to remain as incommensurate and contradictory as Lewis-Fernández proposed. Lambek did not wish to identify himself with a cultural, relativist argument, but neither did he want to argue in support of the essentialist tendency in the formal diagnostic language of the *DSM*. Lambek objected to the criteria for Dissociative Trance Disorder, I believe, precisely because the cultural perspective no longer creatively opposes the formal psychiatric nosology but instead has been enlisted to serve it.

In the same issue of *Transcultural Psychiatry*, Paul Antze (1992) explained why he prefers 'idioms of distress' to those of 'disease' or 'disorder' to describe possession. Unlike Lambek, Antze privileged the cultural context in the *DSM* criteria over the formal nosology because 'the meanings that emerge from such efforts [to grapple with local contextual details] are likely to involve a good deal more than psychopathology' (Antze, 1992, p. 321). Further, he suggested that Cardeña's (1992) argument is unconvincing because Criterion B sets up an impossible task for the diagnostician: how to differentiate between possession trance authorized as a normal part of a collective cultural or religious practice and spontaneous pathological possession trance, which, the criteria suggest, occurs outside normal cultural practice. Antze opposed the wording of Criterion B because, '[t]o the extent that any form of trance is recognized as such by members of a culture and therefore given meaning, it is culturally "authorized", even if only as a form of illness' (Antze, 1992, p. 322).

Janice Boddy has pointed out that, while introducing possession as a disorder into the *DSM-IV* may appear to validate people's distressful experiences by inclusion, it misleadingly suggests that culturally normative possession states are not distressing. Boddy insisted that distress is a regular component of most reported experiences of possession in ethnographic literature. More importantly, she argued that designating possession as a disorder reinforces (if unwittingly) the tendency of those in power to ignore the social and political contexts that precipitate the phenomena of possession (Boddy, 1992, p. 326). I understand this argument to mean that, for example, the suffering of a Sudanese woman possessed by a *zar* spirit carries potential meaning, not only for herself as an individual sufferer, but also for her marriage, her family and her community; the husband, the family and the patriarchal cultural collective need not engage with this suffering if they classify the behaviour as a psychogenic disorder. Anthropologists such as Boddy and Kapferer have demonstrated how so-called dysfunctional distressing possession is often a highly creative, politically informed response to intolerable collective situations. Boddy asked, 'in whose interest would it be, then, to define possession cases as "disorders"?' (1992, p. 326).

Significantly, many of the critics surveyed by *Transcultural Psychiatry* believed that the criteria in the *DSM-IV* for identifying possession trance as a disorder overlook fundamental contemporary issues such as the social construction of personhood or personal identity and the nature of consciousness. Boddy's summary is eloquent: 'Coming to grips with the normality of possession requires us to abandon, or at least re-evaluate Western ideas that in every culture a normal healthy self will be internally coherent and relatively well integrated' (1992, p. 325).

Critiquing the dissociative disorders in the *DSM*

Roland Littlewood, Ian Hacking, and Laurence Kirmayer all critique Western psychiatry as a social discourse which fails to acknowledge and meaningfully contain the variability of mental functioning in individuals. Littlewood (2001, 2004) structures his argument on the classic opposition between sciences and humanities. He describes psychiatry as having over-identified with the biological determinism of the natural sciences and having banished the opposing personalistic models of the humanities to a place outside its frame of reference. As a result, psychiatry has used exclusively naturalistic and mechanistic models to describe mental illness in Western societies and, at the same time, produced, as if unawares, an imperialist-motivated, exotic literature of 'culture-bound syndromes' in other societies, syndromes which the editors of the *DSM-IV* still confine to an appendix.

Recently comparative and cultural psychiatry have attempted to reconcile psychiatric practice with the syndromes which it has relegated to the Other and to the appendices. Still, Littlewood (2004, p. 7) shows that current psychiatric diagnostics persist in 'picking away at a confusing series of cultural and idiosyncratic envelopes [in order] to reveal the real disease'. He points out that academic subjects remain operationally divided into sciences and humanities, despite theoretical critiques of this dualism. Similarly, he argues, clinical psychiatry still employs a nineteenth-century German distinction between form and content in its nosology, even after this distinction has proved ineffective for the artistic disciplines in which it originated. In other words, psychiatry conceptualizes as 'form' the essential pathogenic biological determinants of a mental disorder, which it claims it can explain and address with a treatment strategy, and it conceptualizes as 'content' the personalistic and the cultural elements, which it can seek only to understand. Emphasizing 'form' over 'content' permits psychiatry to defend its nosology as universal and subsume the variability of symptoms into the criteria for a uniform disorder. Extremely important economic and political motivations impel psychiatry to maintain this position and, indeed, to promote its nosology worldwide as biologically rather than culturally based.

Littlewood's premise is similar to my own. Rather than examining idioms of distress characterized by spirit possession through the criteria of a dissociative disorder, he proposes to examine dissociative disorders in Western settings through the idiom of spirit possession. A Sora ritual, he says, is explicitly diagnostic in the sense that an individual seeks through possession to identify the cause of a family member's death. At the same time, and more importantly, the *sonum* or spirit of the dead person is invoked as (what he glosses as) 'memory', 'a set of forces and values perceived as external but which affect the living individual through actually constituting part of his own experiences and personality' (Littlewood, 2004, p. 147). According to the present criteria, Dissociative Trance Disorder would pathologize such a state of 'possession' (particularly if it is 'distressing') because a discrete, bounded, individual self experiences itself as replaced by a disembodied or spiritual agent, not as having activated an internal psychological function. Littlewood proposes the opposite strategy: using the ethnographic literature about Sora rituals and other forms of possession to construct an effective frame within which to interpret and assess certain Western psychopathological phenomena.

Refiguring three examples of psychopathological suffering as 'idioms of distress', Littlewood hypothesizes that they partially critique the Western notion of an integrated self and the biological, mechanistic bias of psychiatry, in much the same way that Boddy characterized the *zar* as critiquing the assumptions of the dominant Sudanese culture. Littlewood classifies Multiple Personality Disorder, domestic siege (that is, most often, fathers taking spouses or children hostage and threatening violence) and anorexia nervosa as three Euro-American psychopathologies which function less like the *DSM*'s disorders and more like the appended culture-bound syndromes. He proposes a three-part social functionalist frame within which to examine them; this frame is similar to I. M. Lewis's social functionalist anthropological descriptions (see Chapter 2). Individuals, often disempowered for reasons of age, gender, personality, or subdominant social position, experience themselves in a particular moment as even more marginalized and powerless than before; then, they enter a phase in which they suffer this further loss of agency as illness; in a third phase, because they are perceived to be not fully responsible for the illness, more powerful others respond and integrate the sufferers back into the everyday.

Littlewood characterizes this tripartite structure of psychopathologized distress as ritualistic. In the light of Kapferer's use of Bourdieu's theory of practice, and Kapferer's and Boddy's use of Turner's theory of ritual (see Chapter 2), I take Littlewood to mean that these idioms of distress induce the collective to engage responsibly with the sufferers in shared acts of social restitution and reintegration. To some extent, then, the sufferers within this three-part practice or ritual submit themselves to the power of the collective, including, in these particular cases, to psychiatry's biological bias and its specific assumptions about selfhood. In addition, this submission, marked by the entrance into the second phase, which is the illness (be it Multiple Personality Disorder, domestic siege, or anorexia nervosa), is synonymous with entering liminality, so that the suffering becomes, paradoxically, both increasingly distressing and disordering and at the same time numinous. But, as Boddy has effectively argued, to the extent that this ritual or practice partakes of the liminoid as well as the liminal, it implicitly criticizes the collective. And this is precisely Littlewood's point: the sufferings diagnosed as Multiple Personality Disorder, domestic siege and anorexia nervosa contest and challenge precisely the medicalizing psychiatric assumptions to which the sufferers have submitted themselves.

For Littlewood, the naturalistic bias of the medical/psychiatric diagnostic frame does not allow for the possibility that, in such sufferings, 'biology is better understood as supplying a repertoire rather than a causality'. He writes:

> If as I argue here those people medicine terms neurotic are playing a game, then (to paraphrase Engels) it is a game whose rules are set by others, and a game in which participation is hardly to be considered a free choice but rather the best available under the circumstances. . . . I prefer here the idea of something akin to the anthropological sense of a ritual – a standardized way of proceeding which represents core idioms and which constrains and transforms the way we experience ourselves but which does allow us to have access to some other power without demanding that we be held fully accountable. And through which ambiguity, our responses reaffirm the meaning of everyday life for our fellows.
>
> (Littlewood, 2004, p. xvi)

Littlewood is not arguing in favour of the personalistic. While he acknowledges that a number of twentieth-century disciplines have attempted to reconcile the naturalistic and the personalistic, including psychoanalysis, phenomenology, and sociobiology, he faults psychoanalysis in particular 'for failing to keep both naturalistic and personalistic knowledge in play'. Littlewood characterizes the psychoanalytic argument as exclusively personalistic, even recuperating the idioms of descriptive psychiatry to use 'as moral metaphors' in a manner which, for example, renders 'neurotic' individuals solely responsible for their suffering, in a way that a sociogenic framework does not. Equally problematic, he says, is the Western postmodern privileging of culture over nature if it promotes a demedicalization of disease as a biological reality. Once psychoanalysis identifies itself only with hermeneutics – an interpretive procedure which seeks to uncover meaning rather than provide a causal explanation of disease – it fails, as psychiatry fails, to do justice to both types of knowledge by reducing one to servant of the other.

Unsurprisingly, Littlewood makes no reference to explicitly personalistic models such as Tobie Nathan's ethnopsychiatry. Building on the work of George Devereux, Nathan initially addressed the phenomenon of migrant peoples in France who suffer chronic disabling syndromes that they attribute to minor physical injuries but that seem to be triggered instead by the sufferers' confrontations with French physicians and medical control authorities. Nathan (1988, 1994, 2001) proposed a psychoanalytically inclined psychotherapeutic technique which aligns itself with the communal orientation of the traditional societies in question and the practices of traditional healing. Nathan had a theoretical tendency to make culture an absolute and to underrate the naturalistic, whereas Littlewood (like Lambek) argues for 'a procedural dualism' in which psychological considerations slip between the naturalistic and the personalistic; his model is necessarily dialogic, since only one mode can be correct at any one time. As a result, he argues, 'It is in the inescapable slippage between naturalistic and personalistic that ... [the experience of] godhood emerges' (Littlewood, 2001, p. 146). This conclusion aligns with Certeau's Lacanian reading of the possession at Loudun, with Jeanne des Anges's testimony of the *réel* as slippage between the theological and a demonized erotic, and also with Schieffelin's reading of the Kaluli séance, of the 'procedural dualism' conveyed by reporting ethnographically the experiences of both the possessed performers and the possessing spirits.

Littlewood's medical anthropological argument contrasts with Ian Hacking's philosophical critique of the *DSM*'s dissociative disorders. Hacking (1995) redefines the dissociative disorders such as Multiple Personality Disorder as 'transient mental illnesses' of a specific time and place. An example (Hacking, 1998) is the epidemic of 'hysterical fugue' that followed Phillipe Tissié's 1887 description of the case of Albert Dadas, the mad gas fitter of Bordeaux. Tissié's 'hysterical fugue' became a disorder during a sudden wave of enthusiasm for mass tourism and a negative obsession with vagrancy, and Hacking uses the metaphor of an ecological niche to explain how such a transient mental illness can embed itself 'in a twoheaded way' into a culture. Tissié, a cycling enthusiast, acted from within a new ecological niche or collective contradiction when he chose Dadas as a patient from the ward to function as his parallel and opposite. Hacking's description of the disorder Dadas exemplified resembles Littlewood's social functionalist description of sufferers of Multiple Personality Disorder, domestic siege and anorexia nervosa, as well as of Boddy's anthropological descriptions of the *zar*-possessed:

> Fugueurs were relatively powerless men who found in the possibility of fugue an escape over which they had no control and for which they had no memory; I do not find in these cases any significant vestige of fraud or shamming; instead their powerlessness which produces temporary mental breakdown finds release in a mental illness which relieves them of responsibility.
>
> (Hacking, 1998, p. 50)

Whereas Boddy finally located in the *zar* in northern Sudan a ritualization of potential feminine re-empowerment, Hacking finds in the Tissié-Dadas case a *folie-à-deux* between doctor and patient that was rendered tragic (at least in part) by the mere medicalization of Dadas's suffering.

Extrapolating from 'hysterical fugue' to the contemporary American clinical scene, Hacking argues from a philosophical position of pragmatism and scepticism that while mental disorders such as schizophrenia are 'real' (that is, they are neurological and/or biochemical dysfunctions), the dissociative disorders in the *DSM* are 'not real'. Hacking proposes an ecological reason for the late twentieth-century 'epidemic' of Multiple Personality Disorder that has two opposing elements: a 'rather romantic' challenge to hegemonic ideas about identity and selfhood that appeared in North American culture after 1970 (what he calls 'the splintering glory of the purely post-modern') and the negative element of child abuse. But Hacking portrays the dilemma at the centre of an argument between the naturalistic and the personalistic (such as Littlewood's) only in terms of the biological versus the social constructionist, and he explicitly refuses to consider whether mental illnesses can be psychogenic, that is, without physiological, chemical or neurological correlates (Hacking, 1998, p. 100). He argues that theorizing about and treating dissociation only leave the sufferers weaker in the long run; he predicts that the dissociative disorders, like other transient mental illnesses, will disappear and (the tone of his argument is difficult to sidestep) the sooner the better.

Laurence Kirmayer (1994, 1996) hypothesizes two reasons for the relatively recent increase in psychiatry's interest in dissociation. 'Hysteria' had been edited out of formal nosology because of the word's popular negative connotation and because of debate concerning its status as a biologically driven disease entity. Whereas Hacking (1998) says that American psychiatry simply succumbed to powerful lobbying by traumatologists such as Donald Spiegel when they legitimized Dissociative Identity Disorder (even grandfathering 'fugue' into the *DSM* as historical justification), Kirmayer argues that psychiatry resisted the renamed dissociative disorders until psychological research established hypnosis as a dissociative phenomenon reproducible in the laboratory and also as a therapeutic technique demonstrably effective in treating somatic problems. More importantly, because psychiatry historically attached dubious morality to dissociative symptoms, both dissociative sufferers and psychiatric research into dissociation gained legitimacy only with the introduction of new categories of dissociative disorder such as Post-traumatic Stress Disorder and Multiple Personality Disorder. In other words, in the late twentieth century, by attaching these labels to suffering attributed to war trauma and physical and sexual abuse in childhood, American psychiatrists manoeuvred their patients around the charge of 'malingering' and the negative term 'self-cause' that attached historically to 'hysteria' and other diagnoses of dissociation. Unlike Hacking, Kirmayer considers this increased use of the category of dissociative disorders to be valid, but he recommends what he refers to as the 'decomposition' of the essentialist concept of dissociation in the *DSM* in order to promote research into the heterogeneous nature of dissociative phenomena.

For Kirmayer, the status of hypnosis in psychological research exemplifies problems associated with current concepts of dissociation. On the one hand, he says, social-psychological theorists argue that hypnosis is a form of strategic social enactment, a kind of sociogenically inspired performance. For these theorists, Janet's work linking hysteria and hypnosis in late nineteenth-century France, like Tissié's work on fugue, demonstrates only how patients collude theatrically with doctors' expectations. On the other hand, cognitive psychologists argue that hypnosis requires specific personality traits and imaginative processes that are distinctively measurable and quantifiable. For instance, Bowers (1991) distinguishes between imaging and dissociating in assessing an individual's capacity to control pain through hypnotic suggestion, a differentiation between two cognitive processes which hitherto had been generalized. Kirmayer also mentions reports on hypnotizability and word recognition on the Stroop task (Sheehan et al., 1988; Nadon et al., 1991; Dixon and Laurence, 1992) as examples of cognitive psychological research which, he says, surpass or even bridge the opposition between these sociogenic and psychogenic models of hypnosis.

Kirmayer proposes his own bridging model of four states of mind that are heterarchical rather than hierarchical: self-consciousness, consciousness of the external world, automaticity and reverie. That is, self-consciousness does not master cognitive processes but is merely one of four modes which can dominate conscious attention but which otherwise work unconsciously in the background. With this model, Kirmayer defines dissociation as any shift to a mode outside of self-consciousness:

> A shift to unself-conscious (i.e., external) awareness is viewed as distraction. A shift to automatic, procedural knowledge is mindlessness (or, if we are adept and retain enough awareness to savor it, *flow*; Csikszentmihalyi, 1990). A shift to reverie is absorption and corresponds to hypnotic trance, at least as the concept is employed by many clinicians.
>
> (Kirmayer, 1994, p. 102)

Kirmayer summarizes research by J. R. Hilgard (1970), E. R. Hilgard (1977) and Evans (1991) to show that individuals demonstrate a single dominant cognitive mode and greater or lesser capacity for and rapidity in shifting between modes. Highly hypnotizable individuals demonstrate cognitive traits which enhance their ability to respond to complex stimuli automatically, without the interference of self-conscious awareness. Interestingly, these same traits render individuals susceptible to dissociative phenomena: experiences of involuntariness, alterations of sense of self, and ruptures of memory in response to emotion or psychological trauma.

Extrapolating from this model and from other research into hypnosis, Kirmayer argues that dissociation is more or less a constant occurrence, apparently concurring with Boddy's critique of the essentializing Western notion of a coherent integrated self and opposing Hacking's portrayal of dissociative experience as 'false consciousness'. Kirmayer charts a succession of processes which smooth over and render tolerable the ubiquitous gaps in the experience of personhood. This succession begins with shifting attention and proceeds, through bridges of cause and consequence, to the weaving of emotional memories into associative narrative constructions and eventually to rehearsing these constructions in a social discourse which sanctions them within a larger-than-individual context. The failures in this complex, multifaceted process of smoothing over 'normal' dissociative experience, Kirmayer believes, cause the 'distresses' which the *DSM* generalizes and renders synonymous with 'disorder'.

Kirmayer's (1992) model of mental functioning employs not only cognitive but also sociogenic aspects, in that society is held responsible for the quality or effectiveness of its rituals and/or discourses. I understand Kirmayer to argue against the criteria for Dissociative Trance Disorder in the *DSM-IV* and even perhaps in favour of privileging the cultural or social contextual readings of Dissociative Trance Disorder over the formal psychiatric nosology. This understanding is prompted by the observation that, like Littlewood, he attributes the dramatic increase in the number of extreme dissociative cases seen in American clinical practice to the collective failure of psychiatry (and Western culture in general) to provide narrative structures and an effective social discourse with which to 'smooth over' and meaningfully contain individuals as they experience their selfhood as disturbingly plural.

Possession, dissociative trance disorder, cognitive research and neuroscience

John Kihlstrom (1987) recommended replacing the psychoanalytic model of the unconscious with a cognitive model. Guy Claxton (2005) employs recent research in neuroscience to take up this argument. He criticizes psychoanalytic theory for employing a 'romantic' discourse skewed by 'inaccurate metaphorical presuppositions' to describe different modes of complex mental functioning which are continual but not necessarily or simultaneously accessible to consciousness. He proposes a functional rather than a metaphorical discourse, asking not 'what is the brain like?' but 'what is the brain for?' Unfortunately, he fails to notice that, in defining a scientific biotechnical unconscious, he himself employs metaphors, perhaps because they are, for the most part and appropriately enough, technological. For example, Claxton follows Kihlstrom in trying to understand or describe increasingly complex conceptions of human mental processes by comparing them to a computer's functions. When he says that the brain is an 'unconscious on-board biocomputer', built to certain 'design specifications', he is putting forward not so much a functional description as a metaphor.

Claxton's proposal to replace the psychoanalytic model of the unconscious with a cognitive model by means of neuroscience merely subsumes the personalistic into the naturalistic. This strategy is as problematic as its opposite: psychoanalysis adopting neuroscience as an idealized science and appropriating it to legitimize itself (see Jonathan Lear (2003) and Freud and Jung's misuses of anthropology, Chapter 2). Still, research that supports the phenomena of a cognitive unconscious in terms of 'automatic processes', 'subliminal perception', and 'implicit memory' has implications for both personalistic descriptions of possession and the naturalistic criteria for Dissociative Trance Disorder in the *DSM*. Consider the following examples:

- When frightening stimuli are flashed subliminally to subjects, the emotional centres of their brains, especially the limbic structures called the amygdala, respond in a characteristic 'fearful' way, though no conscious reason for the reaction is generated (Whalen et al., 1998; Phelps, 2005). This research helps to differentiate, for example, between 'self-consciousness' and 'consciousness of the external world' in Kirmayer's model of dissociation.
- When subjects identify words flashed very briefly, many require an exposure three times as long to 'see' a taboo word as to detect a neutral one. The word is recognized unconsciously, and the brain instantly deploys a pattern of inhibition which raises the threshold of consciousness or prevents certain experiences from rising above the limits of the unconscious (Price, 2001). As well as demonstrating 'external consciousness of the world' functioning independently from 'self-consciousness', this research suggests that inhibitive activity located in the frontal lobes of the brain effectively dissociates 'external consciousness' or retards the relaying of information from it to 'self-consciousness'.
- Changes in test performance by patients exposed to auditory information while anaesthetized show that information is processed even though the patients have no conscious recollection of it (Sebel, 1995, cited in Knox, 2004a). This research supports Daniel Schacter's (1996) hypothesis of implicit memory in which experiences encoded without awareness form unconscious generalized patterns of meaning not available to conscious recall.
- Underlying the frontal lobes, and closely interconnected with them, is an area on each side of the brain called the anterior cingulate. Neuroimaging studies found that, in the right hemisphere, the anterior cingulate became active when subjects heard a real sound and also when they were hallucinating, but not when they imagined the same sound. It would seem, then, that normally this area is inhibited when something is imagined, but in stressful situations it can become disinhibited, rendering what is imagined into a full-blown hallucination (Richard Bentall, cited in Begley, 2001). This research associates inhibitory activity located in the anterior cingulate in the right hemisphere with what Kirmayer might call discrimination between 'external consciousness' and 'reverie'. Claxton points out that cultures vary considerably in their distinction between the real and imaginary. Clearly some cultures ritualize 'stressful situations' in order to promote disinhibition and the mixing of 'consciousness of the external' and 'reverie' in trance and possession states, while other cultures discourage and pathologize hallucinatory experiences. Kirmayer might argue that cultures which devalue a mode of

mental functioning such as 'reverie' will experience it as 'negative rupture' and will require patterns of social discourse to effectively 'smooth over' the imaginary. Littlewood characterizes Multiple Personality Disorder as psychiatry's nosology for a strongly sociogenic idiom of distress which critiques Western psychiatry's own effectiveness in smoothing over such negative ruptures.

• Alterations in the experience of the boundaries of the self are paralleled by a drop in activity in the superior parietal region of the cerebral neocortex. Studies of subjects engaged in transcendental meditation show increased coherence in their EEGs; in other words, feelings of bliss are accompanied by a greater 'joined-up-ness' of the brain's activity (Newberg and d'Aquili, 1999; Newberg et al., 2001, cited in Claxton, 2005). Kirmayer's model of multi-mental functioning, which characterizes dissociative experiences as the norm, is balanced by this research, which characterizes some forms of 'meditation' as the opposite, as a culturally valued, learned behaviour in which 'self-consciousness' is deliberately lowered in order to enhance experiences of 'mind' as a multi-functioning totality.

Neuroscientists and cognitive psychologists place dissociative phenomena at the centre of their theories of cognitive functioning. From their research, Jack Glaser and Kihlstrom conclude that the cognitive unconscious is capable of pursuing meta-cognitive processing goals while monitoring itself and even compensating for anticipated threats to the attainment of these goals. In a departure from common conceptions of the unconscious as passive and reactive, this research suggests an unconscious that is, paradoxically, both separate from consciousness and yet 'aware' (Glaser and Kihlstrom, 2005, p. 190). John Bargh goes so far as to propose that consciousness paradoxically produces its dissociating opposite: he hypothesizes that:

> one of the primary objectives of conscious processing may be to eliminate the need for itself in the future by making learned skills as automatic as possible . . . the evolved purpose of consciousness turns out to be the creation of even more complex nonconscious processes.
>
> (Bargh, 2005, p. 53)

These reports about the ubiquitous nature of dissociative phenomena in cognitive psychological and neuroscientific research may be interpreted as support for psychoanalytic notions of the unconscious, and indeed they appear to do so. However, it must be remembered that cognitive psychologists and neuroscientists regard the psychoanalytic unconscious in much the same way that psychiatry does: as failed science, being neither observable nor measurable. Notable exceptions are Susan Anderson, Inga Reznik and Noah

Glassman (2005), who document how representations of significant others unconsciously influence responses to strangers. Their work provides an empirical demonstration of transference, that is, of the self as a repertoire of relational selves grounded in a web of important interpersonal relationships which operate unconsciously through projection. James Uleman (2005), who characterizes their work as an attempt to render psychoanalytic theory 'empirically tractable', nevertheless dismisses the 'old unconscious' of psychoanalytic theory as 'unfalsifiable'. He concludes that 'it does not provide an influential framework for understanding unconscious processes in academic and scientific circles' (Uleman, 2005, p. 5).

A caveat. While Littlewood criticizes psychoanalysis for employing exclusively a personalistic discourse and for therefore failing as scientific theory, Lear (2003) criticizes psychoanalysis when it attempts to legitimize its personalistic arguments by latching onto and recuperating cognitive psychological and neuroscientific research for its own justification. Lear celebrates the paradox that psychoanalysts strive in practice towards a kind of objectivity in their attempts to facilitate in patients the development of the subject. Rather joyously, he locates psychoanalysis in an ironic personalistic discourse, working to put patients into positions where they can objectively experience themselves as subjects. Psychiatry errs, he says, when, from an objective stance, it characterizes patients as nothing more than biological organisms and proposes to replace psychotherapy with antidepressants, but psychoanalysis errs when it advertises itself as objectively offering a cure for depression.

By implication, the writers of the *DSM* err when they propose to classify a state of possession as a disorder simply by naturalizing it, that is, by describing it according to its mechanism but outside of its cultural context. But I err if I oppose the niche that the writers of the *DSM* reserve for research to promote a naturalistic model of the phenomena of possession as a dissociative state.

Perhaps, then, I should err in the opposite direction by characterizing the 1992 creation of such a niche in the appendix of the *DSM-IV* as a small but potentially significant epistemological break. Gaston Bachelard and Georges Canguilhem defined an epistemological break as a moment of rupture that wrenches a science from its past and allows it to reject that past as ideological. For Bachelard in particular, the history of a science is the history of the overcoming of epistemological obstacles or hindrances to knowledge (Tiles, 1984). According to Bachelard:

An epistemological break is not simply a matter of new empirical discoveries or an accumulation of scientific facts. It is a conceptual reorganization of a whole field of knowledge. Ohm's theory of electrical resistance reformulates in the abstract mathematical terms (Ohm's law) the earlier theory that described the passage of electrical 'fluids' through substances in organicist and almost sensualist terms, and reinscribes them in a new network of concepts.

(Macey, 2000, p. 113)

Littlewood and Kirmayer argue that Western psychiatric nosology has historically generalized normative dissociative functioning and relegated it, along with personalistic contextualizing, to the exotic 'culture-bound' syndromes of the Other. If this is so, then the criteria for Dissociative Trance Disorder represent a recent ironic opportunity, created by psychiatry itself, to confront the psychogenic and sociogenic aspects of the dissociative disorders which its essentializing, naturalistic ideology has wrongly left out. In Chapter 4, I will characterize this potential epistemological break in terms of a Vichian model of language, in which psychiatry's discursive language could become more effective as social discourse by reconnecting to the Western historical concept of 'possession' (as outlined in Chapter 1) and at the same time reinterpreting 'possession' in light of contemporary cognitive research about dissociation. However, if, as Hacking proposes, the current dissociative disorders as transient unreal mental illnesses should disappear from the *DSM* by the time of the next revisions, then, no doubt, disordering dissociative phenomena will intransigently resurface in yet other categories of other appendices until an appropriately influential diagnostic framework and an effective psychiatric discourse are devised to accommodate them.

Jung's theory of complexes: Jung and Jungians on dissociation

Jungian theory can contribute to this discussion of Dissociative Trance Disorder in the *DSM-IV* as a potential epistemological break, as discourse poised in the contradiction between 'nosological completeness' and 'cultural inclusiveness'. Towards the end of his life, Jung issued an epistemological challenge to an international congress of psychiatrists:

It will assuredly be a long time before the physiology and pathology of the brain and the psychology of the unconscious are able to join hands. Till then they must go their separate ways. But psychiatry, whose concern is the total man, is forced by its task of understanding and treating the sick to consider both sides, regardless of the gulf that yawns between the two.

(Jung, 1958, para. 584)

Jung had originally trained as a psychiatrist, so his image of psychiatry straddling a gulf between cognitive research and psychoanalysis in the service of the patient was idiosyncratic as well as paradigmatic. While Jung defended the practice of psychotherapy to an audience of doctors, he also challenged them to reconsider the parameters of the medical field:

It is extremely important, in his own interests, that the psychotherapist should not in any circumstances lose the position he originally held in medicine, and this precisely because the peculiar nature of his experience forces upon him a certain mode of thought, and certain interests, which no longer have – or perhaps I should say, *do not yet have* – a rightful domicile in the medicine of today.

(Jung, 1945b, para. 192, italics mine)

Here Jung defines the epistemological challenge which psychotherapy presents to psychiatry in terms similar to Giambattista Vico's scheme in which a discursive discourse must leap simultaneously backwards and forwards if it is to avoid merely circling within its ideology (see Chapter 4).

Dissociationism as a pre-psychological philosophy and dissociationist psychology have a long history from which psychiatry distanced itself but with which Jung identified, as both psychiatrist and psychotherapist. The dissociative disorders formally entered the *DSM* only in 1980, but Henri Ellenberger (1970) located the often overlooked foundations of dynamic psychiatry in the late nineteenth-century dissociationist work of Jean-Martin Charcot and his students Pierre Janet and Alfred Binet, work eventually eclipsed by the sexual model of psychoanalysis and the reflex model of behaviourism. While Freud paid tribute to Binet and Janet, he replaced dissociationism's spatial metaphor of conflicting co-conscious complexes with a temporal metaphor of sexual stages. Even more important, Freud saw the 'normal' psyche as unified and rendered 'dissociation' synonymous with 'pathology' (Haule, 1984).

Following Ellenberger's argument, John Haule located Jung's psychology of complexes – of autonomous splinter personalities which possess a kind of consciousness, a mutually antagonistic quality and a prospective component – in his French heritage: in Janet, under whom he studied in Paris during the winter semester of 1902–1903, and with Théodore Flournoy, whom he visited in Geneva. According to Haule, Jung's most important contribution to dissociationist theory was to locate within the apparently idiosyncratic splitting described by Janet the possibility of archetypal patterns. These patterns provide the potential for the formation of a psychotherapeutic alliance, for meaning to function as a kind of connection which counters the splitting and which is experienced both transferentially, between the analysand and the analyst, and intrapsychically, within both the analysand and the analyst. 'Like psychoanalysis', Haule said, 'Jungian psychology is a "praxis" of relationship, but it is the archetypal form of dissociationism, while psychoanalysis represents an alternative to dissociationism' (Haule, 1984, p. 257).

In making a place in the next *DSM* for possession as a dissociative disorder, the editors might find as much support in Jungian theory as they do in cognitive psychological and neuroscientific research. Jung's theory of complexes offers a highly differentiated model of multi-mental functioning with which to account for the quotidian experience of dissociation and extreme dissociative pathologies. For example, Jungian theory characterizes the ego as only one of many kinds of consciousness; as one kind of self-awareness associated with a narrative of personal identity, it experiences other autonomous complexes as either complementary or contradictory. Roger Brooke (1991) characterized the ego's function of 'reflecting' about its experience of other complexes in ways that resemble Kirmayer's notion of narratives 'smoothing' the contradictory gaps in cognitive functioning. In the absence of strong and flexible ego consciousness, Brooke said, the autonomy of unconscious complexes is experienced as compulsiveness; that is, the individual ego experiences itself as obsessed or possessed.

Jean Knox (2004b) argues that Jung's theory of complexes accounts for the ordinary phenomena of dissociated mental functioning described by cognitive psychologists and also for psychopathology. She finds support in Sandner and Beebe's description of complexes:

> Jung thought that whatever its roots in previous experience, neurosis consists in a refusal – or inability – in the here and now to bear legitimate suffering. Instead this painful feeling or some representation of it is split off from awareness and the initial wholeness – the primordial Self – is broken. Such splitting 'ultimately derives from the apparent impossibility of affirming the whole of one's nature' (Jung, 1934[a], para. 980) and gives rise to the whole range of dissociations and conflicts characteristic of feeling-toned complexes. This splitting is a normal part of life. Initial wholeness is meant to be broken, and it becomes pathological or diagnosable as illness, only when the splitting off of complexes becomes too wide and deep and the conflict too intense. Then the painful symptoms may lead to the conflicts of neurosis or to the shattered ego of psychosis.
> (Sandner and Beebe, 1982, p. 298)

Knox charts the important parallels between Jung's theory of complexes and psychologist John Bowlby's theory of internal working models, in which key attachment figures are internalized and form unconscious schemas which are automatically employed to anticipate and understand new situations. Contemporary research-based attachment theory corresponds far more closely to the conclusions Jung drew from his word association studies about complexes and the intergenerational transmission of attachment patterns, Knox says, than to Freudian and Kleinian theoretical formulations about 'drives' and the 'death instinct'. Attachment theory research data appears to corroborate Jung's graphs of Word Association Test results of family systems and his conclusions concerning the extent to which, for example, a daughter of an alcoholic father approaches new situations employing the same unconscious schemas as her mother:

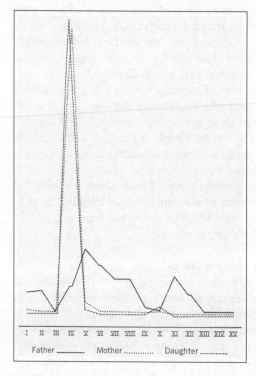

Figure 3.4 Jung's graph of a family's Word Association Test results, showing how the sixteen-year-old daughter's results disturbingly replicate the mother's scores (Figure 8, Tavistock Lectures, 1935). Published by permission from the Stiftung der Werke von C. G. Jung, Zurich, represented by Paul and Peter Fritz AG, Literary Agency, Zurich.

If such a girl comes out into the world as though she were forty-five years old and married to an alcoholic, think what a mess she will get into! This participation explains why the daughter of an alcoholic who has had a hell of a youth will seek a man who is an alcoholic and marry him; and if by chance he should not be one, she will make him into one on account of that peculiar identity with one member of the family.

(Jung, 1935a, para. 156)

John Beebe extends Jung's work on psychological typology by putting forward eight ego-syntonic and ego-dystonic complexes that constitute differentiated functions of consciousness. Beebe (1992) defines 'psychological integrity' in terms of how patients 'become conscious', that is, how they come to experience more and more of that mental functioning in any given moment:

As the notion of good type development moves, both in MBTI [Myers-Briggs Type Indicator] counseling and in Jungian analysis, toward a 'whole type' eight-function model, in which each of Jung's eight types of consciousness is represented within a picture of the person's consciousness that includes both ego-syntonic functions and functions in shadow, the ethical aspects of this development will become ever more evident. Gradually, perhaps, consciousness will realize its potential to become conscience.

(Beebe, 2004, p. 112)

'Wholeness' in this Jungian model is neither essentialist nor progressivist. 'Conscience' and the ethic of Jung's process of individuation are understood as not identifying exclusively with a particular function in a particular moment but as creating coherence out of a multifunctioning experience of self.

Kirmayer (1994, p. 114) finds that Andrew Samuels' post-Jungian notion of a 'plural psyche' complements his own model of treatment for dissociation, and Littlewood also acknowledges this kind of complementarity between himself and Jung:

> The medical interpretation of multiple consciousness, as of the hypnotism and spiritism on which it drew, started from the assumption that in the general run of things there is a single bounded and volitional self which shares a biography with the body which gives rise to it, reflecting and directing in turn the experiences of this body, with a characteristic and enduring identity of personal comportments, responses, habits, sentiments, abilities and memories, all of which are experienced and perceived by others, as hanging together and which are potentially accessible to awareness. . . . But this hanging together becomes unstuck in dreams or in the usual processes of forgetting and inattention, such that chunks of past experience cannot necessarily be recalled simultaneously; and while such split-off 'complexes' (as Jung was to call them) usually include fairly discrete memories and ideas, under appropriate conditions (brain damage, inherited constitution, emotional trauma, hypnosis) the split-off fragments might be so extensive as to actually constitute a parallel secondary self.

(Littlewood, 2004, p. 152)

I mentioned in Chapter 1 how psychopathologists dropped from the word 'obsession' its religious connotation of demons laying siege to a body and employed the word instead to denote particular thoughts, images or impulses which seek to enter the person's mind as well as the characteristic struggle the person feels when trying to keep them out. Similarly, while Criterion A for Dissociative Trance Disorder picks up 'possession' denotatively to signify 'replacement of customary personal identity by a new identity' followed by full or partial amnesia, Criterion B drops from 'possession' its religious connotation and cultural context. Vico's theory of language (see Chapter 4) would identify as typical, even necessary, the process in which discursive language drops the connotative complexity of its mythic and metaphoric origins. This process is inevitable and even progressive but, paradoxically, also impoverishing: it limits the depth, complexity or effectiveness of the social discourses to which the culture has access. Kirmayer and Littlewood regard Western cultures as impoverished in precisely this sense: social discourse no longer effectively and meaningfully smoothes over ordinary experiences of dissociation.

The entry of 'possession' into the *DSM-IV*, stripped of its connotations, seems to parallel an increase in the number of Jungian thinkers (be they classical, post-Jungian or archetypal) who have written about the effect in twentieth-century Western cultures of having lost 'hysteria' as a disease entity in official medical discourse. 'Possession' is not 'hysteria', just as 'hysteria' is not 'dissociation', but they partake of many shared elements. Niel Micklem defines hysteria as:

> a neurotic illness with pronounced features of suggestibility; with an emotional instability and readiness to fall into psychic dissociation, so that conflict is often converted unconsciously into physical symptoms; with a tendency towards flight into illness if things go wrong; with an exaggeration of expression and over-relatedness towards spectators, much of which stems from a desire to be 'at the centre of the stage', cost what it may.
>
> (Micklem, 1996, p. 5)

He reconnects this medical nosology with its connotative and cultural roots, tracking the imagery of hysteria through centuries of Western belief and writing. By reconnecting hysteria to its myth and its history, Micklem comes to defend, among other things, Jung's assessment of hysteria as 'more than a disease to be cured, being a necessary ingredient of the personality and a state that was readily understandable in terms of the psychological complex' (Micklem, 1996, p. 13). Micklem portrays Western cultures as over-identifying with a medical perspective, denying or denigrating hysteria because medicine eliminated it from its discourse as nonbiological. He argues for a paradoxical appreciation of hysteria's distressing and disordering characteristics.

Christopher Hauke (2000) also recognizes Jung's appreciation of value in the apparently pathological fantasies of the hysteric. Hauke extrapolates from Janet's case histories to contemporary examples of anorexia and self-mutilation, which he sees as powerlessness directly expressed through the language of the body. Unfortunately, however, because he relies on I. M. Lewis's social functionalist anthropological argument (see Chapter 2), Hauke himself falls into the trap of essentializing hysteria.

Perhaps more effectively, Greg Mogenson (2003) differentiates between Freud's theory of repression of instinctual drives and Jung's theory of the dissociative tendency of unconscious autonomous complexes, emphatically placing hysteria at the centre of both theories. Mogenson locates what I would call a potential epistemological shift, similar to the introduction of the idiom of 'possession' into the discourse of the *DSM*, in Christopher Bollas's proposal to introduce the word 'spirit' into psychoanalysis:

> Under special circumstances the term 'spirit' should be introduced into psychoanalysis, even though there would be many objections to a term laden with pre-psychoanalytic meanings. If, however, we understand spirit as the expressive movement of an individual's idiom through the course of his or her life, we may say that each of us is a spirit, and that we have spiritual effects upon others – who will indeed carry us as such within themselves, and we in turn will be inhabited by the spirits of others. Spirit is not the same as an internal representation although it does, I think, come very close to what we mean by an internal object: something deeper, more complex, beyond representation, yet there.
>
> (Bollas, 1992, p. 64)

Mogenson characterizes psychoanalytic discourse as positivistic and objectivist (not as personalistic or hermeneutic). Therefore, since psychoanalysis devalues 'spirit' logically as 'negative' in the sense that it is non-empirical, non-material, and purely subjective, Mogenson depicts Bollas's proposal to introduce the word 'spirit' into psychoanalytic discourse as 'a decisive step in leaving empiricism and external reflection' (Mogenson, 2003, p. 116). In the end, Mogenson judges Bollas's epistemological challenge to psychoanalysis as a failure, and he rancorously presents Bollas (2000) as subsequently writing about hysteria not in the subjective terms of 'spirit' but only in terms of object relations. Criticizing Bollas's psychoanalytical approach to hysteria, Mogenson calls for differentiation between a sterile, pathological hysterical character disorder and an anima/animus-inspired hysteria which creatively challenges psychoanalytic and medical discourses. This positive view of hysteria resembles Boddy's description of the *zar*'s liminoid critiquing of the northern Sudanese dominant collective:

> The patient may be regarded as a malignant hysteric when, in fact, the situation is one in which the anima/animus, provoked by the analyst's *mauvaise foi* (and, yet, true to their function for all that) orchestrates an epistemological critique of the analyst and of the theoretical underpinnings of psychoanalysis itself by means of the negative therapeutic reaction. . . . It is a grave omission on the part of the analytic tradition from which [Bollas] speaks . . . to have failed to distinguish between hysterical presentations that are anima/animus-based and the mother-fixated syndromes of hysterical character disorder.
>
> (Mogenson, 2003, pp. 24–25)

For Mogenson, the subjectivist discourse of the archetypal school of analytical psychology is the only Jungian discourse which has not capitulated to
the dominant discourse of positivistic psychoanalysis. He identifies his argument with the archetypal school, turning a blind eye to Jung's interest in
empiricism and to the fact that Jung explicitly positioned his own discourse
between the naturalistic and the personalistic. In fact, Jung was not purely
subjectivist; I would argue much more in favour of Luigi Aurigemma's suggestion that Jung articulated an experience which 'in itself is neither an analytical method nor a scientific method . . . [but which became] the throughline
of numerous decades of therapeutic activity and scientific production'
(Aurigemma, 1992, p. 15, translation mine). Nevertheless, like Micklem and
Hauke, Mogenson argues that, despite its current status, hysteria has a
valuable and legitimate place, a rightful domicile in a medical perspective on
mental disorders, particularly because it would creatively oppose and challenge the parameters of that perspective if permitted to reside within them. In
this sense, a Jungian argument supports the epistemological challenge which
'possession' as a dissociative disorder presents to the inclusive editorial pol-
icies of the *DSM*.

And so, as much as the writers of the *DSM* would find support in Jungian
complex theory for creating a nosological niche for 'possession' as a dissociative disorder, they would also find that Jungian theory emphasizes the cultural context and sociogenic significance of any experience of 'possession'.
Kirmayer and Littlewood characterize Multiple Personality Disorder and
anorexia as culture-bound syndromes that, in part, challenge and critique the
collectives from within which they emerged, in much the same way that
Boddy interpreted the *zar* cult as, in part, challenging and critiquing a recent
patriarchal Islamic overlay on Sudanese culture. Likewise, Jungian theory
would hypothesize not only personal idiosyncratic causes but also the sociogenic aspects of an idiom of distress such as Dissociative Trance Disorder,
aspects which it describes in terms of a collective or cultural unconscious
(Singer and Kimbles, 2004). Jungian theory would seek to assign meaning to
'possession' as at least partly an idiom of distress, in terms of the prospective
function it carries not only for the individual but also for the collective.
Psychotherapy – the method of treatment recommended by the *DSM* for
most dissociative disorders – can be effective, according to a Jungian model,
to the degree that the biological, psychogenic, sociogenic and prospective
aspects of dissociative distress can all be meaningfully synthesized or
integrated.

den 17.Juni 1952.

Herrn Dr.R.J.Zwei Werblowsky,
Dept.of Semitics,
University of Leeds.
Leeds 2.

Lieber Herr Doktor,

    Für die freundliche Zusendung Ihrer kritischen Ueber-
legungen danke ich Ihnen bestens. Sie sind mir wertvoll und in-
teressant als die Reaktionen eines (beinahe) Unbeteiligten. Sie
haben ja von der leichten Berührung mit der Psychologie bereits
einen "goldenen Finger" bekommen und müssen jetzt Ihrer Umwelt
Red' und Antwort stehen. So geht es sogar Leuten, die nur einmal
"Guten Tag" zu mir gesagt haben.

    Ich weiss nicht, ob ich darüber froh sein soll, dass
man meine verzweifelten Versuche, der Wirklichkeit der Seele gerecht zu werden, wenigstens als "geistvolle Zweideutigkeit" wür-
digt. Zum mindesten ist damit meine Anstrengung, die "geistvolle
Zweideutigkeit" der Seele einigermassen adaequat wiederzugeben,
anerkannt.

    Für mich ist die Seele ein beinahe unendliches Phäno-
men. Ich weiss ganz und gar nicht, was sie an sich ist und nur
sehr undeutlich, was sie nicht ist. Auch weiss ich nur in be-
schränktem Masse, was an der Seele einzeln und was allgemein ist.
Sie erscheint mir als ein sozusagen allumfassendes Beziehungs-
system, wobei mir "stofflich" und "geistig" in erster Linie als
Bezeichnungen für bewusstseinstranszendente Möglichkeiten gelten.
Ich kann von nichts sagen, es sei "nur psychisch", denn alles in
meiner unmittelbaren Erfahrung ist psychisch in erster Linie. Ich
lebe in einer perceptual world, aber nicht in einer an sich be-
stehenden. Letztere ist zwar real genug, aber wir haben nur in-
direkte Informationen über sie. Dies gilt sowohl von den "äusse-
ren" Dingen wie von den "inneren" bezw. den stofflichen Existen-
zen und den archetypischen Faktoren, die man auch als
bezeichnen könnte. Ueber was ich immer rede, so spielen beide
Faktoren mehr oder weniger mit herein. Dies ist unvermeidlich
denn unsere Sprache ist ein getreues Abbild des psychischen Phäno-
mens mit seinem Doppelaspekt von "perceptual" und "imaginary".
Wenn ich "Gott" sage, dann ist schon der Doppelaspekt von ens
absolutum und Wasserstoffatom (bezw.von Corpuskel + Welle) gege-
ben. Ich bestrebe mich "neutral" zu reden, d.h. der psychischen
Natur mit ihrem Doppelaspekt gerecht zu werden. (Prof.Pauli würde
sagen: die "neutrale Sprache" zwischen "physikalisch" und "arche-
typisch".) Die Sprache muss zweideutig bezw. doppelsinnig sein.
Ich strebe bewusst und absichtlich nach dem doppelsinnigen Aus-
druck, weil er der Eindeutigkeit überlegen ist und der Natur des
Seins entspricht.

    Ich definiere mich selbst als Empiriker, denn ich muss
doch etwas Anständiges sein. Sie geben ja selber zu, dass ich ein
schlechter Philosoph bin, und ich mag selbstverständlich nicht
gerne etwas Minderwertiges sein. Als Empiriker habe ich wenigstens

Figure 4.1 Jung's letter to Dr. R. J. Zwi Werblowsky, 17 June 1952, in which he defines his equivocal discourse, Jung Collection, ETH Bibliothek, Zurich, published by permission from Stiftung des Werke von C. G. Jung, Zurich, represented by Paul and Peter Fritz AG, Literary Agency, Zurich.

Chapter 4

Reading Jung's equivocal language

> A metaphor can appear to be a gesture of healing – it pulls a stitch through the rift that our capacity for language opens between us and the world. A metaphor is an explicit refusal of the idea that the distinctness of things is their most fundamental ontological characteristic. But their distinctness is *one* of their most fundamental ontological characteristics (the other being their interpenetration and connectedness).
>
> (Jan Zwicky, *Wisdom and Metaphor*, p. 59)

> The Brain – is wider than the Sky –
> For – put them side by side –
> The one the other will contain
> With ease – and You – beside –
>
> (Emily Dickinson, *The Complete Poems*, No. 632)

To analyse Jung's concept of possession, it is important first to place that concept rhetorically in a discourse that he himself described as deliberately equivocal. Vico's privileging of mythopoeic language was a precursor of Jung's argument in favour of ontologically privileging images, and understanding this connection will, I hope, attune readers' expectations when they read Jung's words. A Vichian argument reconnects Jung's concept of possession etymologically with its image, with the embodied notion of being able to sit in one's own seat, and situates this concept in Jung's epistemology of paradox. Tracking the word 'possession' through Jung's Collected Works renders his concept explicit and practicable.

Jung's equivocation

In 1951, Professor R. J. Zwi Werblowsky, a lecturer at Leeds University and at the Institute of Jewish Studies of Manchester, submitted a manuscript entitled *Lucifer and Prometheus* to Jung, asking him to write an introduction. Jung was worried that a psychiatrist's introduction to a study of Milton's

Paradise Lost would appear highly incongruous. Still, he fulfilled the request and wrote a few paragraphs in which he emphasized the clinical relevance to the contemporary reader of the ambiguous figure of Lucifer, explaining just 'how and why the devil [has] got into the psychiatrist's consulting room'.

Jung speaks of Milton's devil as the drive towards selfhood. He argues that the ambiguous, deceiving devil Goethe portrayed in *Faust* a hundred and forty years later was the dark half of the alchemists' *filius*, a manifestation of Mercurius, known to be capable of anything, but by then the *filius* had dwindled into Faust's personal familiar; this devil was a mere shadow of Milton's struggling hero. Jung then cites his own psychological rule: when an archetypal image has lost its metaphysical hypostasis, its substantiality or importance, it becomes identified or fused with the conscious mind of the individual, and, being numinous, produces an inflation. Because the devil had become so diminished, Jung concludes, it is not at all surprising that Goethe dubbed his Faust a Superman and that, through Nietzsche and beyond, the West continues to suffer the collective consequences that one might expect from a demonic possession (Jung, 1952, para. 472).

A few months later, in a letter to Werblowsky, Jung considers his remarks about Milton's ambiguous Lucifer. He mentions that Martin Buber has derided his work as 'Gnosticism' and accused him of an 'ingenious ambiguity', criticism that Jung turns on its ear. Buber's remarks do him credit, he says, since he has always tried to respect the 'ingeniously ambiguous' nature of the psyche. Furthermore, he tells Werblowsky, his language is deliberately equivocal:

> The language I speak must be ambiguous, must have two meanings, in order to do justice to the dual aspect of our psychic nature. I strive quite consciously and deliberately for ambiguity of expression, because it is superior to unequivocalness and reflects the nature of life. My whole temperament inclines me to be very unequivocal indeed. That is not difficult, but it would be at the cost of truth. I purposely allow all the overtones and undertones to be heard, partly because they were there anyway, and partly because they give a fuller picture of reality. . . . That is why I prefer ambiguous language, since it does equal justice to the subjectivity of the archetypal idea and to the autonomy of the archetype. . . . The realm of psyche is immeasurably great and filled with living reality. At its brink lies the secret of matter and of spirit. . . . For me it is the frame within which I can express my experience.
>
> (Jung, 1973, Vol. 2, pp. 69–71)

The 'frame' within which Jung wrote, with its inherent ambiguity, continues to frustrate his readers in both clinical and academic circles. As Jung explains in other letters, he was bitterly aware that this rhetorical frame often stumped people and adversely affected the reception of his writings. But, as his collected correspondence also makes explicit, he continued to defend his decision to write within that frame.

More than linguistic considerations, what Jung calls a 'moral imperative' (Jung, 1916b/1958, p. 68) drives much of his writing. In his memoirs, he describes an early intrapsychic dialogue in the form of a confrontation with an anima-voice who insists that his writing down his fantasies is 'art'. He counters this accusation by saying that recording these fantasies is reporting objective 'nature'; in other words, he portrays himself as tempted by his own inferior function's inclination to both overvalue and undervalue this work by deeming it artistic, and he resists the possible inflation and deflation of his ego by unconscious contents. He argues that, following a moral imperative, he must objectify his experience of psyche onto the page in order to subject it to scientific study (Jung, 1962, p. 186). Encountering his unconscious armed only with artistic intent and aesthetic interpretations, Jung fears that his ego will be overwhelmed, that the psychotherapist will lose the name of action and that the man will lose his psychic equilibrium, even his sanity.

Jung often acknowledges the benefit of the word's ability to depotentiate the power of the mind's unconscious contents, the psychotherapeutic value of objectifying these contents onto paper. But he is equally mindful that this apotropaic effect of words can be hubristically employed as an ego-defence and that words themselves are dangerous. So, for instance, in a letter to a doctor who has sent him an essay on symbology, Jung advises:

> It is very important for your mental health that you should on the one hand concern yourself with psychic material but on the other hand should do so as systematically and accurately as possible, otherwise you are running a dangerous risk! Do not forget that the original meaning of all letters and numbers was a magical one! Hence the perils of the soul!
>
> (Jung, 1973, Vol. 1, pp. 528–529)

According to Jung, the problem with words is both their magical origins and the distance which they can appear to create from that magic. He wants to adopt the terminology of an empiricist as he examines the manifestations of psychic nature within himself and in his patients, but he also finds himself resisting the distancing or reductive effect of a purely clinical terminology. As early as 1909, he wrote to Sándor Ferenczi to protest that Freud's style troubled him, that in an essay on obsessional neurosis, Freud had used the phrase 'symptom of omnipotence', which Jung rejects as 'too clinical'. On the same day, Jung also wrote to Freud: 'We shall not solve the ultimate secrets of neurosis and psychosis without mythology and the history of civilization. . . . Hence my attacks on "clinical terminology" ' (Jung, 1973, Vol. 1, pp. 14–15). And in his late reflections on Freud, Jung evaluated Freudian language as precise but constrictive:

Although, for Freud, sexuality was undoubtedly a numinosum, his terminology and theory seemed to define it exclusively as a biological function. It was only the emotionality with which he spoke of it that revealed the deeper elements reverberating within him. Basically, he wanted to teach – or so at least it seemed to me – that, regarded from within, sexuality included spirituality and had an intrinsic meaning. But his concretistic terminology was too narrow to express this idea. ... He remained unaware that his 'monotony of interpretation' expressed a flight from himself, or from that other side of him which might perhaps be called mystical. ... He was blind toward the paradox and ambiguity of the content of the unconscious and did not know that everything which arises out of the unconscious has a top and a bottom, an inside and an outside.

(Jung, 1962, pp. 152–153)

It seems that, even though Jung's own thinking function wants words that 'get a grip on something' by conceptualizing (Jung, 1973, Vol. 1, p. 212), his intuitive function distrusted philosophical words which, he said, 'curse us with the ability to think a thing and to imagine we possess it while being miles away in reality' (Jung, 1973, Vol. 1, p. 96). To avoid what he regarded as this particularly Western epistemological problem, Jung thought it best to anchor his words in a genuine empiricism, to attach his signifiers to concrete sensate experiences, to hook his terms to observable manifestations of psychic nature. 'As I am thoroughly empirical I never took a philosophical concept for its own sake', he said. 'It was a word to me, which designated something tangible and observable, or it meant nothing' (Jung, 1973, Vol. 1, p. 465).

But as much as Jung wanted to adopt an empirical attitude, his subject matter – fantasies, dreams, visions, parapsychological events, all the irrational manifestations of the inner life – and his psychotherapeutic goal forced him to differentiate himself from other proponents of scientific method in the study of human suffering. This determination was so strong that he declared, 'I have always staked my life on keeping psychotherapy separate from both psychiatry and neurology' (Jung, 1973, Vol. 1, p. 163). Jung's claim that he was an empiricist remains controversial; perhaps the most generous and inclusive position is that, at the time, certain forms of phenomenology, such as William James's idea of 'radical empiricism', extend the empirical to include the subjective (Dourley, 2002).

Disavowing any artistic hope of employing words to paint a picture of life, Jung expressed satisfaction with a workmanlike language of conventional signs (Jung, 1973, Vol. 1, p. 324). His words, he said, were not rational and not systematized but mere names for groups of irrational experientially based phenomena (Jung, 1973, Vol. 2, p. 302):

If I had invented a system, I certainly should have constructed better and more philosophical concepts. ... [But] when things fit together, it is not

always a matter of a philosophical system; sometimes it is the facts
that fit together. Mythological motifs are facts; they never change; only
theories change. There can never be a time which denies the existence of
mythological motifs. . . . Yet the theory about them can change a great deal
at any time.

(Jung, 1973, Vol. 2, p. 192)

Mythological motifs are the facts which Jung chose to investigate in order
to theorize comparative anatomies of the psyche and a corresponding
practice of psychotherapy. He did not repudiate reason; he used it, but he
also wanted to write using a mythopoeic language as equivocal as the oracle
of Delphi or a dream. So, on the one hand, he preferred the term 'the
unconscious' because it 'was coined for scientific purposes' and was 'far
better suited to dispassionate observation which makes no metaphysical
claims'. On the other hand, he found 'the unconscious' to be 'too neutral
and rational a term to give much impetus to the imagination' (indeed, it even
robs it of its power), whereas 'daimon' or 'god' includes or evokes the
emotional quality of numinosity, if only the mythopoeic diction were not so
highly charged that a concept expressed in this language provokes as much
controversy, even fanaticism, as it evokes meaning (Jung, 1962, p. 341). Here,
Jung positions himself somewhat awkwardly in the middle of the cultural
division of his time between the sciences and the humanities. And because he
wanted to write in service of the totality of the psyche – top and bottom,
concrete and abstract, inner and outer, rational and instinctual, scientific and
humanistic – he chose a language of ambiguity and equivocation.

Privileging mythopoeic language in Vico's *New Science*

Jung's vocabulary and epistemology had a precursor in the work of the early
eighteenth-century philosopher and rhetorician Giambattista Vico. An
important critic of the Enlightenment, Vico developed a theory of knowledge
that sees the natural sciences and the humanities as contradictory domains.
Differentiating between observation of the external world and understanding
human experience led Vico to oppose the Cartesian bias of his time; according to Vico, it is fallacious to apply the rules and the language of the natural
sciences to the domain of volition and feeling. He may also have been the first
thinker to recognize the continuing underlying role of mythological motifs
in Western cultures, even as these cultures grew increasingly secularized and
scientifically rationalized, and he was the first to argue that these cultures
need to privilege and rehabilitate mythopoeic language.

At the core of Vico's *New Science* (1725) is his principle of *verum
factum*: truth is made, not perceived. This principle led to his perception of
the difference between *certum*, knowledge from outside (such as the physical

Figure 4.2 Allegorical frontispiece from Giambattista Vico's *Principj di Scienza nuova, d'intorno alla comune natura delle Nazioni*, which compensates for the bias of Descartes's scientific rationalism with a new science of 'imaginative universals' (Naples, 1744).

sciences), and *verum*, knowledge from inside (such as history and pure mathematics). Vico attacked other theorists because their one-sided stance devalued insight or self-knowledge:

> But in the night of thick darkness enveloping the earliest antiquity, so remote from ourselves, there shines the eternal and never failing light of a truth beyond all question: that the world of civil society has certainly been made by men, and that its principles are therefore to be found within the modifications of our own human mind. Whoever reflects on this cannot but marvel that the philosophers should have bent all their energies to the study of the world of nature, which, since God made it, He alone knows; and that they should have neglected the study of the world of nations, or civil world, which, since men had made it, men could come to know.
>
> (Vico, 1744/1948, p. 96)

According to Vico's epistemology, *verum* and knowledge acquired through the faculty of the imagination, through *fantasia*, are the foundation of the human sciences. Vico argued that image and narrative are the primary source of philosophizing, rather than concept (Verene, 1981, p. 180). The important distinction between the two traditional categories of knowledge – the deductive, which includes logic and grammar, and the perceptual, derived from empirical observation – is that the former yields truth independently of what one makes, whereas the latter concerns matters which one perceives as natural events, as external facts. Vico acknowledged the possibility of other kinds of knowledge, such as the metaphysical, which may include the Platonic Forms but which is revealed through faith as embodied in the Church. However, he placed particular emphasis on self-knowledge attained through the faculty of the imagination. Imaginative insight allows for the possibility of establishing a truth based on an inner fact; in this way, he thought, the human sciences can also posit truth, even though such truths do not rely on Cartesian-style pure and fixed ideas. And imagination also permits members of one age or culture to attempt empathetically to enter into the values, ideals, and forms of life of another time or culture, to re-create it from within through its language and its mythology in order to attempt to understand it.

Vico acknowledged that this imaginative faculty renders humans prone to the error of anthropomorphosis, of mistakenly projecting knowledge onto the natural world and then misreading that world in human terms. But he accused Descartes of having committed the opposite error, of dogmatically renouncing the epistemological function of the imagination and of assimilating the human sciences into the non-human realm of nature. This defence of what we today would call self-knowledge makes Vico a crucial (though sometimes neglected) precursor not only of the Romantics, certainly, with their impassioned faith in the imagination, but also of twentieth-century intellectual movements such as psychoanalysis, existentialism and structuralism (Burke, 1985, p. 8).

Vico contextualized the arguments of his philosophical contemporaries by locating rationalism in a three-stage historical cycle. According to his theory, civilizations move through a mythical age of gods, a heroic age of aristocracy, and a demotic age of the people, which is followed by a precarious leap back to the mythical. Leaving aside this historicism, seeing his own times as 'third-stage' allowed him to acknowledge the relative merits of the Enlightenment while at the same time seeing rationalism as part of an intellectual climate: he articulated what its viewpoint was good for, asked what was missing from its perspective, and speculated about the logical end to which it was directing itself. This teleological concern led to his mapping of *corsi e ricorsi*: advancing through time, a civilization either spirals progressively or merely repeats itself, depending on the quality of that leap from the third stage to the first. At its very best, paradoxically, this leap is simultaneously a jumping forward and a jumping backward. With this theory of cycles, Vico portrayed human culture as an intelligible, constantly changing reality which must be intuited, in much the same way as nature must be observed empirically.

In the English-speaking world, Vico's ideas remained fairly well buried until the great mid-twentieth-century thinker and essayist Isaiah Berlin brought them to more public attention. Berlin was of two minds about a tension that exists between Vico's humanistic historicism and his Christian teleology. In one essay, he noted that there is no progress from the imperfect toward perfection in Vico's cyclical image, 'only a flow from new needs created by the satisfaction of the old ones in an unceasing self-creation and self-transformation of men' (Berlin, 2001, p. 348). This world view may be seen as culturally and morally relativistic, but Berlin preferred to read it as pluralistic, since members of one culture, by force of imaginative insight, can understand another (Berlin, 2001, p. 9). But elsewhere, Berlin spoke about the degree to which Vico's phases are not haphazard, are not a sequence of mechanical causes or effects; instead, they reflect stages in a movement towards an intelligible collective purpose. An intelligent divine presence plays a strong role in Vico's world view, a Creator whom Vico may be trying to propitiate when he named that dangerous leap out of the third stage 'Providentia' (Lilla, 1992). At the same time, his dramatizations of the stages of civilization as cumulatively informed by a collective 'mind' can also be read as expressing a more human creativity (Mali, 1992). In any case, Vico was demonstrably a Christian teleologist, portraying religion as the only genuine socially cohesive force and attributing a divine aspect to humans, a 'light' or 'spark' which they collectively value and which paradoxically transforms the darkest aspects of their bestial nature to advantage:

> Out of ferocity, avarice, and ambition, the three vices which run throughout the human race, it creates the military, merchant and

governing classes, and thus the strength, riches, and wisdom of commonwealths. Out of these three great vices, which could certainly destroy mankind on the face of the earth, it makes civil happiness.

(Vico, 1948, p. 62)

Berlin went so far as to identify the beginning of phenomenology in Vico's portrayal of human experience as shaped by unconscious and then progressively conscious ends (Berlin, 2000, p. 55).

More pertinently, Vico suggested that each age within a civilization produces its own kind of language. Thus each culture has recourse to three kinds of verbal expression, which he called the poetic, the heroic, and the vulgar or vernacular. In opposition to Plato and the Neoplatonists, Vico insisted that poetry, not philosophical prose, underlies humanity: a culture develops out of a primary framework of mythological motifs or 'imaginative universals' rather than out of reasoned principles (Vico, 1948, p. 143), and there are no concepts without images:

Poetic style arose before prose style; just as, by the same necessity, the fables or imaginative universals arose before the rational or philosophical universals, which were formed through the medium of prose speech. For after the poets had formed poetic speech by associating particular ideas . . . the peoples went on to form prose speech by contracting into a single word, as into a genus, the parts which poetic speech had associated. Take for example the poetic phrase, 'the blood boils in my heart', based on a property natural, eternal, and common to all mankind. They took the blood, the boiling, and the heart, and made of them a single word, as it were a genus, called in Greek *stomachos*, in Latin *ira* and in Italian *collera*. Following the same pattern hieroglyphs and heroic letters [or emblems] were reduced to a few vulgar letters, as *genera* assimilating innumerable diverse articulate sounds; a feat requiring consummate genius. By means of these vulgar *genera*, both of words and letters, the minds of the peoples grew quicker and developed powers of abstraction, and the way was thus prepared for the coming of the philosophers who formed intelligible *genera*.

(Vico, 1948, p. 154)

Vico privileged the poetic, not only because, according to his historical mapping, images and narrative precede concepts just as poetry precedes prose (Vico, 1948, p. 131), but also because, in order to appreciate and deftly handle concepts, one must track the genus of an image etymologically, philologically and then imaginatively, through its multiple derivations, back to its original image. One of Vico's most revolutionary discoveries is that words, like ideas, are directly determined by things – the sensory, concrete circumstances in which people live – and are therefore the most reliable evidence for them

(Berlin, 2000, p. 67). Vico's sociolinguistic approach to culture was not dif-
fusionist (Vico, 1948, p. 29). He was not much interested in how a notion such
as 'herculean' may have derived from a story that travelled from culture to
culture about a companion of Jason on a expedition to Colchis. Rather, he
accumulated a collection of 'credible impossibilities' in which every culture
has its poetic narration of a Hercules performing impossible labours, and
he suggested that these stories cluster around an imaginative universal that
conveys 'the heroic character of the founder of peoples' (Vico, 1948, p. 45).
What interested Vico were not the imaginative universals *per se* but the evolution of human thought; he used such universals as points of entry for his
etymological and philological investigations, through which he could
approach the unique style or pattern of living of each culture as it reveals
itself in language, myth, and ritual.

The divination of 'poetic logic', Vico said, forms the base upon which a
first-stage culture, lacking the capacity for abstraction, will construct its more
abstract 'rational logic'. Neither 'poetic logic' nor 'reasoned reflection' necessarily redeems Vico's cultures from barbarism; first-stage humans are vigor-
ously and cruelly ignorant, and he portrayed the third-stage humans as living
'like wild beasts in a deep solitude of spirit and will, scarcely any two being
able to agree since each follows his own pleasure or caprice' (Vico, 1948,
p. 424). Certainly Vico's map implies that rational reflection can function as a
progressive force, but *ricorsi* means that a civilization inevitably – providen-
tially, he argued – must return to the brutality of first-stage poetic logic over
and over again, that its vitality somehow resides there. When Vico was formu-
lating his ideas, rationalism had dismissed the domain of knowledge acquired
via the imagination. Therefore, I read in Vico's compensatory argument an
ethical concern: if his contemporaries and future generations continue in this
error, humanity is in danger of merely flinging itself into a compensatory
'first-stage' without retaining the insights of the Enlightenment, a *ricorsi*
that condemns its participants to blind and vicious circling rather than to a
phenomenologically progressive or providential spiral. For the modern
reader, Vico demonstrates the inherent complementarity of poetic and
rational logic, and he shows how a one-sided rationalist language endangers
the human sciences by objectifying its subjects and severing self-knowledge
from its cumulative phenomenological potential.

The implications of Vico's languages
for reading Jung

The Neoplatonic elements in Jung's psychology have been connected with
Renaissance humanists from Plotinus through Ficino to Vico (Hillman,
1975a), and there are affinities between Jung's acausal principle of synchronicity and Vico's metaphysics of the self that encounters itself in repetitions
of history (Verene, 2002). Indeed, the formulation of Jung's thought in terms

of Vico's philosophy of rhetoric demonstrates similarities between Vico and Jung, in particular their rhetorical privileging of poetic logic (Gardner, 2008) and of paradox.

Vico defined three kinds of language – the poetic, the heroic and the vernacular. The first language is mythopoeic and metaphoric. This vocabulary is both highly charged with numinosity and, at the same time, concrete rather than abstract. In its syntax, subject and object are linked by a common power; it is possible to say, 'this is that'. In its ontology, a metaphor claims 'X is Y', when in fact 'X' is not 'Y'; 'X is Y' is not a metaphorical claim unless 'X is not Y' is true (Zwicky, 2003, p. 5). Metaphors show meaning by making states of existence which are not the same intersect. Vico associated this language with insanity but, more importantly, with divination, in which the main operative image is of fusion. In this discourse, 'spirit', with its connection to 'breath', is the entity that uses language, and writing in this language is often 'a series of gnarled epigrammatic and oracular statements that are not to be argued about but must be accepted and pondered, their power absorbed by a disciple or reader' (Frye, 1990, p. 7). If articulating a word can bring about a fused state between subject and object, the value of this language to a collective is clear. To suggest only one example, knowing the name of a god or elemental spirit might give the person who knows this name some special rapport with that god or spirit; the acquisition of the word would empower the speaker with the capacity to invoke.

Heroic language mediates between the divine and the human, and it is analogical and allegorical rather than metaphoric. Heroic language is used not so much by a 'spirit' as by an individual 'soul' which resides 'in' a body. Heroic stories mirror this dynamic of incarnated rather than oracular words; their narratives tell about heroes, many of them born of a conjunction between a god and a human. In heroic language, words bridge rather than fuse, giving outward expression to inner experience; the metaphorical, in which the subject submits to an identification with a life force or power or energy – 'this is that' – is superceded by the metonymic, 'this is put for that'. Words 'put for' thoughts function as outward expressions of an inner reality, and, at the same time, because thoughts residing within are also experienced as indications of a transcendent order 'outside', words function as the bridge to this transcendent reality. Thus humans employ heroic language to imitate verbally a reality both inward and beyond; in other words, metonymic language expresses analogues, parallels, and similarities.

A tension inevitably exists between metaphorical and metonymic discourses. The metaphorical element in indecent and morally paradoxical stories about the gods found in Homer were later deconstructed through allegory, 'a special form of analogy, a technique of paralleling metaphorical with conceptual language in which the latter has the primary authority'. Etymologically, allegory comes from the Greek *allegoria*, from *allos* meaning 'other' and *agoria* meaning 'speaking'. In heroic times, mythic narratives 'defer' to argument; the stories are now placed beside and, at the same time, subjected to conceptual arguments. As a result, a connotation or tone of loss accompanies the wisdom gained. In an allegory, the concept not only parallels but also takes precedence over the metaphorical vocabulary and structure. The concept grips or takes hold of the narrative and incorporates it, rendering it meaningful. The metonymic genre par excellence is, therefore, the commentary.

Vico called his third kind of language 'vernacular'. This is a language of clearly distinct subjects and objects which functions typically by way of simile: 'this is like that'. Here, a true verbal structure is one that is like what it describes, that perfectly or realistically reflects the order of nature. The user of this vernacular language is not so much a 'soul' as a 'mind', and the language neither invokes nor evokes but depicts the real or discerns the real from the illusory. The vernacular disallows the metaphysics of the first stage and the transcendental perspective of the second stage. What is 'objective' is real, because this allows for consensus, while 'subjective' is equivalent to 'unreal' or 'illusory'.

Etymologically, the English word 'subject' carries the political sense of the individual subordinated to the authority of his society or its ruler, but it has come to denote the observer of the objective. To what extent, then, does third-stage language render the speaker subordinate – that is, 'subject' to, or under the control of, the objective world? Critical theorist Northrop Frye used Vico's classification of languages to demonstrate how his epistemology reflected most effectively, not what we think we know, but what we experience:

> Just as myth is not antihistorical but counterhistorical, so the metaphor, the statement or implication that two things are identical though different, is neither logical nor illogical but counterlogical. It presents the continuous paradox of experience, in which whatever one meets both is and is not oneself.
>
> (Frye, 2000, p. 179)

Most modern and contemporary clinical and academic language is 'mind-oriented' conceptual and vernacular prose that expresses 'intelligible universals'. Jung, on the other hand, uses a different language to express 'imaginative universals' (Verene, 1981, p. 69), and this at least partly explains why Jung's writings are denigrated, particularly his later works, which are deemed 'mystical', that is, oriented to 'spirit'.

Jung located his equivocal language in the poetic: his words name and narrate more than they conceptualize or argue. His linguistic orientation, like Vico's, privileges the mythopoeic and metaphoric in an epistemology of paradox. In this epistemology, 'only in paradox are words doing the best they can for us' (Frye, 2000, p. 179); in it, 'X is Y' and 'X is not Y' are both true.

Jung posits something similar to Vico's 'science of narration': 'a science that presents in language the inner form of the life of humanity' (Verene, 1981, p. 165). And like Vico, Jung argues that philosophy and theory come out of myth, but myth does not come out of philosophy or theory. 'I think it most unlikely that philosophy produces mythology', he said. 'Philosophy can produce allegory but not genuine mythology, since this is far older' (Jung, 1973, Vol. 1, p. 55). Metaphorical language does not make new connections; it exposes the interpenetration that was already there.

For neither Jung nor Vico was the mythopoeic romantically sublime; rather, it was the raw stuff from which civilizations must distance themselves and with which they must then find ways to reconnect. Jung translated this collective dilemma into the basis for his method of treating individual sufferers: he recognized that psychotherapeutic possibilities reside in moments when individuals rediscover mythopoeic imagery and metaphorical language, when they repair the broken narrative links between their creativity and their self-knowledge (see Chapter 5).

I do not intend to address here the critical question of whether Jung wrote 'successfully' in an equivocal language. Susan Rowland (2005) evaluates brilliantly, and in great detail, the polyphonic nature of Jung's rhetoric in various essays, appraising it not as a tool of argument but as an effective, authentic narrative demonstration of the way the multitudinous nature of the psyche works. Jung's language, she says, 'more than describing the need for healing, ideally enacts it' (Rowland, 2005, p. 151). Yet Jung himself agonized over having published some of his early experiments with language. About his *Seven Sermons to the Dead*, he said:

> The experience has to be taken for what it was, or as it seems to have been. No doubt it was connected with the state of emotion I was in at the time, and which was favorable to parapsychological phenomena. It was an unconscious constellation whose peculiar atmosphere I recognized as the numen of an archetype. . . . The intellect, of course, would like to arrogate to itself some scientific, physical knowledge of the affair, or preferably, to write the whole thing off as a violation of the rules. But what a dreary world it would be if the rules were not violated sometimes!
>
> (Jung, 1962, pp. 190–191)

This equivocal language renders Jung vulnerable to the racist, fascistic politics into which he admits having 'slipped' and his writings liable to readings (such as Richard Noll (1994) demonstrated) that made his allegorical narrative serve a fundamentalist conceptual argument. Of course, this is precisely Vico's point about the brutal weakness and danger inherent in his first-stage language and logic. In this respect, Berlin described Vico's own style as vulnerable in very similar terms:

[*New Science* is] an amalgam of sense and nonsense, an ill-sorted mass of ideas, some lucid and arresting, others shapeless or obscure, bold and novel thoughts cluttered with trivial fragments of a dead scholastic tradition. . . . [his ideas] prove too heterogeneous, too rich and too self-contained to fall in the scheme provided for them; they fly apart and pursue their own paths through the mass of superfluous and, at times, wildly irrelevant matter with which their author's digressive and intuitive mind is at all times clogged; nevertheless their intrinsic force and uniqueness somehow break through. Add to this Vico's lack of literary talent, his struggle and frequent failure to create adequate terms to convey so much that was novel and wholly out of tune with the spirit of his times . . . if all this is taken into account some of the shortcomings of the *New Science* and its lack of readers are not difficult to account for. Nevertheless it remains a work of genius.

(Berlin, 2000, p. 89)

I find many affinities between Berlin's assessment of Vico's most mature work and my own responses to Jung's *Mysterium Coniunctionis* (1955). I consider it absolutely crucial for readers to orient themselves to the language in which Jung seeks to situate his theorizing, to the peculiar specifications of Jung's texts as objects. Jung risked his reputation as a psychiatrist when he chose to write 'The Psychology of the Transference' (1946) using mythological motifs embedded in alchemical images. But with his epistemology of paradox, Jung was not only compensating in the moment for a collective objectification of psyche in most third-stage psychoanalytic prose, but also gambling on the extent to which readers, having necessarily rationalized their theories about transference, would ethically need to revitalize them by returning again and again to this imagery. Emphasizing that mythological motifs stay the same while theories change, Jung invited us to retheorize continually, in the post-Jungian sense, but in ways and with words that do not exclude and will not damage our capacity to connect and reconnect to the vitality inherent in archetypal images.

When Buber accused Jung of 'ingenious ambiguity', Jung's confidence in mythopoeic language allowed him to turn the accusation to his advantage. He declared that his language names experiences that are objectionable according to the prejudices of the contemporary mind (Jung, 1962, p. 188), and he asked that his equivocations be read as a therapeutic sacrifice of single-mindedness in service of psyche's own inherent evasiveness.

Jung's 'possession': compensatory religious term or equivocation?

Jung first wrote about 'possession' as a historical remnant, using the word to make a connection between mental illness in the past and in the present. As early as 1908, in 'The Content of the Psychoses', he refers to the history of mental illness in Western culture, describing how, during a time when soul was endowed with substance and mental illness was attributed to the work of evil spirits, methods of treatment extended from the language's concrete metaphor of fusion, from the image of the patient suffering 'as one possessed' by another (Jung, 1908, para. 321). Also, in his review of complex theory, he lists examples of archaic or first-stage language which locate psychological suffering in a metaphoric language of spirits:

> 'What's got into him today?' 'He is driven by the devil', 'hag-ridden', etc. In using these somewhat worn metaphors we naturally do not think of their original meaning, although it is easily recognizable and points without a doubt to the fact that naiver and more primitive people did not 'psychologise' disturbing complexes as we do, but regarded them as beings in their own right, that is, as demons.
>
> (Jung, 1934a, para. 204)

For Jung, 'possessed' and 'possession' give historical context to his theory of complexes; these words best convey the psychic fact that unconscious complexes function as 'splinter psyches', acting autonomously:

> I wanted to express the fact that one or other basic instinct, or complex of ideas, will invariably concentrate upon itself the greatest sum of psychic energy and thus force the ego into its service. As a rule the ego is drawn into this focus of energy so powerfully that it identifies with it and thinks it desires and needs nothing further. In this way a craze develops, a monomania or possession, an acute one-sidedness which most seriously imperils the psychic equilibrium. Without doubt the capacity for such one-sidedness is the secret of success – of a sort, for which reason our civilization assiduously strives to foster it. The passion, the piling up of energy in these monomanias, is what the ancients called 'a god', and in common speech we still do the same. Do we not say, 'he makes a god of this or that?' A man thinks that he wills and chooses, and does not notice that he is already possessed, that his interest has become his master, arrogating all power to itself.
>
> (Jung, 1917a, para. 111)

The term 'possession' seemed to Jung to compensate for an inherent danger in a psychologizing terminology. In the 1917 lecture 'The Conception of the Unconscious', he describes the problem: autonomous unconscious complexes turn a man 'into a flat collective figure, a mask behind which he can no longer develop as a human being.' Consciousness must somehow come to terms with these contents, 'firstly in the factual contents of [the] personal unconscious, and then in the fantasies of the collective unconscious' in order to 'get to the root of [the] complexes and in this way rid [oneself] of [the] possession' (Jung, 1917b/1935, para. 387). By the time of the Vision Seminars in 1932, Jung had concluded that the best way to come to terms with these unconscious contents is through a disidentifying from them:

> We should disidentify, we should not identify with those grand powers which were once great gods worshipped in temples. In the past, a man who was possessed by an uncontrollable emotion was always thought of as being possessed, and nobody was mistaken enough to think otherwise, he was just one poor sad victim. But now if a man is angry, we make him responsible. The primitives would be afraid to do that, they would wait until the spirit had left him. And on a higher level the analyst must do the same thing; when a patient gets out of control one must say, 'Now just wait, you are possessed by an evil spirit, a thought that is blinding you; we will wait until the storm has blown over.' I don't make him identify with that thing, because he has to learn that he is not necessarily identical with his emotions.
>
> (Jung, 1997, p. 531)

Jung recommends fostering a respectful, even religious attitude toward the psychic content, and he employs the word 'possessed' to reinforce that stance towards the psyche. In this sense, his use of the word is compensatory. He portrays ego consciousness as misled in part by a Vichian third-stage vocabulary about 'mind' which belies the power of repressed unconscious contents and speaks of them as 'nothing but'. Psychologizing is problematic because concepts expressed in this language misleadingly lack contents; in Vichian terms, these intelligible universals have become detached from the etymological origins that linger only in images:

> Three hundred years ago a woman was said to be possessed by the devil, now we say she has a hysteria. . . . The facts are the same; only the previous explanation, psychologically speaking, is almost exact, whereas our rationalistic description of symptoms is really without content. For if I say that someone is possessed by an evil spirit, I imply that the possessed person is not legitimately ill but suffers from some invisible psychic influence which he is quite unable to control. . . . It behaves exactly like a goblin that is always eluding our grasp.
>
> (Jung, 1931a, para. 710)

Even in the attempt to reconnect the concept to the content – the occupier as goblin – the bias in vernacular language renders it 'only a simile'. Inherent in any comparative construction in this language is an attitude which demotes the image to the merely imaginary. Consequently the language fails to convey the power of the controlling complex over the ego respectfully and skews the ontological claim of the intrapsychic Other. As a result, Jung argues, a third-stage demotic language objectifies but, paradoxically, renders the ego-as-speaker more vulnerable to possession than a first-stage language which includes spirits in its discourse:

> Always, therefore, there is something in the psyche that takes possession and limits or suppresses our moral freedom. In order to hide this undeniable but exceedingly unpleasant fact from ourselves and at the same time pay lip-service to freedom, we have got accustomed to saying apotropaically, 'I *have* such and such a desire or habit or feeling of resentment', instead of the more veracious 'Such and such a desire or habit or feeling of resentment *has me*.' The latter formulation would certainly rob us even of the illusion of freedom. But I ask myself whether this would not be better in the end than fuddling ourselves with words. The truth is that we do not enjoy masterless freedom; we are continually threatened by psychic factors which, in the guise of 'natural phenomena' may take possession of us at any moment. The withdrawal of metaphysical projections leaves us almost defenseless in the face of this happening, for we immediately identify with every impulse instead of giving it the name of the 'other', which would at least hold it at arm's length and prevent it from storming the citadel of the ego.
>
> (Jung, 1938, para. 143, italics in original)

There is more than a little irony in this picture of how psychologizing objectifies psychic experience while rendering the individual more susceptible to psychic infection. For this reason, extrapolating from the individual to the collective, Jung suspects that secularized Western cultures may be more susceptible to collective possession than other cultures which have words and viable, living strategies with which to address the problem. (This is similar to Kirmayer's argument that Western discourse renders the dissociative nature of ordinary cognitive functioning as psychic rupture: see Chapter 3.) As he mentions in his letter to Werblowsky about Milton, Jung regards psychologizing as both appropriate and ineffective: it is an attempt to disidentify from psychic contents, as he himself recommends, by employing a demotic language; but, because the bias in the language devalues the significance or power of the unconscious, the effect can be the reverse. Of course, to relinquish the discriminatory strengths of demotic language for the purely metaphysical bias of poetic logic would be an equally one-sided strategy leading to fundamentalism. For this reason, Jung ultimately wants not a compensatory religious vocabulary but an equivocal one.

Jung uses the word 'possession' to describe psychopathological states, but, for him, it also adequately denotes the dynamic between consciousness and the unconscious in so-called normal psychological experience. The danger that unconscious contents will suppress consciousness prevails in dissociative and schizoid states (Jung, 1939a, para. 501), he observes, and yet he also attempts to normalize his concept of possession by emphasizing the degree to which these pathological symptoms occur in 'normal' psychology:

> They may take the form of fluctuations in the general feeling of well-being, irrational changes of mood, unpredictable affects, a sudden distaste for everything, psychic inertia, and so on. Even the schizoid phenomena that correspond to primitive possession can be observed in normal people. They, too, are not immune to the demon of passion; they, too, are liable to possession by an infatuation, a vice, or a one-sided conviction; and these are all things that dig a deep grave between them and those they hold most dear, and create an aching split in their own psyche.
>
> (Jung, 1934b, para. 287)

So, for Jung, one of the advantages of the word 'possession' is that he can use it with reference to both psychopathological states and common psychological suffering, which is why Jung's non-pathologizing psychological concept of possession is a useful bridge between anthropology and psychology.

Jung finds uses for both psychological and religious connotations of 'possession':

> We are still as much possessed by autonomous psychic contents as if they were Olympians. Today they are called phobias, obsessions, and so forth; in a word, neurotic symptoms. The gods have become diseases; Zeus no longer rules Olympus but rather the solar plexus, and produces curious specimens for the doctor's consulting room, or disorders the brains of politicians and journalists who unwittingly let loose psychic epidemics on the world.
>
> (Jung, 1929, para. 54)

Interpreting Jung's verbal strategy according to Vico's epistemology is enlightening. Vico did not characterize psychological and religious languages as opposites; rather, he linked etymologically the rational concept to the imagistic. When Jung wants to describe the binding incestuous force in transference and countertransference, which is more powerful than analyst and analysand, he uses the word 'possession' because, by virtue of its etymology, it implies the need to adopt an appropriately respectful attitude toward a psychological phenomenon of suffering:

> The existence of the incest element involves not only an intellectual difficulty but, worst of all, an emotional complication of the therapeutic situation. It is the hiding place for all the most secret, painful, intense,

delicate, shamefaced, timorous, grotesque, unmoral, and at the same time, the most sacred feelings which go to make up the indescribable and inexplicable wealth of human relationships and give them their compelling power. Like the tentacles of an octopus they twine themselves invisibly round parents and children and, through the transference, round doctor and patient. This binding force shows itself in the irresistible strength and obstinacy of the neurotic symptom and in the patient's desperate clinging to the world of infancy or to the doctor. The word 'possession' describes this state in a way that could hardly be bettered.

(Jung, 1946, para. 371)

Jung's concept suggests a psychological dilemma of both fusion and disintegration. I have already pointed a number of times towards the etymology of the word 'possession' in order to better appreciate Jung's psychotherapeutic notion of inward relatedness. It is time to make this explicit. In German, *Besessenheit* denotes 'the occupation of something'. In English, 'to possess' denotes 'to hold as property', 'to own', 'to occupy'; like the French *posséder*, it derives from the Latin *possidere*, from *potis* meaning 'able' and *sedere*, 'to sit'. The metaphor in the concept of possession is that a being claims space and sits in a position of capability within or power over the sufferer, and Jung finds the metaphor effective because it personifies an entity occupying that seat after a tyrannical overthrow. The goal of psychotherapy is that the patient should become 'self-possessed'. At its most banal, this suggests that the patient should regain the habit of exercising self-control; at its most profound, it conveys the image of a self able to sit squarely, capably, potently in its own seat (see Chapter 5).

In his essay 'Concerning Rebirth', Jung (1950) enumerates three kinds of psychic contents from which the ego must disidentify in the process of what he calls individuation: the persona, the shadow, and the anima or animus; in the same essay, he also refers to the possession of the ego by an 'ancestral soul' (Jung, 1950, para. 221–224; see also Ancelin Schützenberger, 1998: Chapter 5). His paradoxical concept of possession suggests both a fusion and a disunity: parts of the psyche which have split off from consciousness come to overwhelm or fuse with the ego, with the result that the individual's character appears to be torn apart and selfhood is falsified in the interest of the tyrannizing split-off fragments. Jung suspects that an exclusively clinical stance promotes an anatomizing of parts, but that recognition of these parts doesn't necessarily promote cooperation between them (Jung, 1945a, para. 1374). Similarly, he criticizes conventional organized religion for inadvertently providing 'the inner disunity with an outward vessel without really changing the *disiunctio* into a *coniunctio*' (Jung, 1946, para. 397). What is required, he says, is:

a dialectical procedure, a real coming to terms with them, often conducted by the patient in dialogue form, so that, without knowing it, he puts into effect the alchemical definition of the *meditatio*: 'an inner colloquy with one's good angel'.

(Jung, 1954, para. 85)

Jung's concept of 'possession' must be read equivocally. Situated paradoxically and meaningfully over the chasm between the humanities and sciences, it denotes contemporary psychological experience, but Jung also recognized its connotative roots in the phenomenology of religion. With the concept of possession, he situated his analytical psychology in a problematic of power and personhood and asked the fundamental question: what or who sits in the seat of selfhood?

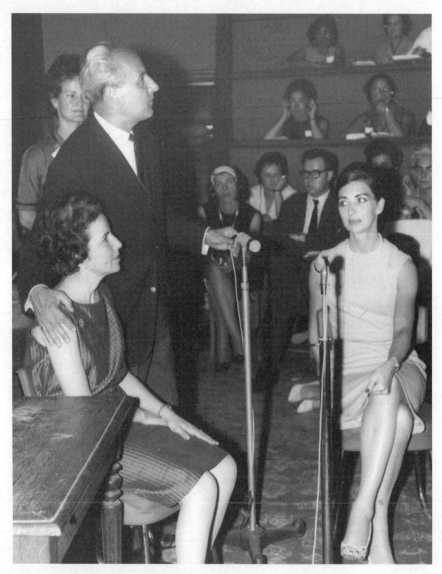

Figure 5.1 Dean Eleftery and Doreen Madden Eleftery demonstrating Moreno's psycho-therapeutic triad, working in the service of a protagonist and the spontaneous emergence of self in roles, at the Paris Congress of Psychodrama, 1964. Published with permission of Doreen Madden Eleftery.

Chapter 5

Jung's concept of possession and the practice of psychotherapy

> Now when one is possessed by the unconscious to a certain extent, when a man is possessed by his anima for instance, he has of course a very difficult time in dealing with it, so as a rule people simply cannot do it alone. One cannot isolate oneself on a high mountain and deal with the unconscious; one always needs a strong link with humanity, a human relation that will hold one down to one's human reality. Therefore, most people can only realize the unconscious inasmuch as they are in analysis, inasmuch as they have a relation to a human being who has a certain amount of understanding and tries to keep the individual down to the human size, for no sooner does one touch the unconscious than one loses one's size.
>
> (C. G. Jung, *Seminar on Nietzsche's Zarathustra*, p. 331)

In the first pages of this book, I promised to show that Jung's concept of possession can be most clearly understood in his writings about psychotherapy. So far, I have located Jung's use of the word 'possession' within the context of the history of religion in Western Europe, as well as within the frame of his own equivocal language. I have shown how Jung borrowed from anthropology, and I have placed beside Jung's concept a number of enriching, even contradicting, images from contemporary anthropological studies of possession in non-Western cultures. And I have argued that, by introducing the concept of possession into its formal nosology, contemporary psychiatry has taken a step towards a potential epistemological break, towards a widening of its frame of reference and its field of knowledge.

Jung's writings about psychotherapy bring his theory down to human size, to the intimate context of a patient and a therapist. Although a good deal of contemporary psychotherapy springs from Freudian psychoanalysis, Jung's concept of possession accounts for some valuable and distinctive aspects of psychotherapeutic practice, aspects with which most psychotherapists are very familiar. Temenos/containment, personification/mimesis, and integration/synthesis are integral components of Jung's particular contribution to contemporary practice. Jung's concept of possession unifies theoretically and carries important implications for these three aspects of psychotherapy.

The concept of possession also functions in two other Western psychotherapeutic approaches. Jung's practice aligns with that of Jean-Michel Oughourlian, a disciple of the thinker René Girard, and with the work of Jacob Moreno, the creator of psychodrama. Moreno's psychotherapeutic triad especially complements Jung's. Comparing and contrasting these three psychotherapeutic practices corroborates the validity of Jung's concept.

Jung's concept of possession and the practice of Jungian psychotherapy

Jung's psychotherapy is a treatment of the psyche in which a patient and a psychotherapist work to bridge the inherently high degree of dissociability that Jung associated with Western consciousness, an association that recent cognitive research appears to corroborate (Wilkinson, 2006). In the terms of Jung's theory of complexes, this dissociability renders the ego susceptible to possession by unconscious contents whenever these complexes are activated. One suffers possession by a complex as both a dissociation and as a fusion of ego and Other; ironically, this works to the detriment of the personality as a whole. Jung described the ego as at times overwhelmed, gripped or inflated by the dissociated, unconscious splinter psyche. 'When the god is not acknowledged', he said, 'egomania develops, and out of this mania comes sickness' (Jung, 1929, para. 55). Through the dialectic between the psyches of the patient and the psychotherapist, symbols from the unconscious emerge that paradoxically facilitate both the detaching of the ego from the unconscious contents and the integrating of some aspects of these contents into consciousness. These emerging symbols carry the potential to free the ego from its fused or possessed state and, at the same time, to provide a bridge by means of which the ego can relate responsibly to the force and the meaning (as well as the meaninglessness) of the unconscious as Other.

Jung deliberately employed an equivocal language to convey the affective and dynamic aspects of many of his psychological concepts. With respect to psychotherapeutic practice, he described the technique of building the psychological container within which the patient and psychotherapist meet and work. He called this contained space a 'temenos', using the classical Greek word for a demarcated precinct within which a god's presence can be felt, a holy place that protects the sacred centre (Jung, 1935b, para.410). Thus he drew attention to a ritualistic aspect of analysis which most psychodynamic psychotherapists now acknowledge. The rhythm of recurring meetings at a specified time each week, the familiarity of the setting, the patterns of gestures which begin and end sessions – all these repetitive features of the analytical encounter produce an experience often called 'the therapeutic frame' (Robert Langs, in Gray, 1994). Melanie Klein and D. W. Winnicott said that psychoanalysis offers the patient an experience of 'containment' which is 'transitional', that is to say, 'illusory but creative' (Winnicott, 1951, p. 232; Laplanche and Pontalis, 1973, p. 465). Jung's notion of temenos adds that the repetitive aspects of the analytic frame create the potential for the therapeutic space to be experienced as ritualistic or ceremonial, as 'liminal' (in Victor Turner's sense: see Chapter 2).

Medical anthropologist Arthur Kleinman's argument that American psychiatry should acknowledge the religious component in the Chinese practice of healing (see Chapter 3) is like Jung's respect for the religious connotation of the liminal in Western psychotherapeutic healing. Jung attempted to normalize the role of the religious function as an instinct from which secularized modern cultures have distanced themselves but which often manifests within the temenos as an aspect of the healing. His concept of temenos embraced this sense of something akin to liminality in the ritualized container of psychotherapy. Indeed, he described the psychotherapeutic healing process contained within the temenos as psychically charged with unconscious possibilities; the ego, he thought, experiences these possibilities as an Otherness tinged with a religious connotation of numinosity. 'We might say, then, that the term "religion" designates the attitude peculiar to a consciousness which has been changed by experience of the numinosum', he said (Jung, 1938, para. 9). To the important concepts of therapeutic frame and psychoanalytic containment, Jung contributed this additional notion of a protected, even sacred, space. Employing the concept of temenos allowed Jung to grant equivocally an equal ontological status to the demarcated unconscious dimension. Thus he avoided the hierarchy that Winnicott implicitly established when describing the 'transitional' as 'illusory'. Jung's perception of this inappropriate hierarchy is similar to anthropologist Edward Schieffelin's perception of the hierarchy in performance theory's description of Kaluli possession as 'theatricalized' (see Chapter 2).

Jung's concept of possession has an ample context in the history of European Christianity, anthropology and psychiatry, and this breadth is also evident in the discerning, respectful attitude that he considered essential toward participants in psychotherapy. Both the analyst and the analysand render themselves receptive in the temenos to 'the god felt within the sacred precinct', to possibilities for change within formidable and unpredictable unconscious processes. Anthropologists shifted from Turner's notion of 'ritual' towards Bourdieu's notion of 'practice' in an attempt to avoid theorizing that renders the phenomena of possession exotic, esoteric or exclusive in cultures which do not exoticise them; their viewpoint also shifted to avoid privileging structure and order over anti-structure and chaos. In much the same way, post-Jungian theorists carefully detach Jung's definition of the religious function in psychotherapy from connotations of an esoteric system of belief, and, at the same time, they defend it from classical psychoanalytic interpretation that sees it as a component of transference phenomena which constitutes resistance and an obstacle to healing. Jung's concept of synchronicity provides an important framework for understanding numinous experiences which are otherwise considered taboo within clinical settings and for considering the interaction of religious and scientific imagery (Main, 2000). There are potential risks within the transference – and for the therapy in general – when this dimension of psychotherapeutic practice is not processed consciously but acted out in the transference and countertransference, or when it is interpreted only reductively, that is, as infantile and illusory (Stein, 2004; Wiener, 2004). With his concept of possession, Jung argued that psychotherapeutic healing depends on the care with which the therapist considers the implications of this religious function when the Otherness of the unconscious manifests in the temenos of the therapeutic encounter.

Looking at possession from a slightly different angle, Jung described the technique of personifying complexes – for instance as animals, persons or gods – and, as a result, of experiencing psychic conflict between antagonistic aspects of the personality. Complexes may be seen as organized sets of ideas and memories that are, for the most part, unconscious but that carry enormous affective power when activated. Even though Freud and Breuer used 'personification' in their early studies of hysteria, its theoretical importance in psychoanalysis can be attributed to Jung's studies in word association; indeed, Freudian psychoanalysis increasingly shunned the term after Jung and Adler placed complexes at the centre of their theories as natural phenomena (Laplanche and Pontalis, 1973, pp. 72–74). For orthodox Freudians, the complex remains a symptom resulting from a failed act of repression. For Jung, having

> complexes does not in itself signify neurosis . . . and the fact that they are painful is no proof of pathological disturbance. Suffering is not an illness; it is the normal counterpole to happiness. A complex becomes pathological only when we think we have not got it.
>
> (Jung, 1942, para. 179)

Jung's concept of possession emphasizes personification as a spontaneous psychological process which plays an important role in psychotherapeutic healing. Whereas psychiatry associates personification with the irrational and pathological hallucinatory phenomena of Dissociative Identity Disorder and psychosis, Jung normalizes it as a natural psychological process through which unconscious contents manifest:

> Every autonomous or even relatively autonomous complex has the peculiarity of appearing as a personality, i.e., of being personified. This can be observed most readily in the so-called spiritualistic manifestations of automatic writing and the like. The sentences produced are always personal statements and are propounded in the first person singular, as

though behind every utterance there stood an actual personality. A naïve intelligence at once thinks of spirits.

(Jung, 1935b, para. 312)

This process is comparable to what Laurence Kirmayer (1999), in his review of cognitive research on dissociation, saw as a component of reverie. He noted a study by Witztum and Goodman (1999), who believed that when their patients addressed their suffering through reverie and a manipulation of symbols, they were effectively reorganizing cognitive schemas, unconscious dynamics and interpersonal interactions. Kirmayer described their psychotherapeutic practice precisely in terms of working with split-off aspects of the self which are experienced as supernatural entities and spirits.

According to Jung, the technique of personifying provides a psychotherapeutic means by which the ego can free itself from the possessing affective power of an unconscious complex. In his memoirs, as well as in his theoretical writings about complexes, he recorded his experiments with the personified image of the complex. He observed that if, rather than simply suffering the active complex's often difficult affect, one deliberately enters a state of reverie and permits the complex to manifest spontaneously to conscious awareness as a personified image, then one takes away its power over ego consciousness and makes interpretation possible:

> The essential thing is to differentiate oneself from these unconscious contents by personifying them, and at the same time to bring them into relationship with consciousness. That is the technique for stripping them of their power. It is not too difficult to personify them, as they always possess a certain degree of autonomy, a separate identity of their own. Their autonomy is a most uncomfortable thing to reconcile oneself to, and yet the very fact that the unconscious presents itself in that way gives us the best means of handling it.
>
> (Jung, 1962, p. 187)

For this reason, an important component in Jung's practice of psychotherapy focused upon supporting the ego of the patient within the temenos to the point that it could experience the autonomy of the unconscious complex as a splinter psyche and eventually reconcile itself to that psychic reality through a personified meeting and confrontation. 'A patient who cannot personify tends merely to personalise everything. Analysis can be seen as an exploration of the patient's relationship to his or her personifications' (Samuels et al., 1986, p. 108).

In the mid-1970s, James Hillman (1975b) described the essential contributions which the technique of personification could make to the practice of psychotherapy. In terms very similar to Roland Littlewood's medical anthropological argument (summarized in Chapter 3), Hillman argued that, by honouring the inherent multiplicity and pluralism of the psyche, Jung's process of personification compensates for the dangers inherent in the one-sidedness of modern Western cultures and the practice of an ego-oriented psychology of self-development. Hillman also proposed that the personification of unconscious contents can provide an effective way to adopt the paradoxical position of, on the one hand, claiming the personified aspects as one's own and, on the other hand, experiencing their autonomy and their distinctness from ego consciousness. Furthermore, Hillman suggested that personification demands a dramatically engaged and lived response to the unconscious as Other, in contrast to intellectualizing and conceptualizing unconscious contents, which will not be psychotherapeutically effective.

Thirty years later, John Beebe demonstrated this therapeutic use of personifying rather than conceptualizing. He differentiated a model of eight mental functions using Jung's theory of psychological types. Within his model, Beebe privileged a differentiation by personified archetypal figure: for example, the tertiary function is the puer/puella; the inferior function, the anima/animus; the opposite attitude to the inferior function, the demonic (Beebe, 2004). In Vichian terms, Beebe expressed his model of mental functioning in both demotic and mythopoeic languages, but I suspect that when he is inside the psychotherapeutic frame or temenos with a patient, he deliberately tips the balance slightly to privilege the mythopoeic, perhaps referring more to the hero than to the superior function. Certainly, I can hypothesize moments when a patient needs to hear 'your anima' and other moments when the same patient needs to hear 'your inferior function', but Beebe's working model provides a space between these two vocabularies, thus making room for the autonomy of the unconscious and for possibilities of change to manifest.

Jung's concept of possession contributed to an understanding of personification and to the effective practice of psychotherapy. He said of the troubled patient:

> Instead of allowing himself to be convinced once more that the daemon is an illusion, he ought to experience once more the reality of this illusion. He should learn to acknowledge these psychic forces anew, and not wait until his moods, nervous states, and delusions make it clear in the most painful way that he is not the only master in his house. His dissociative tendencies are actual psychic personalities possessing a differential reality. They are 'real' when they are not recognized as real and consequently projected; they are relatively real when they are brought into relationship with consciousness (in religious terms, when a cult exists); but they are unreal to the extent that consciousness detaches itself from its contents. . . . The personification enables us to see the relative reality of the autonomous system, and not only makes its assimilation possible but also depotentiates the daemonic forces of life.
>
> (Jung, 1929, para. 54–55)

Pragmatically, from within Jung's epistemology of paradox, the more possessing unconscious contents are really lived and engaged with through personification, the less intensely they are experienced as real. Jung's concept of possession accounts for this ontological paradox and for the psychotherapeutic effect of personification by privileging the reality of the unconscious Other, so undervalued in Western cultures. Jung employed Lévy-Bruhl's concept of *participation mystique* to describe a kind of mental functioning in which the ego perceives contents of the personality projected onto objects with which it then feels compelled to identify, even if only negatively, by devaluing them (see Chapter 2). Klein's concept of projective identification had defined the pathology inherent in this psychodynamic process in terms of object relations: subjects eject into the outside world things which they refuse in themselves (Laplanche and Pontalis, 1973, p. 356). For Jung, projection risked rendering the splinter psyches ontologically 'unreal', to the extent that they are not only disowned but disembodied; at the same time, ironically, unconscious complexes acquire an ontological status that is 'more real than real', since they insistently overwhelm ego consciousness with their reality and unseat the personality:

> The characteristic feature of a pathological reaction is, above all, identification with the archetype. This produces a sort of inflation and possession by the emergent contents, so that they pour out in a torrent which no therapy can stop. Identification can, in favourable cases, sometimes pass off as a more or less harmless inflation. But in all cases identification with the unconscious brings a weakening of consciousness, and herein lies the danger. You do not 'make' an identification, you do not 'identify yourself', but you experience your identity with the archetype in an unconscious way and so are possessed by it.
>
> (Jung, 1934c, para. 621)

Becoming conscious is then synonymous with reversing the process of projective identification, with integrating as much as possible and realizing what has been rendered 'unreal' – in other words, with incarnating what Jung's concept of possession would express in personified form as disembodied spirit. Jung personified unconscious complexes – images and highly charged affects clustering around an archetypal core – as spirits or gods seeking to incarnate because he can thereby convey, not only their affective power over the individual ego, but also their precarious quality as unlived potentialities of the personality that manifest prospectively as impulses towards concrete embodiment in time and space.

Inside the temenos of psychotherapeutic practice, the patient and therapist may experience resistances to this process of personification. One reason for this is the relativizing which the ego must suffer as it confronts a multiplicity of autonomous mental functioning which contradicts its identity and over which it cannot exercise control. Also implicit in Jung's concept of possession is another kind of resistance with which psychotherapists are familiar: the 'emptying' or diminishment which the god, spirit or split-off complex suffers in moving from the grandiosity of its collective or archetypal manifestation into the merely personal. In other words, in addition to the resistance to losing the psychopathological primary gain of the dissociative illness, there is what Jung describes in personified terms as the anima or animus experiencing itself as depotentiated to human size, to the status of a mere psychological function accessible to consciousness (Jung, 1935b, para. 374). In terms very similar to Janice Boddy's ethnological description of marriage as the central metaphor of northern Sudanese *zar* possession practices (see Chapter 2), Jung accounted for both of these aspects of suffering by paradoxically dramatizing the process of individuation – of becoming psychologically whole – as a gradual, painful but propitious marrying of the antagonistic elements of spirit and matter.

As a result, according to Jung's concept of possession, one of the most difficult tasks in psychotherapy is, ironically, to strengthen the ego to the point at which it can endure the truth about itself, the point at which it can not only differentiate itself from unconscious complexes but also abdicate its defensive claim that it is the governing principle of the personality. Jung described the situation this way:

> Consequently if the ego drops its claim to victory, *possession* . . . ceases automatically, . . . for it is certain that when the ego makes no claim to power there is no *possession*, that is to say, the unconscious too loses its ascendancy. . . . This . . . is the desired 'mid-point' of the personality, that ineffable something betwixt the opposites, or else that which unites them, or the result of conflict, or the product of energic tension: the coming to birth of personality, a profoundly individual step forward.
>
> (Jung, 1935b, para. 382)

The ego identity must be sufficiently strengthened to accept that it has only relative autonomy and a relative significance within the psychic structure of the personality. On that basis, Jung characterized the practice of psychotherapy as an attempt within the temenos both to depotentiate the affective power of disparate elements of psyche through personification and to relativize ego consciousness.

The concept of possession accounts for Jung's ideas of temenos and personification, and it also accounts for his notion of psychotherapy as 'synthesis'. He theorized that psychotherapy compensates for the high degree of dissociability of Western consciousness by promoting symbolization as a way in which the psyche can engage naturally in a constructive or synthetic process with the disparate and contradictory elements of self. Western cultures undervalue symbolizing, narrative-making and reverie, which strategically smooth over gaps and conflicts in cognitive functioning; the result is that dissociative phenomena are experienced culturally as ruptures and interpreted as pathologies (see Chapter 3). In Jung's view, psychotherapy works best in cases of dissociative suffering when it is practised more 'synthetically' than 'reductively'. The therapist and patient may interpret a symbol reductively or developmentally to signify, in causal terms, a repeated and inadequate infantile response to a psychological conflict, but they interpret the symbol synthetically when they narrate its emergence into consciousness, in prospective or teleological terms, as an imagistic possibility that surpasses the dilemma or in some way renders it old and irrelevant. Jung aligned a synthetic method with what he saw as an inherent compensatory capacity to symbolize to mediate opposites, to facilitate transitions by generating images which potentially transcend psychological impasses:

> If the mediatory product remains intact, it forms the raw material for a process not of dissolution but of construction, in which thesis and antithesis both play their part. In this way it becomes a new content that governs the whole attitude, putting an end to the division and forcing the energy of the opposites into a common channel.
>
> (Jung, 1921, para. 827)

These symbolic propositions are ephemeral, vulnerable to either chaotic dissolution, if left to unconscious processes, or rigidification, if overintellectualized by merely rendering the unconscious conscious (Cambray and Carter, 2004). Recognizing this danger, Jung emphasized the need for an adequate psychotherapeutic approach, an approach that would remain balanced between privileging either artful expressiveness or intellectual meaningfulness. 'We could say that aesthetic formulation needs understanding of meaning, and understanding of meaning needs aesthetic formulation. The two supplement each other to form [what I call] the transcendent function' (Jung, 1916b/1958, para. 177).

As a result, Jungian analytic methods technically privilege the circumambulatory amplification of images and the application of the expressive arts to psychotherapy; personified figures are dialogued with, and emerging images are sometimes painted, sculpted, soliloquized, or mimed in dance (Chodorow, 1997, 2004). Jung's concept of possession orients the patient and the therapist by casting the problem of individuation less in terms of assigning meaning than in terms of incarnating and embodying spirit as an aspect of self, 'the goal of the individuation process [being] the synthesis of the self' (Jung, 1941b, para. 278).

Jung characterized the effective practice of psychotherapy as privileging the integrating aspects of mental functioning, such as personifying, narrating, and symbolizing, that Western cultures devalue. He did this precisely because these aspects compensate for the biases inherent in Western consciousness that bring about its high degree of dissociability. Within the ritualized container of the temenos and through the personification of complexes and the dialectical process engendered between the psyches of the patient and the psychotherapist in the transference and countertransference, Jung believed, symbols may emerge from the transcendent function. These symbols potentially synthesize conflicts between consciousness and the unconscious by casting them in a new and different light. Jung's concept of possession characterizes these psychotherapeutic tasks of containing, personifying, and synthesizing as a process of incarnating and embodying spiritualized psychological potentialities.

It is important to exercise caution lest comparison between different cultural practices tip into essentializing. Nevertheless, it is illuminating to look at analogies between Jung's concept of possession, as it informed his practice of facilitating the emergence and embodiment of symbols, and therapeutic strategies which address suffering caused by possession in non-Western cultures. It is easy to observe parallels between Jung's practice and the Galle Sinhalese possession ceremony described in Chapter 2. The lighting of the demon palace alters the sufferers' perceptions of their suffering, not so much by exorcising a tyrannical spirit as by paradoxically 'illuminating' it and thereby granting the demonic an ontological legitimacy; at the same time, the ceremony places the demon contextually within a pantheon of lesser and greater deities. The analogies are obvious between Jung's possessing anima/animus figures (which can be integrated) and shadow figures (which pose a moral problem that the sufferer consciously endures rather than integrates) and the Sinhalese deities and demons, and also between Jung's animus/anima and shadow figures and the northern Sudanese *zar* spirits (which adepts marry) and black *jinn* (which are exorcised). Such analogies are evocative and important because they contribute to constructing what Jung called comparative anatomies of the psyche.

In the context of the historical material reviewed in Chapter 1 and the anthropological material reviewed in Chapter 2, Jung's concept of possession holds together and renders coherent the techniques of Jungian psychotherapy such as temenos, personification and synthesis. The concept of possession addresses the ontological significance of Jung's practice and contrasts with a classical psychoanalytic practice which refers materialistically to what transpires in the container as 'creative but illusory'. More to the point, Jung's concept of possession inscribes the fundamental problems of Western consciousness in terms not so much of how individual identity is analysed but of how selfhood is embodied.

Oughourlian's 'interdividual psychology' and the concept of mimetic desire

Jean-Michel Oughourlian (1991) based his 'interdividual' psychology on a psychosocial theory of imitative or 'mimetic' desire developed by the cultural critic and theorist René Girard. According to Girard (1974, 1987), all human beings tend to imitate unwittingly the actions, attitudes and desires of others. Girard argued that Freud essentialized human desire into mandatory patterns such as the Oedipal longing of the boy to possess his mother, the woman's envy of the phallus, and the death instinct, whereas his own research showed that desire is universally mimetic: one learns what to desire by watching the desiring of others.

Girard's theorizing about selfhood as desire is wide-ranging. For instance, he described scapegoating as a mechanism by which an outbreak of undifferentiated mimetic desire shifts the victimizers' escalating hostility towards each other as rivals into fellowship and shared hostility against a common victim. Girard depicted societies as founding themselves on the restriction of conflict and rivalrous desires by ritualistically celebrating memories of the victimizers' common cause against an evil scapegoat, thereby perpetually transferring onto a third party the violence that would otherwise be unleashed within the small group:

> Where only shortly before a thousand individual conflicts had raged unchecked between a thousand enemy brothers, there now reappears a true community, united in its hatred for one alone of its number . . . all the differing antagonisms now [converging] on an isolated and unique figure, the surrogate victim.
>
> (Girard, 1974/1977, p. 79)

Oughourlian applied Girard's theory of mimetic desire to the psychology of possession, hysteria and hypnosis, arguing that these phenomena are best understood as expressions of mimetic behaviour. Oughourlian argued that mimetic desire is not inherently pathological, although it creates rivalries and dependencies which lead to serious psychological problems. He characterized demonic possession in Christianity as problematic because it rejects mimetic desire as pathogenic and chronic, whereas, he proposed, African possession is effectively therapeutic and cathartic because it recognizes the mimetic basis of desire and the interdividual basis of self. Oughourlian proposed a psychosocial interpretation of cultures based on their collective responses to the reality of mimetic desire; this proposal resembles Lévi-Strauss's division of societies into the cannibalistic, which ingest or integrate the Other, and the anthropemic, which vomit out or expel the Other. And, more explicitly than Lévi-Strauss, Oughourlian favoured the former.

Basing his psychosocial argument on anthropological evidence from the early twentieth-century summaries of Oesterreich and the ethnomusicological work of Gilbert Rouget (1980), Oughourlian proposed the term 'adorcism' to refer to the preferable process of invoking rather than denying or exorcising mimetic desire:

Adorcism is therapeutic because it recognizes the reality of mimetic desire and humbly acknowledges the universality and power of the inter-dividual relation. It is therapeutic because such recognition of alienation has the power to de-alienate, because such humility has the power to raise one up, because such humble submission to psychological reality has the power to heal: possession is acted out as 'possession by' the Other, but that Other, when called on, invoked, prayed to, also lets itself be appropriated, in a sense, by being imitated or identified with. On the other hand, exorcism is by definition pathogenic: it seeks to expel the Other as if it were possible to deny otherness as such . . . to cure human beings radically of their humanness.

(Oughourlian, 1991, pp. 76–77)

From a Girardian position, Oughourlian presented his argument as a critique of Freud's theory of desire and his concept of the unconscious. Desires do not originate from within an autonomous self, Oughourlian said, but in the unwitting imitation of some other self endowed with greater reality, power or ontological status than one feels one holds oneself. He characterized Freud's theory as a strategic misinterpretation of this social psychology of desire; the theory masks the mechanisms of mimetic desire and perpetuates the myth that desires originate from within. Freud merely replaced the medieval myth of demonic possession (which exteriorizes and personalizes the Other as evil) with the modern myth of the unconscious (which interiorizes and depersonal-izes the Other as sexual). Oughourlian's interdividual relation located experi-ences of self in an inherently psychosocial process, in a field of interplaying mimetic forces:

Consciousness is an attribute of the self, a product of desire which is mimetic; there is no truly independent human self, there is never any self except in relation to another. Each dialectic of desire produces a psycho-genesis, a memory, and thenceforth a self.

(Oughourlian, 1991, p. 230)

For this reason, Oughourlian characterized the ritualization of possession as a healthy cultural acknowledgement of the interdividual relation and the mimetic character of desire, and he defined hysteria, not in terms of a psychi-atric illness, but as possession's opposite – as a culturally determined form of the misunderstanding, or even denial, of interdividual psychology. In this way, he aligned himself in the history of French social psychology with Hippolyte Bernheim, the nineteenth-century neurologist who supported the psychotherapeutic concept of suggestibility as a normal and general phe-nomenon, as opposed to Charcot's notion of suggestibility as inherently pathological (Ellenberger, 1970, p. 86), and also with Gabriel Tarde's seminal 'The Laws of Imitation' (Tarde, 1890). Following Bernheim's line of thought,

Oughourlian said that, on the one hand, the possessed deliberately submit to the external Other, taking on the Other as the model and origin of desire, identifying with collective beliefs located in that Otherness, and replacing the realization of desires with their representation, often expressed through theatricalization. On the other hand, hysterics strive in a pathogenic manner to annihilate the desire of the Other; lacking the capacity to identify, they insist on their own precedence over the Other and on a private representation of conflict and disorder.

In his ethnographic description of an advanced *zar* initiate in northern Ethiopia, Oughourlian defined optimal psychological health according to his mimetic theory of interdividual psychology:

> To behave all day long as if possessed by various *zars* is to manifest the highest degree of initiation: in full consciousness, Malkam Ayyahu recognizes explicitly the otherness in each of her desires, the mimetic origin of each of her psychological motivations. She names them and represents them. The absence of alteration in the state of consciousness and the permanence of the representation confer a theatrical aspect on this phenomenon, even if one must still call it possession. On this level of initiation and mastery, it is as much a matter of manifesting inspiration as of living a possession.
>
> (Oughourlian, 1991, p. 128)

Oughourlian emphasized not merely the psychotherapeutic efficacy of acknowledging the mimetic character of desire but, more to the point, the importance of an active invoking and submitting to the interdividual relation inherent in the experience of desiring.

The review of anthropological literature on possession in Chapter 2 reveals obvious weaknesses in Oughourlian's argument. Working from the early summaries of Oesterreich, as well as relying almost exclusively on the research of only one ethnographer, the ethnomusicologist Gilbert Rouget, Oughourlian essentialized the phenomena of possession. In other words, he oversimplified and misrepresented its complexity in order to make possession serve his theory of interdividual psychology. He generalized all African possession as healthy and integrative, setting it up in opposition to possession in Western cultures, which he characterized as negative and synonymous with hysteria. He made no distinction between various African cultures or between different possession traditions within one culture, for example, between the integrative rituals of *zar* possession and the exorcisms of possessing black *jinn*, which, Boddy showed, exist concomitantly in the northern Sudanese village of Hofrayat (see Chapter 2). In a similar way, Oughourlian argued that hysteria is culturally determined, but then he generalized it as possession's pathogenic opposite without describing its cultural particularities. More disappointingly, Oughourlian did not clearly outline the implications of his mimetic theory for Western practices of psychotherapy, beyond citing the description of the Ethiopian *zar* initiate and proposing a few suggestions such as: 'To become cured of the desire that takes possession of us, it is sufficient to mime the mimesis, which is to say, to recognize it for what it is' (Oughourlian, 1991, p. 140).

Fortunately, more recent Girardian scholarship seeks to provide supporting arguments for Girard's mimetic theory and Oughourlian's interdividual psychology. Tom Pace and Rusty Palmer (1995) situate mimetic theory in relation to object relations theory. They praise Oughourlian's refusal to attribute a psychological crisis to unconscious causes or factors from a patient's upbringing and his effort to identify how the conflict has emerged in contemporary adult relations. And in a survey of learning theory and neurological research, Scott Garrels (2004) points out how the recent identification of mirror neurons in the premotor cortex of the human brain gives credence to Oughourlian's psychological concept of mimetic desire. Mirror neurons are both motor and sensor neurons; first identified in monkeys, they respond both when an individual performs a particular motor movement, such a putting a peanut in its mouth, and when it observes another monkey performing the same movement (Rizzolatti and Sinigaglia, 2008; Rizzolatti et al., 1996, 2002), and research indicates that comparable neurons exist in humans (Vilayanur Ramachandran, in Kandel, 2006). Garrels uses this research on mirror neurons to support Girard and Oughourlian's argument concerning the fundamentally mimetic nature of desire and the interdividual origins of the experience of self. 'The activation of these neurons is automatic', Garrels says, 'and independent of the individual performing or observing the action, creating an immediate and shared experience' (Garrels, 2004, p. 14). He argues that mimetic reciprocity becomes functional in the earliest moments of the mother–infant dyad (apparently much earlier than Jean Piaget had thought) and facilitates experience-dependent neurocognitive development; it remains the most important organizing characteristic of adult mental representation, language processing, and intersubjective experience.

Unfortunately, Girard and Oughourlian claimed that mimetic theory radically critiques Freud's psychoanalytic unconscious; Oughourlian went to the extreme of using the word 'unwitting' to avoid the word 'unconscious'. This emphasis discouraged the forging of links with other researchers, among them Daniel Stern, whose psychoanalytic-based infant research included descriptions of 'affective attunement', a kind of transmodal mirroring during the first six months. In this 'affective attunement' (not to be confused with empathy), parents mirror their infants unawares, almost automatically (Stern, 1985, p. 145). This rejection of the unconscious in mimetic theory is also unfortunate because both Oughourlian's interdividual psychology and Jung's analytical psychology locate their theorizing and the implications for their psychotherapeutic practices in concepts of possession. Conceptually, there is a good deal of potential complementarity between them. For instance, as

psychotherapists, both Oughourlian and Jung favoured a paradoxical conscious submission of the sufferer to the power of something Other: for
Oughourlian, the invoking and identifying with the origins of desire outside
oneself, and for Jung, the ego's recognition of its function relative to the
autonomy of unconscious complexes and the teleology of the personality
as a whole. Also, both Girardians and Jungians characterize the psychotherapeutic process of becoming conscious as working against nature, even
though Oughourlian located this dialectic with the Other exclusively outside
the individual and Jung allowed for its manifestations intrapsychically, interpersonally and transferentially. At the same time, Jung privileged the interior
process, claiming that it manifests externally as fate only if the prior inner
integrative process is avoided.

In an address entitled 'Cultures of Eros', read at the Eranos conference in
1997, Girardian scholar Eugene Webb emphasized the differences between
Jung's Eros principle and Girard's mimetic theory of desire, rather than
exploring any similarities. Webb located Jung in a Spinozist tradition of theorizing about 'a fundamental vital Eros that expresses itself as simultaneously corporeal and spiritual' (Webb, 1999, p. 9), while he located Girard
in a Hobbesian and Freudian tradition of distrusting Eros. This distinction
led Webb, in his conclusions, to identify himself more with Jung than with
Girard:

> The problem this represents for our present consideration of 'Cultures of
> Eros' is that a culture that condemns human desire as inherently egoistic
> and disorderly is likely to overlook or deny the [more positive] possibility
> of what I have called existential Eros. Fortunately, as I hope I have
> shown, the latter also has some persuasive advocates. Although I deeply
> appreciate the powerful insights that Becker and Girard, like Freud and
> Hobbes before them, offer into the dark side of our humanity, I neverthe-
> less believe that the patterns of thought represented by such thinkers as
> Karl Jaspers, Carl Jung, Eric Voegelin, Bernard Lonergan, Jean Piaget,
> Lawrence Kohlberg, and Robert Kegan offer us the best hope we have of
> raising that darkness into light – by which I mean not just bringing our
> more sinister impulses under control but transforming them through the
> elucidation and education of desire.
>
> (Webb, 1999, p. 47)

As a Girardian scholar and Oughourlian's translator, Webb argued authori-
tatively about the extent to which Girard resides within a Freudian paradigm
of rendering desire darkly sinister, but his reading of Jung's Eros principle
tends too strongly towards the simplistic and bright. Certainly Jung characterized Eros as a principle of desire or psychic relatedness, and this Jungian
principle has been defined in both human and archetypal contexts (that is,
manifesting as spirits and gods) in terms of loving, creativity and involvement

(Guggenbühl-Craig, 1999, p. 25). And Webb correctly associates Jung's concepts of psychological integration and individuation with Eros, with 'a force of truth that actively seeks, by hounding us, to come into consciousness (as compared with the Freudian idea of the unconscious as setting up obstacles to consciousness)' (Webb, 1999, p. 9). But Jung also discussed more sinister aspects of desire. He argued that, logically, the opposite of love is hate, and the opposite of Eros may be Phobos or fear (which, in Webb's thesis, concurs precisely with the darker philosophical positions of both Girard and Ernest Becker); however, 'psychologically, the opposite of Eros is the will to power' (Jung, 1917a, para. 78). Unconscious Eros inevitably finds expression in a power drive (Samuels et al. 1986, p. 55). With his concept of possession and his application of Girard's mimetic theory to interdividual psychology, Oughourlian approached a similar observation when he described hysteria as 'unwitting' suffering caused by a power-driven incapacity to submit to and positively identify with one's own Otherness.

Despite these similarities, I have to concur with Webb's arguments about the fundamental differences between Girard's theory of mimetic desire and Jung's Eros principle. In the end, Oughourlian's Girardian concept of possession and Jung's concept of possession differ with regard to the implications they bring to bear on the practice of psychotherapy. For Oughourlian, 'miming the mimesis' signified seeing desire for what it is. Girard's interpretation of the Christian revelation best exemplifies this recognition: Jesus deliberately enacts the scapegoat mechanism, thereby revealing the Otherness of desire in the experience of self and rendering conscious the violent, irrational, non-altruistic sacrifice upon which human sociability is constructed. Translating this into the terms of psychotherapeutic practice, Oughourlian recommended, on the one hand, seeking mimetically to understand the desire that a symptom expresses, and, on the other hand, renouncing the experience of Other as rival and obstacle in order to keep it only as a model (Oughourlian, 1991, p. 245).

Mimesis was also fundamental to Jung's practice of psychotherapy. The concept of mimesis has a long and significant history in Western cultural traditions, but it is most familiar as the foundational issue of 'imitation' in discussions about the representational nature of the arts (see Auerbach, 2005). In Book III of *Republic*, Plato defined all the arts and sciences as mimetic to the extent that they imitate the ideal or Platonic forms. In *Poetics*, Aristotle defined mimesis as a characteristic of poetry that represents humans in action. He identified the expression of the instinct to imitate as the source of both knowledge and pleasure, whereas Plato denigrates it as potentially dangerous to societal distinctions, since any individual can mimic any other. In the twentieth century, mimetic realism in the arts was attacked by, among others, Brecht in the theatre, the New Critics in literature, and the post-Saussurean linguists, who stress the arbitrary nature of the sign which does not imitate an external reality (Macey, 2000). At the same time, mimesis has been valued by many others, including the psychologist and cognitive neuroscientist Merlin Donald (1991) and the anthropologist Michael Taussig (1992), who both propose that mimesis, not language, continues to provide the basis for human cultural evolution.

In Jungian terms, Oughourlian's notion of 'miming the mimesis' would involve personifying the complex (see Donfrancesco, 1995). Imaging would render conscious the autonomy and the affect of the possessing spirit or god or splinter psyche, thereby stripping the complex of its power and draining away the ego's will to power. But Jung would add, I think, that the dialectic process of psychotherapy – personifying the complex and incarnating the possessing god through active imagination inside the temenos of the transference–countertransference relationship – does not educate the unconscious complex; rather, it gradually transforms both aspects of the self. This sensibility informs Jung's psychological interpretation of incarnation in the Christian tradition, as well as his radical thesis concerning the psychological significance of the dialectical process between God and man narrated in the Book of Job. For this reason, Webb is wrong to suggest that, like Jaspers, Piaget, Kohlberg and Kegan, Jung argues in favour of the education and elucidation of desire. Webb is justified in attributing a 'comic' or romantic teleology to Jung's concept of possession, in opposition to Girard and Oughourlian's 'tragic' concept, if only in the sense that Jung's concept of possession as an Eros-directed process of marrying spirit and matter favours both, not one or the other. In other words, for Jung, emerging symbols, phenomenological evidence of the transcendent function, characterize the principle of Eros as desire engaged in the synthetic process of transcending oppositions; psychic relatedness moves in the direction of a wholeness. This is why Webb associates Jung's Eros principle with Spinoza. However, because the metaphor of marriage may imply too bright a tone and too comic or romantic an outcome for the Jungian practice of psychotherapy, it is useful to note that, for Jung, this process of personifying and incarnating spirit and enduring opposites was also existentially comparable to a crucifixion (Jung, 1946, para. 470).

Moreno's psychotherapeutic triad and the principle of spontaneity

Jacob L. Moreno, perhaps the most influential and underestimated thinker about psychotherapeutic practice of the twentieth century, opposed Freud's theories of self as early as 1912, before he graduated from medical school in Vienna. Unlike Freud, he attempted to make psychotherapy effective by addressing the individual's psychosocial problems. According to Moreno, the self emerges through the roles one plays in relation to others, rather than the roles emerging from the self. Moreno located the experience of selfhood in an external field of interrelatedness, an idea that Oughourlian would develop sixty years later in his interdividual theory of psychology. Moreno delineated laws of social gravity from the patterns that emerge when individuals interact spontaneously, and he proposed a triad of psychotherapeutic practices – group psychotherapy, sociometry, and psychodrama – which addresses the loss of spontaneity in the otherwise naturally continuous emergence of self.

Moreno said that his three-part psychotherapeutic model had been informed by several precursors. Among others, he mentioned Henri Bergson's principle of *élan vital*, the life force passing from one generation to the next, which is best intuited and reflected upon rather than intellectualized, and Hyppolite Bernheim's principle of social suggestibility and his study of groups and crowds. As well, Moreno credited the principle of spontaneity implicit in Freud's use of free association, although he believed the psycho-analytic practice of free association to be merely 'preliminary' to his own therapeutic approach. 'Instead of searching after past experiences', he said, 'the subject turned his mind to the present, to immediate production. Instead of free association we sought the full release of the subject, his mental and mimic expression' (Moreno, 1934, pp. 5–8).

In other words, in his practice of psychotherapy, Moreno did not employ the principle of spontaneity in order to analyse backwards towards a past trauma; rather, he analysed the present performance of the individual self as it manifested in roles to support or enhance the individual's spon-taneity (Moreno, 1960, p. 5). Marx's economic–materialist argument, with its emphasis on symbolic memberships in collectivity, was another precursor, but Moreno dismissed Marx for disregarding both the individual as a psycho-logical entity and society as 'continuously pressed by psychological currents and the networks they form' (Moreno, 1934, p. 9). Moreno's model of psychotherapy was an attempt to synthesize elements from all of these thinkers.

Moreno addressed the suffering of the individual self in problems of role. Rejecting concepts such as personality or ego as metapsychological, he pro-posed instead to work with the psychosocial concept of the self as it mani-fests interpersonally. He evaluated the effectiveness of a role according to its fusion of individual and collective elements and the degree of spontaneity and creativity operating in the interpersonal relation. 'Role-playing is an act, a spontaneous playing; role-taking is a finished product, a role conserve', Moreno (1960, p. 84) said. 'Role-taking', for him, meant confinement to a finished, fully established, scripted interaction that would not permit the individual any degree of spontaneity or creativity, whereas 'role-playing' would permit some degree of both, and 'creating a role' permitted both to the highest degree. Possession enters Moreno's model in the sense that possessed individuals over-identify or fuse with a role and therefore suffer from a loss of self, and this fusion manifests as the inability to interact spontaneously and creatively. The emergence of self is threatened to the extent that a 'role conserve' as a unit of conserved behaviour eliminates possibilities for spontaneous and creative interaction.

Moreno observed the human inclination to resist the continual process of spontaneous emergence of the self in interpersonal experiences, and he identified this resistance as a source of suffering. He argued that the notion of self as a finished, perfected product is a comforting illusion reinforced by our tendency to prefer pre-scripted role-taking to confronting the unknown in role-play, a tendency which the cultural conserves of groups and societies reinforce:

> There is a shrewd motive in this procedure . . . because if only one stage of a creative process is a really good one, and all the others are bad, then this chosen stage substituting for the entire process can be memorized, conserved, eternalized, and can give comfort to the soul of the creator and order to the civilization of which he is a part.
>
> (Moreno, 1934, p. 363)

Moreno developed his three-part practice of psychotherapy to compensate for this inclination to create conserves. It would, he thought, render accessible once more the inherent spontaneity of the individual self and of the human society within which individual selves locate their selfhood.

In Moreno's practice of group psychotherapy, individuals experienced selfhood in terms of their capacity to participate spontaneously and creatively within a field of interpersonal relations. In the encounter engendered by the presence of others, the individual learned to distinguish experiences of projection from what Moreno called experiences of *tele*, a concept he derived partly from Bergson's *élan vital*. Etymologically, 'to project', derived from Latin, means 'to throw in front of', whereas *tele* is a Greek prefix denoting 'from a distance'. Projections throw in front of the engaged individuals a set of fixed or conserved roles to which they are then confined. The effective practice of group psychotherapy, in Moreno's view, provided a safe container within which the individual could witness and, as much as possible, work to withdraw projections and their illusory effects. But Moreno emphasized that group psychotherapy should also provide experiences of role-play and 'flow' between people – authentic here-and-now exchanges of attraction and repulsion. His notion of *tele* identified a non-rational, nonverbal processing (as if 'from a distance') of interpersonal relationships and the bonds which hold groups together:

> Group cohesiveness, reciprocity of relationships, communication, and shared experiences are functions of *tele*. *Tele* is the constant frame of reference for all forms and methods of psychotherapy. . . . Neither transference nor empathy could explain in a satisfactory way the emergent cohesion of a social configuration.
>
> (Moreno, 1960, p. 17)

Moreno emphasized that the effective practice of group psychotherapy would provide opportunities both for minimizing the projective aspects of interpersonal relationships and for optimizing the authentic communication of *tele* (Bradshaw-Tauvon, 1998a, pp. 33–35).

Sociometry, the second element of Moreno's psychotherapeutic practice, is a phenomenological study of an individual or a group's interpersonal choices. It maps and evaluates networks of existing and preferred relationships. For instance, an individual's social map would include representations of family members, friends, neighbours, and work colleagues, with each interpersonal relationship situated according to its distance from a nuclear self; in this sense, the emergent self is momentarily observed in time and space as manifesting in all its roles. Group psychotherapists could also use sociometry to track psychological mechanisms, such as scapegoating, within the group dynamic. In other words, they could chart the group's need to reinforce cohesion by creating and expelling an isolate. At the same time, such maps could anticipate the extent to which a specific individual's repertoires of roles or selfhood might incline him or her towards a collusive desire to take on the conserved role of scapegoat for the group. In the case of scapegoating, Moreno said, the effective practice of group psychotherapy depends on the capacity to measure the collective desire to isolate an individual member of the group as it sparked and shifted and to re-integrate potential isolates into the natural cohesiveness of the group's *tele*. Thus the therapist could employ sociometry to ensure that no particular individual over-identified with the role of sacrificial Other and that no group succeeded in banishing or dissociating its own integral Otherness from its midst.

In psychodrama, the third component of Moreno's psychotherapeutic practice, psychodramatists guided mimetic activities to examine problems, explore new role possibilities and, most importantly, revitalize stale role conserves (Moreno, 1960, p. 85). Psychodramatic sessions began with the identification of an individual as the protagonist in whose service the group agreed to work. Then the protagonist's problem would be incarnated through dramatic action including role doubling, role reversing, mirroring, and soliloquizing. The sessions ended with observation and shared reflection, the goal of which was to facilitate a synthesis of spontaneous insights experienced verbally and nonverbally during the action phase by the protagonist and by the other role-players, observers and therapists. Psychodrama was ritualistic or ceremonial in the sense that these sessions would often be highly structured, moving through clearly identifiable phases that could be demarcated both temporally and spatially.

Practitioners of Moreno's three-part psychotherapy have examined the extent to which they – and Moreno himself – emphasize or privilege certain components of the triad over others. In some psychodramatic groups, dramatic action could take precedence over group psychotherapy and sociometry to the extent that not to perform psychodrama within a session meant failure to meet the criteria of the group (Bradshaw-Tauvon, 1998b, p. 293). From another viewpoint, Moreno deliberately privileged group psychotherapy over the other two components because he explicitly described psychodrama as an extension of group psychotherapy (Elefthery and Elefthery, 1966; Moreno and Elefthery, 1975). In this case, moving from group psychotherapy to the spontaneous and potentially volatile action phase of a psychodramatic session is justifiable only in terms of the need of an individual who functions as protagonist and never in terms of the director's or the group's needs. For this reason, sociometry should be used to assess the group dynamic in psychodrama – for example, measuring the degree to which a director or a group is inclined, often unawares, to produce a protagonist and a psychodrama in order to avoid individual and collective processing of the attractions, repulsions, and conflicts engendered within the group encounter itself (Doreen Elefthery, personal communication, 27 October 2005).

Moreno defined his practice of psychodrama according to a psychosocial model in which mimesis served a central synthesizing function. Like Oughourlian sixty years later, Moreno identified a social tendency for mimesis to shift into mere conformity, for roles to become conserves. It is not clear to what extent Oughourlian enacted as well as described or discussed the practice of 'miming the mimesis' – to what degree the psychotherapeutic practice of interdividual psychology requires an action phase. Certainly, for Moreno, the elements of enacting and observing were both crucial for setting up the possibility of psychotherapeutic synthesis. Individual insight resides potentially in the spontaneity and creativity of the action, but in the structure of a psychodramatic session, insights can be incorporated into the protagonist's repertoire of roles and emerging sense of self only through reflection and a reintegration into the group process. 'It took the theorist and practitioner in one, a theory which grew out of and with practice, a synthesis of actor and observer, to give the new methodologies the peculiar concrete shape they have', Moreno (1960, p. 86) said. In other words, Moreno found the structure of the psychodramatic container necessary for facilitating both action and observation.

Like Jung (and like Oughourlian later), Moreno characterized the practice of psychotherapy as socially compensatory as well as a way of addressing individual psychosociological suffering. In this respect, he believed that his model of action and observation addressed not only the psychotherapeutic healing of the individual self but also the revitalizing of cultural conserves:

> The system of relations and codes that unite actors and the system of relations that can be observed among organisms constitute two different areas. The actorial system depends upon the consensus that can take place only in an encounter of actors. This secret and imminent consensus is of essential significance in the actualization of the ongoing research. And often even this is not enough. The observers have to participate in

the process of production and turn into actors in order to attain an unbroken, integrated social system.

(Moreno, 1960, p. 130)

Moreno's model emphasized and accounted for psychosocial phenomena such as scapegoating as mechanisms which groups unwittingly exercise in the interest of reinforcing cohesion, but to their detriment: by sacrificing the scapegoat as Other, they sacrifice *tele*. This idea resembles Oughourlian's interdividual psychology, based on Girard's theory of mimetic desire, but Moreno was not as concerned as Oughourlian to avoid psychoanalytic terminology such as 'unconscious' and 'transference'. Yet, because Moreno, too, located the self externally (that is, psychosocially in roles), he criticized both Jung and Freud for defining the self in terms of the individual psyche. Furthermore, Moreno considered Jung's concept of the collective unconscious to be flawed, to leap from a personal to a universal context without sufficiently taking into account the psychology of the group and the positive phenomenon of *tele*:

> We must look for a concept which is so constructed that the objective indication for the existence of this two-way process does not come from a single psyche but from a still deeper reality in which the unconscious states of two or several individuals are interlocked with a system of 'co-unconscious' states. Jung postulated that every individual has, besides a personal, a collective unconscious. Although the distinction may be useful, it does not help in solving the dilemma described. Jung does not apply the collective unconscious to the concrete collectivities in which people live. There is nothing to be gained in turning from a personal to a 'collective unconscious' if by doing this the anchorage to the concrete, whether individual or group, is lost. Had he turned to the group by developing techniques like group psychotherapy or sociodrama, he might have gained a concrete position for this theory of the collective unconscious, but, as it is, he underplayed the individual anchorage but did not establish a safe 'collective anchorage' as a counterposition. The problem here is not the collective images of a given culture or of mankind, but the specific relatedness and cohesiveness of a group of individuals.

(Moreno, 1960, pp. 116–117)

Even so, Jung's practice of psychotherapy posited a concept of possession by complexes and a principle of relatedness and intrapsychic equilibrium which answers to it; similarly, Moreno's practice posited a concept of possession by role conserves, as well as principles of spontaneity and creativity that manifest interpersonally to heal co-consciousness and co-unconscious states. 'The longer a synthetic group endures', he said, 'the more it begins to resemble a natural group, to develop and share an unconscious life, from which its members draw their strength, knowledge and security' (Moreno, 1960, p. 117). In Moreno's terms, the paradoxical emergence of the individual self from within the roles of actor and observer not only heals the individual from the suffering of possession by role conserves but also challenges and revitalizes cultural conserves with the spontaneity and the genuine social cohesiveness of *tele*.

A problematic of possession, desire and power

Jung, Oughourlian, and Moreno all propose practices of psychotherapy located in a problematic of possession, desire and power. For Jung, the psychological opposite of Eros or the principle of relatedness is a will to power. The possessed ego suffers both a fused and a dissociated state relative to

Figures 5.2, 5.3, 5.4
Three practitioner-thinkers who worked with concepts of possession at the borders of dissociation and self, Eros and power: Carl Gustav Jung (top left), René Girard (top right), and Jacob L. Moreno (bottom). Yousuf Karsh photo of Jung published with permission of Camera Press London.

autonomous unconscious contents, and the unconscious complex as Other 'suffers' from the ego's wilful resistance, as well as from its own impulse to incarnate rather than remain split off and unembodied. Jungian practice proposes a dialectical process engendered in the temenos between the psyches of the patient and the psychotherapist; by means of this process, symbols spontaneously emerge from the transcendent function. Personifying these symbols, narrating the dreams in which they appear, and analysing the transferences and countertransferences in which they manifest all work against the inherent dissociability of Western consciousness, relativizing ego consciousness and re-imaging the possession as a marrying and embodying of disparate elements.

For Oughourlian, possession as hysteria or dissociation is 'unwitting' suffering caused by a power-driven incapacity to submit to and positively identify with Otherness. Oughourlian presented ritualized possession enacted in non-Western cultures as dramatically exemplifying his concept of an interdividual self which experiences desire as a wish to absorb what it perceives to be the greater power of other people. The practice of 'miming the mimesis' paradoxically involves submitting to the reality of mimetic desire and, at the same time, consciously renouncing the experience of the more powerful Other as a rival and an obstacle, thereby metamorphosing desire and incorporating the meaning of the Other into an experience of self.

For Moreno, dissociative suffering arises when powerful cultural conserves block spontaneity and creativity in the expression of selfhood in interpersonal roles. 'What conserved creativity truly represents, at best, is power, a means of expressing superiority when actual superiority has ceased to be available', Moreno (1960, p. 13) said. Moreno's three-part practice of psychotherapy seeks to address the problem of possession by cultural conserves, freeing individuals as paradoxical actor-observers to experience selfhood in the genuine interplay of desire and repulsion which constitutes *tele*.

It would be misleading to overstate these similarities. Fundamentally, Oughourlian and Moreno saw their psychosocial theories as critiques of psychoanalytic and psychodynamic concepts such as Jung's that locate individual selfhood intrapsychically. And Jung indeed privileged the intrapsychic over the interpersonal, arguing that what is not intrapsychically integrated is only then experienced externally as fate. With regard to the practice of psychotherapy informed by a psychosocial concept of self, Jung suggested that 'group therapy is only capable of educating the social human being' (Jung, 1973, Vol. 2, p. 219); it addresses only the problems of the 'persona' as a social role within which the self meets an external Other. Still, Jung's diagrams of complexes and their relationship to ego consciousness compare strikingly with Moreno's sociometric mapping of a cultural conserve and its effect on a social network. The terrain of both is a similar problematic of possession, but Jung, from an introverted perspective, privileges an intrapsychic map of the self, whereas Moreno, from an extraverted perspective,

privileges an interpersonal map. Jung's and Moreno's practices of psychotherapy, while dissimilar, seem inherently complementary.

Emphasizing the concepts of possession which inform the psychotherapeutic practices of Jung, Oughourlian, and Moreno is a way to arrive at
this notion of their complementarity through theorizing. But a good deal of
the difficult work of forging complementarity from the oppositions between
an introverted intrapsychic model and more extraverted interpersonal models
has already been accomplished, not theoretically, but in the laboratory of
psychotherapeutic practice. A number of practitioners have hammered out
effective ways to work in such contradictory spaces; they might even say their
work is more effective because they locate their practices in such inclusive
spaces. Four of the most noteworthy are Dean Elefthery and Doreen Madden
Elefthery, who both trained with Moreno, and Helmut Barz and Ellynor
Barz, Jungian analysts who trained with the Eleftherys.

Doreen Elefthery has demonstrated why psychodrama as an intervention
should be introduced only as an extension of group psychotherapy. Unless
the group psychotherapy aspect of Moreno's triad is prioritized, the interven-
tions of the director or the group members can slip unwittingly into power
rather than expressing the spontaneous creative expression of *tele*, and the
protagonist can become possessed, colluding with the group's needs and acting out of a stultifying role conserve rather than insightfully experiencing in
action the emergence of self. Employing both intrapsychic and interpersonal
models provides Elefthery with a means to contain and process the projections, her own countertransferences, and the interpersonal dynamics between
group members, as well as synchronistic and collective experiences (such as
political events) that occur outside the therapeutic dimension. By constantly
mapping and interpreting all of these (and by discerning which of these to
share), she can create a safe enough space in which to work psychotherapeutically with possibilities that emerge spontaneously and creatively from the
transcendent function and/or the transpersonal *tele*. Elefthery's method is
that strict and that inclusive.

Jungian analyst Helmut Barz described how Moreno's psychodrama provides analysands with insight not only in introverted reflection but also in
catharsis, not only in observation but also in embodied action:

> I have become convinced that it is rewarding to employ this tool as a
> complement to individual analysis, because it makes possible something
> which all too often in analysis receives short shrift: the experience of total
> effect through the symbol. The valid work of analysis is in making
> conscious the symbol to be interpreted in its finest ramifications, using
> speech as the essential tool. Moreno . . . tried to find precisely a way out
> of the logical and syntactical form of communication, as he formulated
> it. We have him to thank for making possible the visualization of
> symbolic images personified, to experience them directly in bearing,

mimicry, gesture and voice, and to convince ourselves that they are not a product of a private dream analysis but are rather present and effective in us all.

(Barz, 1990, p. 438)

Barz drew attention to the therapeutic value of the action phase of a psychodrama, to personifying or miming complexes and symbols in role-playing as a form of what Jung called 'active imagination', recognizing the 'total effect' of actively incarnating symbols as complements to the analytical practice of reflecting on them.

As a group psychotherapist, psychodramatist and student of Moreno, Anne Ancelin Schützenberger (1998, p. 6) noted a complementarity between Jung's theory of complexes and her own psychotherapeutic work on the transgenerational transmission of unresolved role conflicts. Jung had described family constellations as identifications between parents and children which he could measure empirically using the Word Association Test; I have already mentioned (in Chapter 3) one memorable case history of a sixteen-year-old girl whose results on the test produced a profile of complexes so similar to her mother's that Jung imagined her reproducing the mother's life experiences, including marriage to an alcoholic (Jung, 1935a, para. 155–159). Jung also described the possession of the ego, not by the shadow or anima/animus, but by transgenerational family history,

by something that could perhaps most fitly be described as an 'ancestral soul' by which I mean the soul of some definite forebear. For all practical purposes such cases may be regarded as striking instances of identification with deceased persons.

(Jung, 1939c, para. 220–224)

Elsewhere, Jung referred to unresolved family conflicts passing unconsciously from generation to generation like the curse of the house of Atreus (Jung, 1931c, para. 88). Extrapolating from this complementarity between Jung's theory of complexes and Moreno's theory of the self in roles, Ancelin Schützenberger theorized about how unconscious loyalties to previous generations may cause synchronistic repetitions and unwitting re-enactments of important family dates and ancestral events, to the detriment of the self. Chantal Nève-Hanquet, who trained both as a psychodramatist with Ancelin Schützenberger and as a Jungian analyst, extends this work, using genograms to map sociometrically how transgenerational family systems trap individuals in unconscious complexes and role conserves, and psychodramatic techniques to provide compensatory experiences of a spontaneously emerging selfhood (Nève-Hanquet and Pluymaekers, 2008).

Another Jungian analyst and psychodramatist, Wilma Scategni, employs the Jungian term 'temenos' to denote the necessary quality of containment which group members require during psychodramatic sessions before they can risk expressing their spontaneity and creativity:

> It allows people to outline an area, or a perimeter inside which there are no intervening forces or foreign influences [from outside], where feelings, thoughts and emotions can emerge in a chaotic form, settle, take shape, and express themselves. . . . At the same time, the group holds in the [inner] destructive forces, allows them to show themselves, and frees up the energy locked inside the complexes by giving them the chance to be expressed and worked out.
>
> (Scategni, 2002, p. 28)

Scategni documents dreams of group members and interprets them to demonstrate how the group functions ritualistically as a protected analytical space in which the transcendent function can spontaneously and creatively manifest.

Using the concept of possession, Jung's, Oughourlian's, and Moreno's practices of psychotherapy can be located theoretically in a similar problematic, and making this problematic explicit may enable such theorizing to provide an additional context within which to understand the challenges of working in these opposing but potentially complementary practices. The phenomena of possession play out as problems of power, of being overpowered by spirits, complexes, or cultural conserves. The practices of psychotherapy under consideration address these problems through a relativizing process in which ego consciousness becomes more supple or flexible, detaching from and yet relating to various acting and observing roles. The fluidity and plurality of self come to be experienced, not as dissociative rupture, but as mimetic flow and circumference. The risks that arise in these psychotherapeutic processes are difficulties inherent in the ontological predicament of how to give equal weight to both the enacted and the reflected realities and how to process synthetically an individual protagonist's intrapsychic complex as well as the interpersonal *tele* of a group.

So, for example, Jung's practice of active imagination may be understood within the context of transferences and countertransferences – within the group of two (Schaverien, 2005), and active imagination should then be understood as an extension of the analytical relationship, located within the temenos. This idea resembles the understanding that psychodrama is an extension of group psychotherapy rather than a practice in itself. Considering active imagination in terms of Jung's concept of possession highlights the need to structure and contain the ontological predicament it poses, which, for the participants, could resemble psychosis. Jungian practitioners should recognize the importance of interpreting aspects of transference in the work of active imagination; such recognition can actually strengthen the temenos and prevent the possibly numinous or transpersonal quality of the transcendent function from manifesting as power.

By keeping the concept of possession in mind, practitioners of these kinds of therapies can identify potential problems more clearly. Before therapists decide to move into the action phase of a psychodrama as a therapeutic intervention, for instance, they should map the group dynamic sociometrically, attempting to discern to what extent protagonists are possessed by the group's needs or even the director's needs to do psychodrama. Similarly, when therapists bear witness to active imagination, they must grapple with the ontological paradox of allowing patients to both act and be acted upon. For precisely this reason, they must work to keep the temenos sealed and to reintegrate the patients back from liminality into time and space, finding the right moment to interpret all three aspects of interrelatedness or Eros – the intrapsychic, the interpersonal/psychosocial, and the transferential. The concept of possession emphasizes the potential, at many points in all these practices, for the therapeutic process to slip, and such slippage turns what Jung calls Eros, what Moreno calls *tele*, and what Oughourlian calls mimetic desire into power.

It is also possible for therapeutics to slip into the esoteric; Jung's concept of possession, in particular, can be misread as inscribed in religious doctrine. On the contrary, locating Jung's concept of possession in terms of clinical practice differentiates it from the concept articulated by ethnopsychiatrist Tobie Nathan (1988, 1994, 2001). Nathan's practice is explicitly and unapologetically 'esoteric': Western practitioners position themselves outside a doctrine and privilege the intelligibility of those who are within it. As a psychotherapist working with immigrants from non-Western cultures who seek assistance for psychological suffering in Western clinical settings, Nathan argues that Western psychotherapy can only provide effective containers (what Jung calls temenos) within which these individuals can work in search of healing. In these containers, their gods and 'exotic' beliefs (that is, their systems of belief originating outside the cultures in which they now reside) can safely manifest themselves. Similarly, Jung argued that therapists should repatriate sufferers who have been attached to a Western system of belief such as Roman Catholicism back into their faith and doctrine (Jung, 1939d, para. 618) before attempting psychoanalytic psychotherapy. He differentiated the esotericism of a belief system which is intelligible and effective for the initiated from his 'exoteric' psychological interest in the purposiveness of what individuals who are outside a system of belief or creed suffer as 'possession'.

For this reason, I disagree with Adam Crabtree's clinical use of Jung's concept of possession. Crabtree (1985, 1997) recommended a therapeutic intervention for Multiple Personality Disorder which consisted of interviewing possessing entities or separate personalities in a manner that resembles Jung's technique of personifying complexes. Crabtree (1985, p. 409) also referred to Jung's concept of a collective unconscious to account for dissociative experience with features which are not immediately attributable to a personal anamnesis. He described reaching therapeutic resolutions through dialogic encounter between therapist and spirit (and eventually sufferer and spirit) in which the misplaced spirit would leave the body of the sufferer and locate itself more appropriately. But Jung did not locate his psycho-therapeutic techniques of personification and synthesis in this kind of eso-teric practice. Jung's concept of possession led him to identify a sacred or liminal quality in psychotherapeutic containment and attach a numinous aspect to the experience of the transcendent function, and this theorizing is easy to misread. In fact, Jung inscribed his concept of possession in an epistemology of paradox; he hypothesized synthetic clinical possibilities for healing in the prospective process of giving an equal but contradictory onto-logical status to the autonomous complex/spirit and to ego consciousness, and then enduring the ensuing conflict consciously within the temenos of the transference–countertransference relationship. This is what he meant when he spoke of the attempt in analysis to bring an individual who has been touched by the unconscious down to human size.

Although his concept of possession equivocally connotes the esoteric, Jung differentiated his practice of psychotherapy from esoteric practice and dem-onstrated its fundamental position, poised at the edge of the epistemological chasm which characterizes contemporary Western consciousness. Rather than identifying Jung's concept of possession as esoteric, I would align it with the complementary psychosocial concepts of possession informing the psy-chotherapeutic practices of Oughourlian and Moreno. For all three theorists, the concept of possession accounted for both the suffering of the individual whose identity has been 'unseated' and the efficacy of using mimesis – Rizzolatti might say, of engaging mirror neurons (Rizzolatti and Sinigaglia, 2008) – to personify Otherness and incorporate aspects of such experience within the temenos into the dynamics of personhood. Clearly, Oughourlian and Moreno's view that personhood resides in interpersonal roles opposes Jung's intrapsychic model, in which self resides in complexes with a collective aspect and an archetypal core and individuation means synthetically incar-nating selfhood. Even so, the concept of possession renders their practices of psychotherapy cogent, coherent and complementary. In particular, Jung's concept of possession focuses attention on the ontological significance of what all three practitioners identify as problematical and pathological in con-temporary Western consciousness.

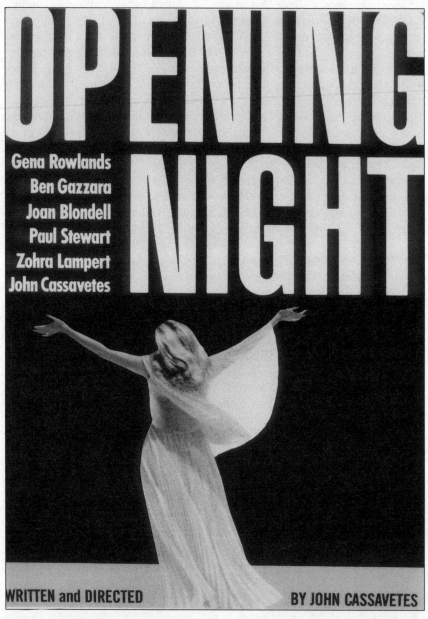

Figure 6.1 An *Opening Night* poster, 1977. John Cassavetes employed possession as an idiom of distress in a film which is neither a melodrama about theatre and madness nor a supernatural thriller. Published with permission of Al Ruban, Faces Distribution Corporation.

Chapter 6

The suffering of Myrtle Gordon

Cassavetes's *Opening Night* and Chaikin's Open Theatre

[Vico's] *New Science* teaches that from the moment human beings began to think humanly, they have believed that through their dying the dead return to a realm of origins from which both the living and the unborn draw life. This is the awesome, anachronic realm of the progenitors to whom the living remain beholden for their houses, their harvests, their laws, their customs, their patrimonies, their wisdom, and everything else that keeps their societies from relapsing into an inhuman barbarism. Herein lies the authority of the dead and the charisma of the ancestor. By passing from the realm of the engendered into that of the engendering, the dead become the authors and proprietors of life, personifying all that transcends and yet at the same time generates human society.

(Robert Pogue Harrison, *The Dominion of the Dead*, p. 94)

It's somewhat daunting to reflect that Hell is – possibly – the place where you are stuck in your own personal narrative for ever, and Heaven is – possibly – the place where you can ditch it, and take up wisdom instead.

(Margaret Atwood, *Negotiating with the Dead*, p. 174)

In 1977, John Cassavetes released his film *Opening Night* in Europe; it was ignored in America until after his death. In the film, Myrtle Gordon (played by Gena Rowlands), a celebrated stage actress, rehearses a new play with a familiar circle of professional colleagues: Manny Victor, the director (Ben Gazzara); Maurice Aarons, the male lead and her former lover (John Cassavetes); and David Samuels, her producer (Paul Stewart). But Myrtle finds herself resisting the character she is playing and resenting the drama, entitled *The Second Woman*, written by the sixty-five-year-old playwright Sarah Goode (Joan Blondell). After witnessing the death of a young fan, Nancy Stein, who had been struck by a car outside the theatre, Myrtle rebels against what she perceives as the complacency of both the play and her peers. She sabotages the New Haven tryouts and teeters dangerously close to alienation, depression and madness.

Cassavetes, who was also the screenwriter and director, had this to say about the protagonist of *Opening Night*:

> I picked a woman who has a career, a job. She's not interested in children, she's not interested in men, even if she still is capable of romantic feelings. Myrtle has a job to do, a career, and that's the most important thing for her. Her whole life is acting, being an actress. . . . [And] Myrtle is alone and in desperate fear of losing the vulnerability she feels she needs as an actress. . . . You never see her as a stupendous actress. . . . She didn't want to expose herself in certain areas. So when she faints and screams on the stage, it's because it's so impossible to be told you are this boring character, you are aging and you are just like her. . . . When you have a problem as an actor people want to know why your feelings are different from theirs. And if you can't explain it to them, they attack you. And this woman can't resist the attacks – attacks coming not from her enemies but her friends. They are more threatening because they can destroy her image of herself. . . . It's very brave on her part to try, then, to follow her idea of herself. She is special in that she's completely honest with herself, very stubborn and very alone.
>
> (Cassavetes, 2001, pp. 412–413)

Opening Night can be understood as Cassavetes's subversive version of a backstage melodrama about theatre and midlife, about acting and being, about illusion and reality explored in the context of ageing. He schematizes the problem as three generations or three ages of women:

> Here's an old lady, Joan Blondell, who still has all her life and sexual feelings, which you can see though we don't go into them; and Gena, who's a few decades down from Joan; and the young girl, who is really seventeen years old.
>
> (Cassavetes, 2001, p. 407)

Cassavetes encapsulates the midlife predicament of his protagonist in the film's brief prologue. We see Myrtle enter the stage, playing the role of Virginia. Maurice, Myrtle's former lover, is playing Marty, Virginia's partner, a photographer. Myrtle, the protagonist, and Virginia, her character, stand between two of Marty's blown-up images on the living-room wall, one of a young girl's face, which Marty describes as cruel, and the other of an old woman's face, which he sees as worldly wise. Myrtle's future predicament is depicted here physically: she will find herself trapped between the cruel but vibrant hunger of the ghost-teenager, Nancy, and the hopeless, defeatist vision of the resigned older woman, Sarah Goode.

Cassavetes encouraged an interpretation of *Opening Night* as a reworking of the famous film *All About Eve* (1950), having originally written the part of the playwright Sarah Goode for the actress Bette Davis, who played the middle-aged protagonist in the earlier film. At the same time, he admitted to deliberately undermining the conventions of such theatrical melodrama with the formality of his camerawork. As both screenwriter and director, he worked technically to prevent his audience from empathizing too much with Myrtle:

> I don't want [people] to identify with the performers, with backstage theatricality, to the point where they become just as mundane as everybody else. So we didn't use those strengths that we know can create loneliness: long shot, then tight shot, key lighting and everything else. We shot it much more conventionally. Everything was normally lit and nothing was really explained. She came in drunk, we didn't know quite why she'd decided to drink, we didn't know quite why she smoked a lot of cigarettes, we didn't know quite why she didn't like the play.
>
> (Cassavetes, 2001, pp. 419–420)

With great subtlety, while formally distancing his audience from the performers and the melodrama, Cassavetes introduced the idiom of possession to describe the suffering of his protagonist. In response to the professional and personal crises in which she finds herself, Myrtle seeks consolation with a seventeen-year-old self, the ghostly figure of the autograph-seeker Nancy, killed by a car in front of the theatre. Unfortunately, Myrtle discovers during increasingly violent episodes that the spirit Nancy rebels as much against her as she rebels against the cast and crew of the play. 'Here's a theatrical story', Cassavetes said, 'and suddenly this apparition appears – and I start giggling. Everybody knows I hate that spooky-dooky stuff and they said, "Are you going to leave that in?" ' (Cassavetes, 2001, p. 410).

'I'm not acting', Myrtle insists, when Manny, her director, finds her bruised and exhausted after having wrestled with Nancy during the night. On the one hand, horrified to witness Myrtle sabotaging the play in rehearsal and performance, her colleagues indulge her by taking her to a spiritualist, but Myrtle walks out of the séance and rejects the esoteric solution of exorcism. On the other hand, when Sarah Goode witnesses the divided Myrtle pummelling her own head against a bedroom door frame, she concludes that the actress is self-harming and certifiably insane. In this sense, *Village Voice* critic Dennis Lim described Cassavetes as gleefully tipping his theatrical melodrama into a 'supernatural thriller' (Lim, 2005).

There is, of course, a tradition into which Cassavetes tapped here. The two best literary examples that come to mind are Henry James's story, 'The Turn of the Screw' (1898), and James Hogg's novel, *The Private Memoirs and Confessions of a Justified Sinner* (1824). James's fictional protagonist is a governess who comes to believe that the malevolent spirits of the former servant and governess, Peter Quint and Miss Jessel, seek to possess her young charges, Miles and Flora. The story has been filmed many times, perhaps best by Jack Clayton, with a screenplay entitled *The Innocents* (1961), co-written by Truman Capote; it has also been adapted as an opera by Benjamin Britten. Hogg's protagonist, possibly possessed by an uncanny stranger or doppelgänger named Gil-Martin, commits a series of crimes including the murder of his estranged brother; Hogg set the pivotal epiphanic confrontation between the brothers at the end of a climb up to Arthur's Seat, a setting that foreshadows the brutal unseating of self. Both writers employed distancing narrative structures and styles which prevent the reader from establishing definitively whether the possessing spirits are more than delusions. Similarly, Cassavetes introduced possession as the idiom within which Myrtle experiences her distress, but his screenplay and his camera work explicitly undermine any esoteric interpretation that would legitimize Nancy's spirit, as well as any psychiatric reading of Myrtle's behaviours which would suggest a diagnosis of Dissociative Identity Disorder.

Oddly enough, Cassavetes did write an anthropemic argument into the *Opening Night* press release. In it, he described Myrtle as eventually having to kill Nancy, and the standard critical interpreters of the film have aligned their comments with the director's intention:

> Although she resists facing them, Myrtle must finally accept and resolve the dilemmas which lie not only at the core of the play she is doing but which reflect the basic realities of her own existence, from which she has heretofore fled, aided by alcohol, men, professional indulgences – and fantasy! The character is left in conflict, but she fights the terrifying battle to recapture hope. And wins! In and out of life, the theme of the play haunts the actress until *she kills the young girl in herself*.
> (Cassavetes, 2001, pp. 424–425, italics in original)

Cassavetes expert Ray Carney, who consistently interpreted Cassavetes's films autobiographically (Carney, 2001, p. 409), and Dennis Lim have both followed Cassavetes's lead: 'Nancy is savagely exorcised [and] a euphoric Myrtle turns up at Maurice's apartment with a new approach to the play' (Lim, 2005). Granted, we do watch Myrtle attempting to overpower and kill off Nancy, but if this strategy addresses Myrtle's suffering successfully, then why does she continue to sabotage the play, arriving late for the opening night too drunk to walk?

Perhaps the beginning of an answer can be found in Freud's commentary on demonological neurosis (see Chapter 1) in the case of Christoph Haitzmann; after nine years of suffering, this possessed artist from Bavaria sought help to exorcise a persecutory devil. According to Freud, the exorcisms and a subsequent commitment to enter a monastic order constituted a neurotic evasion rather than a cure, since, once cloistered, the man succumbed to drinking (Freud, 1923a). Similarly, Cassavetes portrayed his possessed protagonist savagely wrestling her demon to the floor, but in subsequent scenes, she still finds herself victimized and overpowered. Arriving late on opening night, she falls through the backstage door and crawls on her hands and knees along the corridors. If we did not know she was drunk – and Cassavetes chose not to show her drinking beforehand – then we would see her still ridden and pummelled by Nancy, still submerged and wrestling to find her way out of a fused state. Her peers throw the disoriented actress out onto the opening-night stage, sacrificing her to their own needs and to the audience's or, perhaps a little more optimistically, to the Dionysian. In this sense, the idiom of possession which Cassavetes would weave into the film overrides and alters the otherwise melodramatic clichés of an ageing star and the show that must go on.

Interpreting the setting of *Opening Night* as 'some vertiginous inner space where acting and reality have long ago lost their differentiating, ritual borders', a setting that invites 'not a vulgar, but a very sophisticated psychoanalysis, drawing on many interpretative possibilities' leads to a fundamentally different reading of the film (Martin, 2001). The regression into which Myrtle falls and the liminality through which she must manoeuvre resembles the accounts of possession of Nicole Obry, Sister Marthe, and Christoph Haitzmann, which I surveyed in Chapter 1. These historical sufferers all attempted to engage in conversation with their uncanny intimate dead, and they discovered that the conventional discourses of families, priests, and authorities trapped them rather than providing any effective code or language or practice with which they could safely confront these figures from their underworlds. They found themselves and these Others confined exclusively to an anthropemic narrative of exorcism which turns negotiating with the dead into warring against them.

This is not to suggest that the figure of Nancy, for whom Myrtle chooses to make a space, is benign. In 1634, Father Jean-Joseph Surin made a terrifying sacrifice when he created a space within his own psyche for the diabolised erotic Other, constellated by the death of the father confessor, who possessed Jeanne des Anges (see Chapter 1). Among the Hofriyati of Sudan, both the black *jinn* which must be exorcised and the *zar* spirits with whom sufferers may come to relate as if in marriage, are experienced as distressing, as an affliction. In Niger, the Songhay work to free themselves from states of fusion, flinging down the symbolic millet pieces at the crossroads and fleeing back to the safety of the demarcated social space of the compound (see Chapter 2). Laying these readings over Cassavetes's images brings into focus just how much the dead Nancy distresses and afflicts Myrtle.

It is illuminating to analyse this disordering irrational space. In the case of Haitzmann, Freud began his classical psychoanalytic argument by describing the son's task of grieving the dead father consciously, of integrating into ego consciousness a repressed grief and fear, of realizing what has been rendered 'unreal' and 'uncanny', and of working towards living bereft in an adult state of separateness from the dead. Cassavetes sent Myrtle off to a memorial gathering held by Nancy's family. She wants to learn what Nancy's death means to her, but the grieving father quickly intuits her self-centred motive and tells her that she should not have come, that she has no place in the objective reality of mourning rites for the young woman struck by the car. Thus Cassavetes quickly eliminated any interpersonal interpretation of Myrtle's distress. Nor was he interested in presenting any reductive psychoanalytic anamnesis of Myrtle's case history: she never speaks of her own father or mother or other family members.

Perhaps part of the problem for Myrtle is that she herself regards the spirit reductively, as a private fantasy like an imaginary friend that she can manipulate according to her needs. When Jung personified unconscious complexes as gods or spirits of the dead, he thereby conveyed not only their precarious quality as unlived potentialities of personhood but also their affective power over the suffering individual ego. Phenomenologically they strike at us, they throttle us and push us around, they are 'forces'; 'the dead want blood' (Atwood, 2002, p. 166). They manifest teleologically, Jung said, as mad impulses seeking concrete embodiment in time and space. In his concept of possession, an unconscious complex can be rendered conscious only through incarnating what has been experienced as unembodied spirit. The ego must sacrifice the personal narrative in which it assigns itself the seat of the personality, while the autonomous and numinous archetypal aspect must suffer diminishment, a kind of stripping down to the profane particularity of the here and now. At the same time, theoretically, the archetypal aspect of the complex offers the possibility of wisdom through a collective connection within individual suffering; via the archetype, a shared meaning might be found in terrible individual suffering. This would suggest that, like Jeanne des Anges, who drew crowds from all over Europe to the exorcisms at Loudun, who re-enacted on the cathedral stage for six years both a personal erotic problem and a problematic, Myrtle wrestles with not only a repressed fantasy but also a collective dilemma.

In Vichian terms, humanity's living, earthy present exists only to the extent to which that present inhabits the traces of the dead. In his story 'The Dead' (1914), James Joyce expressed his narrator's epiphany as he watches the separate snowflakes blanketing Ireland like an accumulation of individual fallen lives. In this contract of mutual indebtedness between the living and the dead, the living give the dead a future so that the dead may give the living a past:

> In the human realm the dead and the unborn are native allies, so much so that from their posthumous abode – wherever it be – the former hound the living with guilt, dread, and a sense of responsibility, obliging us, by whatever means necessary, to take the unborn into our care and to keep the story going, even if we never quite figure out what the story is about,

what our part in it is, the end toward which it's progressing, or the moral it contains.

(Harrison, 2003, p. ix)

Vico traced the etymology of *humanitas* to *humando*, 'burying'; the term *homo sapiens* designates us as a species, but our humanity is defined by our mortality, not so much by our own death as by our relationship with our dead. Vico's thesis about the three different kinds of language to which a society has recourse (see Chapter 4) carries implications for a society which no longer employs its languages effectively but privileges one over the others. He depicted both the dark 'barbarism of sense', in which a fundamentalist concretization of metaphor prevails, and the malicious 'barbarism of reflection', in which words no longer evoke and invoke the dead but merely describe what the dead once were (Verene, 1981, p. 194).

Similarly, and contrary to Cassavetes's press statement, *Opening Night* argues through narrative and image that killing the ghost will not suffice. Instead, the film presents a triad of interrelated questions which Myrtle must suffer and embody. First, there is the accidental death of Nancy outside the New Haven theatre: of what does Myrtle become conscious when she witnesses the death of Nancy and the complacent responses of her colleagues, who refuse to stop their limousine to help? Second, there's the prison of the script: to what extent does an older woman's vision of the feminine, in which there is neither hope nor redemption nor life, tyrannize Myrtle just as cruelly as the grandiose but ghostly unlived potential of the seventeen-year-old girl? Third, there is the problem of the masculine: Myrtle feels abandoned by Maurice, her co-star, who, at the beginning of the film, chastises her: 'You're not a woman to me any more. You're a professional'. Also, she feels manipulated by Manny, her director, who tries to meet her suffering by sharing anecdotes about how he mismanaged his own midlife crisis. Feeling so much at a loss, she nevertheless rejects the men's advice as well as the older woman's insistence that she capitulate. She rejects the esoteric solution of exorcising her seventeen-year-old antagonist as well as the psychiatric judgement that she is insane. Instead, she puts all her suffering into the vessel of the theatre production and fights for the integrity of her character within the play. Even if Myrtle is not a very good actress, she still knows something about how to inhabit herself as a fiction, to sacrifice her ego's personal narrative in deference to a differentiated Other. Perhaps for this reason she has a fighting chance.

I have aligned the idiom of possession as expressed in European religious history, anthropology, psychiatry, critical theory and psychotherapy with Jung's concept of possession, not to totalize the phenomena of possession but to see how gathering approximative comparative anatomies of psyche makes certain aspects spring into focus. Keeping all these strands in mind, I would like to introduce one last strand to this reading of Cassavetes's film. It comes, appropriately enough for Myrtle, from the American theatre. The actor-director Joseph Chaikin repeatedly employed the idiom of possession in the liminal and liminoid vessel of Western theatre in his attempt to reconnect actors and audiences with *humanitas*, to use Vico's term for the relationship of the living with the dead. For Chaikin, reality can be fathomed in the archaic literal sense of 'encircled with the arms', and it can be 'sounded' (Chaikin, 1987, p. 8). He defined his theatrical method explicitly in terms of possession: actors in his exploratory workshops must permit themselves to become 'obsessed' and 'possessed' by themes in an attempt to discern whatever demands to be embodied or given voice (Blumenthal, 1984, p. 140). Stage notes for the Open Theatre's 1974 production of his play *Terminal* make this explicit:

> To be possessed is to make oneself available to the unknown. At the moments when the dead come through, everything is altered – ideas about life, attitudes toward death, rhythms, sounds, movements. The form of the piece itself must stretch to accommodate these unfamiliar energies.
>
> (Yankowitz, 1974, p. 48)

In 1977, Chaikin directed a production of the classic Yiddish play *The Dybbuk*, in which a rabbinical court attempts and fails to appease the spirit of a brilliant Talmudic scholar that possesses a young bride-to-be. In *Terminal* (1974), his actors create rites with which to address 'the graves beneath this house', 'the bones beneath this floor', working to construct a bridge between the dead and the living (Blumenthal, 1984, p. 102). This attempt is also investigated in *Tongues*, written and performed by Chaikin and Sam Shepard (1978), in which voice and percussion make spaces for 'Voice from the Dead' or 'Voice to One About to Die'. Seated facing the audience, Chaikin explored the conditions inherent in a series of such voices or texts, as well as the moments of transformation from one character to another, incarnated without transitional action. At the same time, Shepard performed with his back to Chaikin, playing an assortment of drums, maracas, chains, and bells, his arms extending above and on either side of Chaikin's chair. In his late struggles with aphasia and his own mortality, Chaikin as performer radically altered the way in which we now listen to the texts of Samuel Beckett; in the same way, Chaikin as director radically altered the criteria of contemporary theatrical performance, demanding that a play function as an 'opening' and that, above all, actors must be paradoxically 'present' within their roles, consciously embodying the contradictions between ego and Otherness.

Opening Night includes several scenes from the play *The Second Woman*, in which Myrtle searches desperately for Chaikinesque moments of opening and presence. In one of these scenes, Marty slaps Virginia. The scene is

Figures 6.2, 6.3
The Open Theatre production of *Terminal*, 1971 (left), and Joseph Chaikin and Sam Shepard in a performance of *Tongues/Savage Love*, 1978 (below): actors renewing our humanity by embodying our dead. Published with permission of the Max Waldman Archive and Dr. Ted Shank, respectively.

enacted in three different ways. First, Myrtle, as Virginia, screams, falls to the floor and refuses to stand up again. Second, Myrtle breaks the vessel of the play by coming out of character and saying to her leading man, in front of the preview audience, 'You're a wonderful actor, Maurice'. Finally, at the end of the film, on opening night, Myrtle abandons the script and subverts the moment of the slap, forcing Maurice (as Marty) to search for a new way to meet her fictionally. Like that seventeen-year-old with whom she has been wrestling, Myrtle declares a kind of open war-game with Maurice:

should either actor fail in the improvisation which she imposes, then all will be lost for both of them. What they come to find is a simple 'leg-shake' gesture, what Chaikin would call an 'emblem', a new attitude incarnated between the two actors in a subtle and spontaneous symbolic gesture (Chaikin, 1987, p. 113). Chaikin describes the process of emblem-hunting as identifying the genuine contact points, the places at which an improvised sound-and-movement story touches more than the storyteller, and then removing all the superfluities to let the emblems resonate in the empty spaces. Until such emblematic actions and sounds are delineated, an initial improvisation (such as Myrtle and Maurice enact on the opening-night stage) might be highly evocative, but it will die when repeated. Once distilled, the emblems set up a series of meetings between the actor and the observer. The succinct, fragmentary nature of the presentation necessitates the imaginative participation of the audience and opens a space for an authentic moment of meeting between the actors and the spectators (Joseph Chaikin, quoted in Blumenthal, 1984).

Joan Blondell said that Cassavetes left her on her own to ponder how her character, playwright Sarah Goode, felt about the opening night improvisation, and he did not instruct the extras playing the theatre audience how to react to the play they were watching, either. It was up to Blondell to decide if the improvisation was a triumph or a failure. On the one hand, Cassavetes's press release described Myrtle as 'winning'. On the other hand, Gena Rowlands called the play within the film a 'disaster' and a 'flop'; the improvised ending, she said, figured its 'ruination' (Cassavetes, 2001, p. 424). After all, the play has been completely jettisoned, and the audience has felt moved without really knowing what it has witnessed.

Jung's concept of possession is rooted in an epistemology and a therapeutics of paradox, similar to what Moreno located in the ontological role-reversal of observer and actor (see Chapter 5). Isaiah Berlin identified this contradictory place – the space between the perspective of the actor and that of the external observer – as 'the deepest chasm which divides historical from scientific studies' (Berlin, 1998, p. 53). Both Schieffelin, the anthropologist of possession, and Jung, the psychotherapist with his concept of possession, position themselves over that chasm. Myrtle, Cassavetes's possessed protagonist, exists precisely in that place. At the beginning of the film, Nancy embraces Myrtle at the stage door, just before she is struck by the car and becomes a ghost. By the end of the film, Cassavetes had shifted his focus from the three women, Nancy, Myrtle, and Sarah, to include a fourth: Dorothy, the director's wife (Zohra Lampert), who applauds Myrtle's improvised performance and comes backstage to embrace her. Throughout the film, Dorothy has been the mostly silent, sometimes jealous but increasingly appreciative observer of Myrtle's active struggle. If there is a victory in *Opening Night* – and Cassavetes says there is one – it has little to do with exorcising Nancy and less to do with a successful opening night on Broadway. The

Figures 6.4, 6.5 Myrtle Gordon (Gena Rowlands) embraced by the autograph-seeker Nancy (Laura Johnson) in *Opening Night* (above), just before Nancy is killed by a car and becomes a ghost. Myrtle and Dorothy (Zohra Lampert) (below), actor and observer, embrace over an epistemological chasm. Published with permission of Al Ruban, Faces Distribution Corporation.

victory has to do with the final image of the film, Myrtle and Dorothy embracing, actor and observer balanced in a precarious moment over an epistemological chasm, embodying both contradiction and connection in an experience of selfhood.

Figure 7.1 Open Theatre actors Raymond Barry and Paul Zimet enact 'The Journey' from *The Mutation Show*, 1974. Published with permission of Mary Ellen Mark.

Chapter 7

Closing

The overarching ideas that have influenced my work and fuelled my interest in conscious and unconscious memory derive from a perspective on mind that psychiatry and psychoanalysis opened up for me. Thus, my initial career as an aspiring psychoanalyst was hardly a detour; rather, it was the educational bedrock of all I have been able to accomplish since. . . . One should not be afraid to try new things, such as moving from one field to another or working at the boundaries of different disciplines, for it is at the borders that some of the most interesting problems reside.

(Eric Kandel, *In Search of Memory*, p. 426)

The existence of complexes throws serious doubt on the naïve assumption of the unity of consciousness.

(C. G. Jung, 'A Review of the Complex Theory', p. 96)

The more uncertain I have felt about myself, the more there has grown up in me a feeling of kinship with all things. In fact it seems to me as if that alienation which so long separated me from the world has become transferred into my own inner world, and has revealed to me an unexpected unfamiliarity with myself.

(C. G. Jung, *Memories, Dreams, Reflections*, p. 359)

The religious, psychological, intellectual and political complexity of the demonic possessions at Loudun still has not been fully explored, even after almost four centuries of scrutiny. From before those possessions in the 1630s to the present day, the phenomena of possession have preoccupied thinkers in many fields, especially, in the past century, anthropologists and psychologists. In the first half of the twentieth century, Jung developed a concept of possession that was both deep and broad. Anatomizing it today in terms of temenos, personification and synthesis reinvests Jungian psychotherapy with its positive potential for practice. Analogizing it – lining it up comparatively beside fragments of late medieval theology, anthropology, psychiatry, critical theory, film criticism and theatre history – leads, not to a naive syncretism, but to possibilities for illumination along the borders of these disciplines. Jung's concept of possession, refreshed with new insights, offers a conceptual bridge between psychology and anthropology, it supports psychiatry's recent shift towards a culturally contextualized classification of disorders, and it carries important implications for psychotherapists who want to improve their work with their patients and enhance its meaning in the professional field.

Jung's concept of possession is etymologically and imagistically precise: it speaks of personhood sitting in its own seat, and it addresses how to accommodate the suffering that occurs when personhood experiences itself as unseated, overthrown by tyrannical Otherness. Thus it challenges theories that imagine personhood defined by consciousness alone, positing instead a much more fluid, pluralistic and embodied notion. It is illuminating to apply Vico's paradoxical epistemology, his sense of moving forward and backward at the same time, to Jung's memoirs and case histories. Enriched with imagery from medieval Catholicism, ethnographic description of possession in other cultures, current cognitive and neuroscientific research, the complementary psychotherapeutic practices of Oughourlian and Moreno, and especially Cassavetes's film *Opening Night* and Chaikin's Open Theatre, Jung's concept of possession has much to say about important contemporary problematics of presence and embodiment, dissociation and self, Eros and power.

Our Western habits of mind and impoverished vernaculars set us up to experience the dissociative tendencies of normal cognitive functioning as psychological ruptures. To master this dissociation, only the activities of the intellect have been favoured, while the discomfort or distress caused by dissociative phenomena has been increasingly pathologized. Practitioners compensate for this impoverishment and these ruptures by adhering even more closely to the singularizing coherence that they find in psychiatry's definitions of mental disorders. For this reason, the 1992 introduction of 'possession' into the *DSM* could bring about a recuperation of the term that would be negative and destructive because the essentializing nosology of twentieth-century psychiatry cannot accommodate its multifaceted nature. On the other hand, including the term in the *DSM* may open the way for an epistemological break in which twenty-first-century psychiatry reflects on its limits as a cultural practice, evaluates its failure to address meaningfully its own 'cultural syndromes', and gradually incorporates some aspect of the Otherness formerly relegated to the appendices of its diagnostic manual.

Jung positions himself, in his predicament as analytical psychologist, at the intersecting point of a double perspective on Western consciousness: he assigns an ontological reality to split-off autonomous complexes as unembodied spirits, as unconscious Other, that is equal to the reality of the suffering, possessed ego-identity. By characterizing his practice of psychotherapy as compensating for Western conceptual impoverishment, Jung attempts within the psychotherapeutic context to privilege the reality of image and/or spirit. Looked at from another angle, Jung's mimetic and synthetic approach can also be characterized as compensatory for the extent to which Western cultures favour the anthropemic 'vomiting out' of the Other. Within the transferential context of therapy, patients and Jungian therapists work towards psychological containment, consciously reorienting themselves to the presence of unconscious factors, personifying, embodying and thereby incorporating images of that Otherness into the experience of selfhood.

For Jung, embodying an unconscious image paradoxically both acknowledges and depotentiates the complex. The embodiment honours and yet limits the complex's ontological claim, expressing it yet confining it to time and space. Its archetypal or collective dimension is individualized while the suffering it causes is rendered collectively meaningful. Jung's therapeutic practice of personification or mimesis promotes not so much a mimetic identification with the Other as a differentiation from and relationship with the Other. Images from anthropological investigations into the phenomena of possession enrich, extend, and challenge the implications of Jung's concept of possession. They reinforce the importance of discernment as crucial to the Jungian practice of psychotherapy: differentiating between organic and psychogenic causes of suffering; differentiating between personal unconscious complexes, which can be integrated, and the moral problem of what Jung called the shadow, which can only be endured; differentiating between the transferences of the patient and the countertransference issues evoked in the therapist; differentiating between morbid aspects of the patient's personality which must be 'cauterized with the acid of analytical understanding' and healthy aspects which should be protected from the analytical gaze (Jung, 1973, Vol. 1, pp. 30–32).

Just as anthropological performance theory is betrayed by the cultural bias that equates 'theatricalization' with 'shamming', Jung's concept of possession is betrayed by the cultural bias that denigrates it as 'esoteric'. Anthropologists manoeuvre around the twin problems inherent in performance theory – that it appears both to devalue possession and to render it exotic – by reframing their observations. When describing his concept of possession, Jung himself slips into essentializing it, primitivizing it, or rendering it esoteric, but the concept should not be rejected on the grounds that its originator was a man of his time and place. When he locates his concept of possession in a psychotherapeutic context of clinical practice that privileges the intrapsychic Other as 'spirit' and as 'complex' (and slightly more as 'spirit' than as 'complex'), he rectifies his own theorizing. When he embeds his description of the psychology of transference in alchemical images, he enacts in his text how to right psychologizing by reinvesting theory in poetic logic, by reconnecting to the counter-rational paradoxical logic of metaphor.

Jung's concept of possession is rooted in an epistemology and a therapeutics of paradox. Isaiah Berlin (1998) called this contradictory place – the space between the perspectives of the actor and the observer – 'the deepest chasm which divides historical from scientific studies'. Berlin identified the Enlightenment as the moment when Western cultures over-identified with factual knowledge and the gathering of like terms, and he saw Vico as one of its best critics, who came to defend knowing as understanding and interpretation. Jung's concept of possession is a precarious bridge over a similar epistemological chasm. Jung attempted, not a reactionary, regressive identification of complexes with spirits, but an image-based theory and psychotherapeutic practice which look backwards and forwards at the same time, producing more effective narratives and social discourse and enough irrational spaces within which to come to terms with the Otherness inherent in selfhood.

The introduction to this book ended with an image that has accompanied me throughout my research and writing: a young Canadian speaking to a journalist about the death of her older brother by fire and about the painful contradiction she endures: she wants to sniff gasoline in order to not lose her connection with the spirit of her brother, who tells her not to sniff gasoline. In closing, I wish for her the integrity with which Myrtle Gordon comes to address her suffering in the temenos of playing a role and with which Chaikin inhabits theatrically over and over again the paradox of presence. I wish she might find enough irreducible space in which to manoeuvre until she can respond to the loss and the contradictions she articulates, taking up ways to be and to move in her journey while sitting in self.

Bibliography

Abram, D. (1996) *The Spell of the Sensuous*, New York: Vintage.

American Psychiatric Association (APA). (2000) *Diagnostic and Statistical Manual of Mental Disorders*, Fourth Edition, Washington, DC: APA.

Ancelin Schützenberger, A. (1998) *The Ancestor Syndrome: Transgenerational Psychotherapy and the Hidden Links in the Family Tree*, trans. A. Trager, London: Routledge.

Anderson, S., Reznik, I. and Glassman, N. (2005) 'The Unconscious Relational Self', in R. R. Hassin, J. S. Weman and J. A. Bargh (eds) *The New Unconscious*, Oxford: Oxford University Press.

Anges, J. des. (1886) *Soeur Jeanne des Anges, supérieure des Ursulines de Loudun: Autobiographie d'une hystérique possédée*, edited by G. Legué and G. de la Tourette, preface by Charcot, Paris: G. Charpentier, Collection Bourneville.

Antze, P. (1992) 'Possession Trance and Multiple Personality: Psychiatric Disorders or Idioms of Distress?', *Transcultural Psychiatric Research Review*, 24, 4: 319–322.

Atwood, M. (2002) *Negotiating with the Dead*, Cambridge: Cambridge University Press.

Aubin, N. (1693) *Histoire des diables de Loudun*, Amsterdam: Abraham Wolfgang.

Auerbach, E. (2005) *Mimesis: The Representation of Reality in Western Literature*, trans. W. Trask, Princeton, NJ: Princeton University Press.

Aurigemma, L. (1992) *Perspectives jungiennes*, Paris: Albin Michel, trans. C. Stephenson (2008) *Jungian Perspectives*, Scranton, PA: Scranton University Press.

Bachelard, G. (1934/1999) *Le Nouvel Esprit scientifique*, Paris: Presses Universitaires de France.

Barbano, R. (2000) 'Un asunto satánico que se basa en la historia familiar', in *Clarín*, 2 April.

Bargh, J. (2005) 'Bypassing the Will: Toward Demystifying the Nonconscious Control of Social Behaviour', in R. R. Hassin, J. S. Uleman and J. A. Bargh (eds) *The New Unconscious*, Oxford: Oxford University Press.

Barz, H. (1990) 'Dream and Psychodrama', in R. Papadopoulos (ed.) *Carl Gustav Jung: Critical Assessments*, London: Routledge, 3: 425–440.

Beebe, J. (1992) *Integrity in Depth*, College Station, TX: Texas A&M University Press.

Beebe, J. (2004) 'Understanding Consciousness through the Theory of Psychological Types', in J. Cambray and L. Carter (eds) *Analytical Psychology: Contemporary Perspectives in Jungian Analysis*, Hove: Brunner-Routledge, 83–115.

Begley, S. (2001) 'Religion and the Brain', in *Newsweek*, 7 May, 52–7.

Berlin, I. (1998) 'The Concept of Scientific History', in *The Proper Study of Mankind*, edited by H. Hardy and R. Hausheer, London: Pimlico, 17–58.

Berlin, I. (2000) *Three Critics of the Enlightenment*, Princeton, NJ: Princeton University Press.

Berlin, I. (2001) *Against the Current: Essays in the History of Ideas*, Princeton, NJ: Princeton University Press.

Bion, W. (1961) 'Group Dynamics: A Review', in *Experiences in Groups and Other Papers*, New York: Basic Books, 141–192.

Bishop, P. (2008) 'The Timeliness and Timelessness of the "Archaic": Analytical Psychology, "Primordial" Thought, Synchronicity', *Journal of Analytical Psychology*, 53, 4: 481–499.

Blumenthal, E. (1984) *Joseph Chaikin: Exploring at the Boundaries of Theatre*, Cambridge: Cambridge University Press.

Boas, F. (1910) 'Psychological Problems in Anthropology', in G. Stocking (ed.) (1989) *The Shaping of American Anthropology, 1883–1911: A Franz Boas Reader*, Chicago, IL: University of Chicago Press, 243–254.

Boas, F. (1911) *The Mind of Primitive Man*, New York: Macmillan.

Boddy, J. (1989) *Wombs and Alien Spirits: Women, Men and the Zar Cult in Northern Sudan*, Madison, WI: University of Wisconsin Press.

Boddy, J. (1992) 'Comment on the Proposed DSM-IV Criteria for Trance and Possession Disorder', *Transcultural Psychiatric Research Review*, 24, 4: 323–329.

Boddy, J. (1999) 'Embodying Ethnography', in M. Lambek and A. Strathern (eds) *Bodies and Persons: Comparative Perspectives from Africa and Melanesia*, Cambridge: Cambridge University Press, 252–273.

Bollas, C. (1992) *Being a Character: Psychoanalysis and Self Experience*, London: Routledge.

Bollas, C. (2000) *Hysteria*, London: Routledge.

Bourdieu, P. (1972) *Esquisse d'une théorie de la pratique, précédé de trois études d'éthnologie kabyle*, Geneva: Librarie Droz; trans. R. Nice (1977) *Outline of a Theory of Practice*, London: Cambridge University Press.

Boureau, A. (2004) *Satan hérétique: Naissance de la démonologie dans l'Occident Médiéval 1280–1330*, Paris: Odile Jacob; trans. T. L. Fagan (2006) *Satan the Heretic: The Birth of Demonology in the Medieval West*, Chicago, IL: University of Chicago Press.

Bowers, K. S. (1991) 'Dissociation in Hypnosis and Multiple Personality Disorder', *International Journal of Clinical and Experimental Hypnosis*, 39: 155–176.

Bradshaw-Tauvon, K. (1998a) 'Principles of Psychodrama', in M. Karp, P. Holmes and K. Bradshaw-Tauvon (eds) *The Handbook of Psychodrama*, London: Routledge, 29–46.

Bradshaw-Tauvon, K. (1998b) 'Psychodrama and Group-Analysis Psychotherapy', in M. Karp, P. Holmes and K. Bradshaw-Tauvon (eds) *The Handbook of Psychodrama*, London: Routledge, 277–296.

Bran, M. (2005) 'Il fallait chasser le démon du corps de Maricica', *Le Monde*, 20 June, 1.

Brémond, H. (1920, 1967) 'Surin et Jeanne des Anges', in *Histoire littéraire du sentiment religieux en France, depuis la fin des guerres de religion jusqu'à nos jours*, Paris: Bloud & Gay, 5: 178–251.

Brooke, R. (1991) *Jung and Phenomenology*, London: Routledge.

Brown, K. M. (1991) *Mama Lola: A Vodou Priestess in Brooklyn*, Berkeley, CA: University of California Press.

Burke, P. (1985) *Vico*, Oxford: Oxford University Press.

Burleson, B. (2005) *Jung in Africa*, London: Continuum.

Cambray, J. and Carter, L. (2004) 'Analytic Methods Revisited', in J. Cambray and L. Carter (eds) *Analytical Psychology: Contemporary Perspectives in Jungian Analysis*, Hove: Brunner-Routledge, 116–148.

Cardeña, E. (1992) 'Trance and Possession as Dissociative Disorders', *Transcultural Psychiatric Research Review*, 24, 4: 287–300.

Carmona, M. (1988) *Les Diables de Loudun: Sorcellerie et politique sous Richelieu*, Paris: Fayard.

Carney, R. (ed.) (2001) *Cassavetes on Cassavetes*, London: Faber & Faber.

Carson, A. (1995) 'The Anthropology of Water', in *Plainwater: Essays and Poetry*, Toronto: Vintage, 113–260.

Cassavetes, J. (2001) *Cassavetes on Cassavetes*, edited by R. Carney, London: Faber & Faber.

Certeau, M. de. (1970) *La Possession de Loudun*, Paris: Julliard; trans. M. B. Smith (2000) *The Possession at Loudun*, Chicago, IL: University of Chicago Press.

Certeau, M. de. (1975) *L'Ecriture de l'histoire*, Paris: Gallimard; trans. T. Conley (1998) *The Writing of History*, New York: Columbia University Press.

Certeau, M. de. (1982) *Le Fable mystique*, Paris: Gallimard; trans. M. B. Smith (1992) *The Mystic Fable*, Chicago, IL: University of Chicago Press.

Chaikin, J. (1987) *The Presence of the Actor*, New York: Atheneum.

Chodorow, J. (ed.) (1997) *Encountering Jung: On Active Imagination*, Princeton, NJ: Princeton University Press.

Chodorow, J. (2004) 'Inner-Directed Movement in Analysis: Early Beginnings', in *Cambridge 2001: Proceedings of the Fifteenth International Congress for Analytical Psychology*, Einsiedeln, Switzerland: Daimon, 323–324.

Clarke, D. (2006) *Descartes: A Biography*, Cambridge: Cambridge University Press.

Claxton, G. (2005) *The Wayward Mind: An Intimate History of the Unconscious*, London: Little, Brown.

Clayton, J. (1961) *The Innocents*, London: British Film Institute.

Connidis, K. (2004) 'A Dream of Dirty Hands', in D. C. Thomasma and D. N. Weisstub (eds) *The Variables of Moral Capacity*, Dordrecht, The Netherlands: Kluwer Academic, 95–111.

Crabtree, A. (1985) *Multiple Man: Explorations in Possession and Multiple Personality*, Toronto: Somerville.

Crabtree, A. (1997) *Trance Zero*, New York: St Martin's Press.

Csikszentmihalyi, M. (1990) *Flow: The Psychology of Optimal Experience*, New York: Harper.

Demaitre, L. (1982) 'Treatment of Insanity', in *Dictionary of the Middle Ages*, New York: Charles Scribner's Sons, 6: 489–493.

Descartes, R. (1999) *Discourse on Method and Related Writings*, trans. D. M. Clarke, London: Penguin.

Dickinson, E. (1890/1970) *The Complete Poems*, edited by T. H. Johnson, London: Faber & Faber.

Dixon, M. and Laurence, J. R. (1992) 'Hypnotic Susceptibility and Verbal

Automaticity: Automatic and Strategic Processing Differences in the Stroop Color-Naming Task', *Journal of Abnormal Psychology*, 101, 344–347.

Donald, M. (1991) *Origins of the Modern Mind*, Cambridge, MA: Harvard University Press.

Donfrancesco, F. (1995) 'Mimesis', *Harvest: Journal of Jungian Studies*, 41, 1: 9–26.

Dosse, F. (2002) *Michel Certeau: Le Marcheur blessé*, Paris: Découverte.

Dourley, J. (2002) 'Response to Barbara Stephens's "The Martin Buber–Carl Jung Disputations: Protecting the Scared in the Battle of the Boundaries of Analytical Psychology" ', *Journal of Analytical Psychology*, 47, 3: 484–485.

Duncan, M. (1634) *Discours sur la possession des religieuses de Loudun*, Saumur, France: Bibliothèque Nationale, 16 Lb. 36.3961.

Elefthery, D. G. and Elefthery, D. M. (1966) 'Our Psychodrama Demonstration in the Permanent Theater of Psychodrama', *Group Psychotherapy*, 19: 17–21.

Ellenberger, H. (1970) *The Discovery of the Unconscious: The History and Evolution of Dynamic Psychiatry*, New York: Basic Books.

Evans, F. J. (1991) 'Hypnotizability: Individual Differences in Dissociation and the Flexible Control of Psychological Processes', in *Theories of Hypnosis: Current Models and Perspectives*, New York: Guilford, 144–168.

Ferber, S. (2004) *Demonic Possession and Exorcism in Early Modern France*, London: Routledge.

Ferber, S. and Howe, A. (2003) 'The Man Who Mistook his Wife for a Devil: Exorcism, Expertise, and Secularization in a Late Twentieth-Century Australian Criminal Court', in H. de Waardt, J. M. Schmidt and D. Bauer (eds) *Demonic Possession: Interpretations of a Historico-Cultural Phenomenon*, Bielefeld, Germany: Verlag für Regionalgeschichte.

Figuier, L. (1860/1881) *Histoire du merveilleux dans les temps modernes: Les diables de Loudun*, Paris: Hachette.

Flower, S. (2006) 'What's in a Word – Projective Identification and Participation Mystique', paper presented at IAJS Greenwich Conference, London, July.

Foucault, M. (1961) *Histoire de la folie*, Paris: Plon; trans. R. Howard (1965) *Madness and Civilization: A History of Insanity in the Age of Reason*, New York: Vintage.

Freud, S. (1911) 'Psychoanalytic Notes on an Autobiographical Account of a Case of Paranoia (Dementia Paranoides) (Schreber)', in *Pelican Freud Library: Case Histories II*, Volume 9, London: Penguin, 1979, 129–223.

Freud, S. (1913) 'Totem and Taboo', in *Pelican Freud Library: The Origins of Religion*, Volume 13, London: Penguin, 1985, 43–224.

Freud, S. (1917) 'Mourning and Melancholia', in *Pelican Freud Library: On Metapsychology: The Theory of Psychoanalysis*, Volume 11, London: Penguin, 1984, 245–268.

Freud, S. (1919) 'The Uncanny', in *Pelican Freud Library: Art and Literature*, Volume 14, London: Penguin, 1985, 335–376.

Freud, S. (1923a) 'A Seventeenth-Century Demonological Neurosis', in *Pelican Freud Library: Art and Literature*, Volume 14, London: Penguin, 1985, 377–423.

Freud, S. (1923b) 'On the History of the Psychoanalytic Movement', in *Pelican Freud Library: Historical and Expository Works on Psychoanalysis*, Volume 15, London: Penguin, 1986.

Frye, N. (1990) *The Great Code*, Toronto: Penguin.

Frye, N. (2000) 'The Double Vision', in *Northrop Frye on Religion*, Toronto: University of Toronto Press, 166–235.

Gardner, L. (2008) 'C. G. Jung and Giambattista Vico: An Exploration in Rhetoric', unpublished PhD thesis, Colchester: University of Essex.

Garrels, S. (2004) 'Imitation, Mirror Neurons, and Mimetic Desire: Convergent Support for the Work of René Girard', Pasadena, CA: Fuller Theological Seminary.

Gayot de Petaval, F. (attributed to) (1735) *Histoire d'Urbain Grandier, condamné comme magicien et comme auteur de la possession des religieuses Ursulines de Loudun*, Amsterdam.

Geertz, C. (1973) *The Interpretation of Cultures*, New York: Basic Books.

Geertz, C. (1988) *Works and Lives: The Anthropologist as Author*, Stanford, CA: Stanford University Press.

Geertz, C. (2000) *Available Light: Anthropological Reflections on Philosophical Topics*, Princeton, NJ: Princeton University Press.

Girard, R. (1974) *La Violence et le sacré*, Paris: Bernard Grasset; trans. P. Gregory (1977) *Violence and the Sacred*, Baltimore, MD: Johns Hopkins University Press.

Girard, R. with Oughourlian, J.-M. and Lefort, G. (1987) *Things Hidden since the Foundation of the World*, trans. S. Bann and M. Metteer, Stanford, CA: Stanford University Press.

Glaser, J. and Kihlstrom, J. (2005) 'Compensatory Automaticity: Unconscious Volition is not an Oxymoron', in R. R. Hassin, J. S. Weman and J. A. Bargh (eds) *The New Unconscious*, Oxford: Oxford University Press.

Gray, A. (1994) *An Introduction to the Therapeutic Frame*, London: Routledge.

Guggenbühl-Craig, A. (1999) *The Emptied Soul: On the Nature of the Psychopath*, trans. G. V. Hartman, Woodstock, CT: Spring.

Hacking, I. (1995) *Rewriting the Soul: Multiple Personality and the Sciences of Memory*, Princeton, NJ: Princeton University Press.

Hacking, I. (1998) *Mad Travelers: Reflections on the Reality of Transient Mental Illnesses*, Charlottesville, VA: University Press of Virginia.

Hallowell, A. I. (1955) *Culture and Experience*, Philadelphia, PA: University of Pennsylvania Press.

Harrison, R. P. (2003) *The Dominion of the Dead*, Chicago, IL: University of Chicago Press.

Hauke, C. (2000) *Jung and the Postmodern: The Interpretation of Realities*, London: Routledge.

Haule, J. (1984) 'From Somnambulism to the Archetypes: The French Roots of Jung's Split with Freud', *Psychoanalytic Review*, 71, 4: 635–659; reprinted in R. Papadopoulos (ed.) (1992) *Carl Gustav Jung: Critical Assessments*, London: Routledge, 238–260.

Hédelin, M. (1637) 'Relation de M. Hédelin, abbé d'Aubignac, touchant les possédées de Loudun au mois de Septembre 1637', in R. Mandrou (1968) *Possession et sorcellerie*, Paris: Plon, 134–194.

Henderson, J. (2003) *Transformation of the Psyche: The Symbolic Alchemy of the Splendor Solis*, London: Brunner-Routledge.

Hilgard, E. R. (1977) *Divided Consciousness: Multiple Controls in Human Thought and Action*, New York: Wiley.

Hilgard, J. R. (1970) *Personality and Hypnosis: A Study of Imaginative Involvement*, Chicago, IL: University of Chicago Press.

Hillman, J. (1975a) 'Plotinus, Ficino, and Vico as Precursors of Archetypal Psychology', in *Loose Ends: Primary Papers in Archetypal Psychology*, Dallas, TX: Spring.

Hillman, J. (1975b) *Re-visioning Psychology*, New York: HarperCollins.

Hogg, J. (1824) *The Private Memoirs and Confessions of a Justified Sinner*, Oxford: Oxford University Press, 1969.

Horwitz, A. and Wakefield, J. (2008) *The Loss of Sadness: How Psychiatry Transformed Normal Sorrow into Depressive Disorder*, Oxford: Oxford University Press.

Huxley, A. (1952) *The Devils of Loudun*, London: Penguin.

James, H. (1898) 'The Turn of the Screw', in *Complete Short Stories 1892–1898*, New York: Library of America, 1996.

Joyce, J. (1914) 'The Dead', in *Dubliners*, New York: Alfred Knopf/Everyman Library, 1991, 199–256.

Jung, C. G. (1902) 'On the Psychology and Pathology of So-Called Occult Phenomena', in *Psychiatric Studies*, Collected Works 1, Princeton, NJ: Princeton University Press, 1957, 1970, 3–88.

Jung, C. G. (1908) 'The Content of the Psychoses', in *The Psychogenesis of Mental Disease*, Collected Works 3, Princeton, NJ: Princeton University Press, 1960, 153–178.

Jung, C. G. (1913) 'The Theory of Psychoanalysis', in *Freud and Psychoanalysis*, Collected Works 4, Princeton, NJ: Princeton University Press, 1961, 83–226.

Jung, C. G. (1916a) 'Psychoanalysis and Neurosis', in *Freud and Psychoanalysis*, Collected Works 4, Princeton, NJ: Princeton University Press, 1961, 243–251.

Jung, C. G. (1916b/1958) 'The Transcendent Function', in *The Structure and Dynamics of the Psyche*, Collected Works 8, Princeton, NJ: Princeton University Press, 1960, 67–91.

Jung, C. G. (1917a) 'On the Psychology of the Unconscious', in *Two Essays on Analytical Psychology*, Collected Works 7, Princeton, NJ: Princeton University Press, 1953, 3–119.

Jung, C. G. (1917b/1935) 'The Relations between the Ego and the Unconscious', in *Two Essays on Analytical Psychology*, Collected Works 7, Princeton, NJ: Princeton University Press, 1953, 123–241.

Jung, C. G. (1920) 'The Psychological Foundations of Belief in Spirits', in *The Structure and Dynamics of the Psyche*, Collected Works 8, Princeton, NJ: Princeton University Press, 1960, 301–318.

Jung, C. G. (1921) *Psychological Types*, Collected Works 6, Princeton, NJ: Princeton University Press, 1971.

Jung, C. G. (1929) 'Commentary on *The Secret of the Golden Flower*', in *Alchemical Studies*, Collected Works 13, Princeton, NJ: Princeton University Press, 1968, 1–56.

Jung, C. G. (1930) 'The Complications of American Psychology', in *Civilization in Transition*, Collected Works 10, Princeton, NJ: Princeton University Press, 1960, 502–514.

Jung, C. G. (1931a) 'Analytical Psychology and *Weltanschauung*', in *The Structure and Dynamics of the Psyche*, Collected Works 8, Princeton, NJ: Princeton University Press, 1960, 358–381.

Jung, C. G. (1931b) 'Foreword to Aldrich: *The Primitive Mind and Modern Civilization*', in *The Symbolic Life*, Collected Works 18, Princeton, NJ: Princeton University Press, 1954, 1980.

Jung, C. G. (1931c) 'Introduction to Wickes's *Analyse der Kinderseele*', in *The Development of Personality*, Collected Works 17, Princeton, NJ: Princeton University Press, 1954, 37–46.

Jung, C. G. (1931d) 'Mind and Earth', in *Civilization in Transition*, Collected Works 10, Princeton, NJ: Princeton University Press, 1960, 29–49.

Jung, C. G. (1934a) 'A Review of the Complex Theory', in *The Structure and Dynamics of the Psyche*, Collected Works 8, Princeton, NJ: Princeton University Press, 1960, 92–106.

Jung, C. G. (1934b) 'The Meaning of Psychology for Modern Man', in *Civilization in Transition*, Collected Works 10, Princeton, NJ: Princeton University Press, 1964, 134–156.

Jung, C. G. (1934c) 'A Study in the Process of Individuation', in *The Archetypes and the Collective Unconscious*, Collected Works 9i, Princeton, NJ: Princeton University Press, 1959, 290–354.

Jung, C. G. (1935a) 'The Tavistock Lectures', in *The Symbolic Life*, Collected Works 18, Princeton, NJ: Princeton University Press, 1954/1980.

Jung, C. G. (1935b) 'The Relations between the Ego and the Unconscious', in *Two Essays on Analytical Psychology*, Collected Works 7, Princeton, NJ: Princeton University Press, 1953.

Jung, C. G. (1936) 'Yoga and the West', in *Psychology and Religion: West and East*, Collected Works 11, Princeton, NJ: Princeton University Press, 1958, 529–537.

Jung, C. G. (1937) 'The Realities of Practical Psychotherapy', in *The Practice of Psychotherapy*, Collected Works 16, Princeton, NJ: Princeton University Press, 1954, 1966, 327–338.

Jung, C. G. (1938) 'Psychology and Religion (The Terry Lectures)', in *Psychology and Religion: West and East*, Collected Works 11, Princeton, NJ: Princeton University Press, 1958, 3–106.

Jung, C. G. (1939a) 'Conscious, Unconscious and Individuation', in *The Archetypes and the Collective Unconscious*, Collected Works 9i, Princeton, NJ: Princeton University Press, 1959, 275–289.

Jung, C. G. (1939b) 'In Memory of Sigmund Freud', in *The Spirit in Man, Art and Literature*, Collected Works 15, Princeton, NJ: Princeton University Press, 1966, 41–52.

Jung, C. G. (1939c) 'Concerning Rebirth', in *The Archetypes and the Collective Unconscious*, Collected Works 9i, Princeton, NJ: Princeton University Press, 1959, 113–150.

Jung, C. G. (1939d) 'The Symbolic Life', in *The Symbolic Life*, Collected Works 18, Princeton, NJ: Princeton University Press, 1954, 1980.

Jung, C. G. (1941a) 'The Psychological Aspects of the Kore', in *The Archetypes and the Collective Unconscious*, Collected Works 9i, Princeton, NJ: Princeton University Press, 1959, 182–206.

Jung, C. G. (1941b) 'The Psychology of the Child Archetype', in *The Archetypes and the Collective Unconscious*, Collected Works 9i, Princeton, NJ: Princeton University Press, 1959, 151–181.

Jung, C. G. (1942) 'Psychotherapy and a Philosophy of Life', in *The Practice of Psychotherapy*, Collected Works 16, Princeton, NJ: Princeton University Press, 1954, 76–83.

Jung, C. G. (1945a) 'Marginalia on Contemporary Events', in *The Symbolic Life*, Collected Works 18, Princeton, NJ: Princeton University Press, 1954, 591–602.

Jung, C. G. (1945b) 'Medicine and Psychotherapy', in *The Practice of Psychotherapy*, Collected Works 16, Princeton, NJ: Princeton University Press, 1954, 84–93.

Jung, C. G. (1945c) 'Definition of Demonism', in *The Symbolic Life*, Collected Works 18, Princeton, NJ: Princeton University Press, 1954, 648.

Jung, C. G. (1946) 'The Psychology of the Transference', in *The Practice of Psychotherapy*, Collected Works 16, Princeton, NJ: Princeton University Press, 1954, 163–321.

Jung, C. G. (1948) 'On Psychic Energy', in *The Structure and Dynamics of the Psyche*, Collected Works 8, Princeton, NJ: Princeton University Press, 1960, 3–66.

Jung, C. G. (1950) 'Concerning Rebirth', in *The Archetypes and the Collective Unconscious*, Collected Works 9i, Princeton, NJ: Princeton University Press, 1959, 113–150.

Jung, C. G. (1952) 'Foreword to Werblowsky's *Lucifer and Prometheus*', in *Psychology and Religion: West and East*, Collected Works 11, Princeton, NJ: Princeton University Press, 1958, 311–315.

Jung, C. G. (1954) 'Archetypes of the Collective Unconscious', in *The Archetypes and the Collective Unconscious*, Collected Works 9i, Princeton, NJ: Princeton University Press, 1959, 3–41.

Jung, C. G. (1955) *Mysterium Coniunctionis*, Collected Works 14, Princeton, NJ: Princeton University Press, 1963.

Jung, C. G. (1958) 'Schizophrenia', in *The Psychogenesis of Mental Disease*, Collected Works 3, Princeton, NJ: Princeton University Press, 256–271.

Jung, C. G. (1961) 'Symbols and the Interpretation of Dreams', in *The Symbolic Life*, Collected Works 18, Princeton, NJ: Princeton University Press, 1954, 1980, 185–266.

Jung, C. G. (1962) *Memories, Dreams, Reflections*, New York: Random House.

Jung, C. G. (1973) *Letters*, Volumes 1 and 2, Princeton, NJ: Princeton University Press.

Jung, C. G. (1984) *Dream Analysis: Notes of the Seminar Given in 1928–1930*, Princeton, NJ: Princeton University Press.

Jung, C. G. (1997) *Visions: Notes of the Seminar Given in 1930–1934*, edited by C. Douglas, Princeton, NJ: Princeton University Press.

Jung, C. G. (1998) *Jung's Seminar on Nietzsche's Zarathustra*, edited by J. Jarrett, Princeton, NJ: Princeton University Press.

Kandel, E. (2006) *In Search of Memory: The Emergence of a New Science of Mind*, New York: W.W. Norton.

Kapferer, B. (1983/1991) *A Celebration of Demons: Exorcism and the Aesthetics of Healing in Sri Lanka*, Oxford: Berg and Smithsonian Institution Press.

Kapferer, B. (1997) *The Feast of the Sorcerer: Practices of Consciousness and Power*, Chicago, IL: University of Chicago Press.

Kenny, M. (1992) 'Notes on Proposed Revisions of the Dissociative Disorders Section of DSM-III-R', *Transcultural Psychiatric Research Review*, 24, 4: 337–340.

Kihlstrom, J. F. (1987) 'The Cognitive Unconscious', *Science*, 237, 1445–1452.

Kirmayer, L. J. (1992) 'Taking Possession of Trance', *Transcultural Psychiatric Research Review*, 29, 4: 283–286.

Kirmayer, L. J. (1994) 'Pacing the Void: Social and Cultural Dimensions of Dissociation', in D. Spiegel (ed.) *Dissociation: Culture, Mind and Body*, Washington, DC: American Psychiatric Press, 91–122.

Kirmayer, L. J. (1996) 'Landscapes of Memory: Trauma, Narrative and Dissociation', in P. Antze and M. Lambek (eds), *Tense Past: Cultural Essays on Trauma and Memory*, London: Routledge, 173–198.

Kirmayer, L. J. (1999) 'Myth and Ritual in Psychotherapy', *Transcultural Psychiatry*, 36, 4: 451–460.

Kleinman, A. (1980) *Patients and Healers in the Context of Culture*, Berkeley, CA: University of California Press.

Knox, J. (2001) 'Memories, Fantasies, Archetypes: An Exploration of Some Connections between Cognitive Science and Analytical Psychology', *Journal of Analytical Psychology*, 46, 4: 613–636.

Knox, J. (2004a) 'Developmental Aspects of Analytical Psychology: New Perspectives from Cognitive Neuroscience and Attachment Theory', in J. Cambray and L. Carter (eds) *Analytical Psychology: Contemporary Perspectives in Jungian Analysis*, Hove: Brunner-Routledge, 56–82.

Knox, J. (2004b) 'From Archetypes to Reflective Function', *Journal of Analytical Psychology*, 49, 1: 1–19.

Koopmans, J. (1997) *Le Théâtre des exclus an Moyen Age: Hérétiques, sorcières et marginaux*, Paris: Imago.

Kugler, P. (1997) 'Psychic Imaging: A Bridge between Subject and Object', in P. Young-Eisendrath and T. Dawson (eds) *The Cambridge Companion to Jung*, Cambridge: Cambridge University Press, 71–88.

Lacan, J. (1966/1977) *Ecrits: A Selection*, trans. A. Sheridan, London: Tavistock/Routledge.

Lakoff, G. and Johnson, M. (1980/2003) *Metaphors We Live By*, Chicago, IL: University of Chicago Press.

Lambek, M. (1981) *Human Spirits: A Cultural Account of Trance in Mayotte*, Cambridge: Cambridge University Press.

Lambek, M. (1989) 'From Disease to Discourse: Remarks on the Conceptualization of Trance and Spirit Possession', in C. Ward (ed.) *Altered States of Consciousness and Mental Health: A Cross-Cultural Perspective*, London: Sage, 36–61.

Lambek, M. (1992) 'Discreteness or Discretion?', *Transcultural Psychiatric Research Review*, 24, 4: 345–347.

Lane, C. (2007) *Shyness: How Normal Behaviour Became a Sickness*, New Haven, CT: Yale University Press.

Laplanche, J. and Pontalis, J.-B. (1973) *The Language of Psychoanalysis*, London: Karnac.

Lear, J. (2003) *Therapeutic Action: An Earnest Plea for Irony*, New York: Other Press.

Legué, G. (1874) *Documents pour servir à l'histoire médicale des possédées de Loudun*, Paris: Delahaye.

Legué, G. (1880) *Urbain Grandier et les possédées de Loudun*, Paris: Baschet.

Lévi-Strauss, C. (1955) *Triste Tropiques*, Paris: Plon; trans. J. Weightman and D. Weightman (1973) *Sad Tropics*, London: Jonathan Cape.

Lewis, I. M. (1971/1989) *Ecstatic Religion: A Study of Shamanism and Spirit Possession*, London: Routledge.

Lewis, I. M. (1976) *Social Anthropology in Perspective: The Relevance of Social Anthropology*, Cambridge: Cambridge University Press.

Lewis, I. M. (1986) *Religion in Context: Cults and Charisma*, Cambridge: Cambridge University Press.

Lewis-Fernández, R. (1992) 'The Proposed DSM-IV Trance and Possession Disorder Category: Potential Benefits and Risks', *Transcultural Psychiatric Research Review*, 24, 4: 301–318.

Lilla, M. (1992) *G. B. Vico: The Making of an Anti-Modern*, Cambridge, MA: Harvard University Press.

Lim, D. (2005) 'The Play's the Thing', in *John Cassavetes: Five Films* [DVD], New York: Optimum Releasing.

Littlewood, R. (2001) *Religion, Agency, Restitution: The Wilde Lectures in Natural Religion, 1999*, Oxford: Oxford University Press.

Littlewood, R. (2004) *Pathologies of the West: An Anthropology of Mental Illness in Europe and America*, London: Continuum.

Lurker, M. (1987) *Dictionary of Gods and Goddesses, Devils and Demons*, London: Routledge & Kegan Paul.

Macey, D. (2000) *The Penguin Dictionary of Critical Theory*, London: Penguin.

Main, R. (2000) 'Religion, Science and Synchronicity', *Harvest: Journal of Jungian Studies*, 46, 2: 89–107.

Mali, J. (1992) *The Rehabilitation of Myth: Vico's 'New Science'*, Cambridge: Cambridge University Press.

Martin, A. (2001) 'John Cassavetes: Inventor of Forms', *Senses of Cinema*, 16, September–October.

Masquelier, A. (2001) *Prayer has Spoiled Everything: Possession, Power and Identity in an Islamic Town in Niger*, Durham, NC: Duke University Press.

Merleau-Ponty, M. (1945/2002) *Phenomenology of Perception*, London: Routledge.

Michaëlis, S. (1613) *Histoire admirable de la possession et conversion d'une penitente, Seduite par un magicien, la faisant Sorciere & Princesses des Sorciers au pays de Provence, conduite à la S. Baume pour y estre exorcizee l'an MDCX au mois de Novembre, soubs l'authorité du R. P. F. Sebastien Michaelis ... Ensemble la Pneumalogie ou Discours du susdit. P. Michaelis*, Paris: Charles Chastellain.

Micklem, N. (1996) *The Nature of Hysteria*, London: Routledge.

Mogenson, G. (2003) *The Dove in the Consulting Room: Hysteria and the Anima in Bollas and Jung*, Hove: Brunner-Routledge.

Moreno, J. L. (1934) *Who Shall Survive? A New Approach to the Problem of Human Interrelations*, Washington, DC: Nervous and Mental Disease Publishing.

Moreno, J. L. (1960) *The Sociometry Reader*, Glencoe, IL: Free Press.

Moreno, J. L. and Elefthery, D. G. (1975) 'An Introduction to Group Psychodrama', in G. Gazda (ed.) *Basic Approaches to Group Psychotherapy and Group Counseling*, Springfield, IL: Charles C. Thomas.

Nadon, R., Laurence, J. R. and Perry, C. (1991) 'The Two Disciplines of Scientific Hypnosis: A Synergistic Model', in *Theories of Hypnosis: Current Models and Perspectives*, New York: Guilford, 485–519.

Nathan, T. (1988) *Le Sperme du Diable*, Paris: Presses Universitaires de France.

Nathan, T. (1994) *L'Influence qui guérit*, Paris: Odile Jacob.

Nathan, T. (2001) *La Folie des autres: Traité d'ethnopsychiatrie clinique*, Paris: Dunod.

Nève-Hanquet, C. and Pluymaekers, J. (2008) 'Psychodrama with Landscape

Genogram in the Training of Family Therapists', in *Psychodrama: Studies and Applications*, 40 Years Elefthery Psychodrama Conference Papers, Leuven, Belgium.

Newberg, A. and d'Aquili, E. (1991) *The Mystical Mind: Probing the Biology of Religious Experience*, Minneapolis, MN: Augsburg Fortress Press.

Newberg, A., Alavi, A., Baime, M. J., Pourdehnad, M., Santanna, J. and d'Aquili, E. (2001) 'The Measurement of Regional Cerebral Blood Flow during the Complex Cognitive Task of Meditation: A Preliminary SPECT Study', *Psychiatry Research: Neuroimaging*, 106, 2: 113–122.

Noll, R. (1994) *The Jung Cult*, Toronto: Simon & Schuster.

Obeyesekere, G. (1970) 'The Idiom of Demonic Possession: A Case Study', *Social Science and Medicine*, July: 97–112.

Obeyesekere, G. (1981) *Medusa's Hair: An Essay on Personal Symbols and Religious Experience*, Chicago, IL: University of Chicago Press.

Obeyesekere, G. (1990) *The Work of Culture: Symbolic Transformation in Psychoanalysis and Anthropology*, Chicago, IL: University of Chicago Press.

Odermatt, M. (1991) *Der Fundamentalismus: Ein Gott, eine Wahrheit, eine Moral? Psychologische Reflexionen*, Zurich: Benzinger.

Oesterreich, T. K. (1921/2002) *Possession: Demonical and Other*, London: Kegan Paul.

Oughourlian, J.-M. (1991) *The Puppet of Desire: The Psychology of Hysteria, Possession and Hypnosis*, trans. E. Webb, Stanford, CA: Stanford University Press.

Pace, T. and Palmer, R. (1995) 'The Usefulness of Mimetic Theory in Clinical Practice: Interdividual Psychology and the Puppet of Desire: Revisited, Revered, Revised – and Applied', in *First Things*. Retrieved from: http://theol.uibk.ac.at/cover/bulletin/xtexte/bulletin17-3.html.

Pagels, E. (1995) *The Origin of Satan*, New York: Random House.

Papadopoulos, R. (1991) 'Jung and the Concept of the Other', in R. Papadopoulos and G. Saayman (eds) *Jung in Modern Perspective*, Bridport: Prism Press, 54–88.

Phelps, E. (2005) 'The Interaction of Emotion and Cognition: The Relation between the Human Amygdala and Cognitive Awareness', in R. R. Hassin, J. S. Uleman and J. A. Bargh (eds) *The New Unconscious*, Oxford: Oxford University Press.

Pike, K. L. (1954) 'Emic and Etic Standpoints for the Description of Behavior', in *Language in Relation to a Unified Theory of the Structure of Human Behaviour*, The Hague: Mouton.

Pike, K. L. and Jankowsky, K. R. (1996) *The Mystery of Culture Contacts, Historical Reconstruction and Text Analysis: An Emic Approach*, Washington, DC: Georgetown University Press.

Price, M. (2001) 'Now You See It, Now You Don't: Preventing Consciousness with Visual Masking', in P. G. Grossenbacher (ed.) *Finding Consciousness in the Brain: A Neurocognitive Approach*, Chichester: Wiley.

Rapley, R. (1998) *A Case of Witchcraft: The Trial of Urbain Grandier*, Montreal: McGill-Queen's University Press.

Rizzolatti, G. and Sinigaglia, C. (2008) *Mirrors in the Brain: How our Minds Share Actions and Emotions*, trans. F. Anderson, Oxford: Oxford University Press.

Rizzolatti, G., Fadiga, L., Gallese, V. and Fogassi, L. (1996) 'Premotor Cortex and the Recognition of Motor Actions', *Cognitive Brain Research*, 3: 131–141.

Rizzolatti, G., Fadiga, L., Gallese, V. and Fogassi, L. (2002) 'From Mirror Neurons to

Imitation: Facts and Speculations', in A. Meltzoff and W. Prinz (eds) *The Imitative Mind*, Cambridge: Cambridge University Press, 247–266.

Rouch, J. (1954) *Les Songhay*, Paris: Presses Universitaires de France.

Rouget, G. (1980) *La Musique et la transe: Esquisse d'une théorie générale des relations de la musique et de la possession*, Paris: Gallimard; trans. B. Biebuyck (1985) *Music and Trance: A Theory of the Relations between Music and Possession*, Chicago, IL: University of Chicago Press.

Rowland, S. (2005) *Jung as a Writer*, London: Routledge.

Sacks, O. (1985) 'Possessed', in 'Excesses', *Granta: Science*, 16, 17–22.

Said, E. (1978) *Orientalism*, New York: Random House.

Samuels, A. (1989) *The Plural Psyche: Personality, Morality and the Father*, London: Routledge.

Samuels, A., Shorter, B. and Plaut, F. (1986) *A Critical Dictionary of Jungian Analysis*, London: Routledge & Kegan Paul.

Sandner, D. and Beebe, J. (1982) 'Psychopathology and Analysis', in M. Stein (ed.) *Jungian Analysis*, LaSalle, IL: Open Court.

Saussure, F. de. (2002) *Écrits de linguistique générale*, Paris: Gallimard; trans. C. Sanders and M. Pires (2006) *Writings in General Linguistics*, edited by S. Bouquet and R. Engler, Oxford: Oxford University Press.

Scategni, W. (2002) *Psychodrama, Group Processes, and Dreams: Archetypal Images of Individuation*, trans. V. Marsicano, Hove: Brunner-Routledge.

Schacter, D. (1996) *Searching for Memory: The Brain, the Mind, and the Past*, New York: Basic Books.

Schaverien, J. (1995) *Desire and the Female Therapist*, London: Routledge.

Schaverien, J. (2005) 'Art, Dreams, and Active Imagination: A Post-Jungian Approach to Transference and the Image', *Journal of Analytical Psychology*, 50, 2: 127–154.

Schieffelin, E. (1976) *The Sorrow of the Lonely and the Burning of the Dancers*, New York: St Martin's Press.

Schieffelin, E. (1996a) 'On Failure and Performance: Throwing the Medium Out of the Séance', in C. Laderman and M. Roseman (eds) *The Performance of Healing*, London: Routledge, 59–90.

Schieffelin, E. (1996b) 'Evil Spirit Sickness, the Christian Disease: The Innovation of a New Syndrome of Mental Derangement and Redemption in Papua New Guinea', *Culture, Medicine and Psychiatry*, 20, 1: 1–39.

Schmitt, J.-C. (1982) 'Western European Magic and Folklore', in *Dictionary of the Middle Ages*, New York: Charles Scribner's Sons, 8: 25–31.

Sebel, P. (1995) 'Memory during Anaesthesia: Gone but not Forgotten', *Anaesthesia and Analgesia*, 81, 4: 668–670.

Segal, R. (2007) 'Jung and Lévy-Bruhl', *Journal of Analytical Psychology*, 52, 5: 635–658.

Shamdasani, S. (1996) 'Introduction: Jung's Journey to the East', in *The Psychology of Kundalini Yoga: Notes of the Seminar Given in 1932 by C. G. Jung*, Princeton, NJ: Princeton University Press.

Shamdasani, S. (2003) *Jung and the Making of Modern Psychology: The Dream of a Science*, Cambridge: Cambridge University Press.

Sheehan, P. W., Donovan, P. and MacLeod, C. M. (1988) 'Strategy Manipulation and the Stroop Effect in Hypnosis', *Journal of Abnormal Psychology*, 97: 455–460.

Shore, B. (1996) *Culture in Mind: Cognition, Culture and the Problem of Meaning*, Oxford: Oxford University Press.

Singer, T. and Kimbles, S. (2004) 'The Emerging Theory of Cultural Complexes', in J. Cambray and L. Carter (eds) *Analytical Psychology: Contemporary Perspectives in Jungian Analysis*, Hove: Brunner-Routledge, 176–203.

Solomon, H. M. (2004) 'The Ethical Attitude in Analytic Training and Practice', in J. Cambray and L. Carter (eds) *Analytical Psychology: Contemporary Perspectives in Jungian Analysis*, London: Routledge, 249–265.

Sprenger, J. and Kramer, H. (1486/1968) *Malleus Maleficarum (The Hammer of Witchcraft)*, trans. M. Summers, London: Folio Society.

Stein, M. (2004) 'Spiritual and Religious Aspects of Modern Analysis', in J. Cambray and L. Carter (eds) *Analytical Psychology: Contemporary Perspectives in Jungian Analysis*, Hove: Brunner-Routledge, 204–222.

Stern, D. (1985) *The Interpersonal World of the Infant: A View from Psychoanalysis and Developmental Psychology*, New York: Basic Books.

Stocking, G. (ed.) (1974) *The Shaping of American Anthropology, 1883–1911: A Franz Boas Reader*, Chicago, IL: University of Chicago Press, 1989.

Stoller, P. (1989) *Fusion of the Worlds: An Ethnography of Possession among the Songhay of Niger*, Chicago, IL: University of Chicago Press.

Stoller, P. (2004) *Stranger in the Village of the Sick: A Memoir of Cancer, Sorcery and Healing*, Boston, MA: Beacon Press.

Surin, J.-J. (1966) *Correspondance*, edited by M. de Certeau, Paris: Desclée de Brouwer.

Tarde, G. (1890) 'The Laws of Imitation', in *On Communication and Social Influence: Selected Papers*, Chicago, IL: University of Chicago Press, 1969.

Taussig, M. (1987) *Shamanism, Colonialism and the Wild Man: A Study in Terror and Healing*, Chicago, IL: University of Chicago Press.

Taussig, M. (1992) *Mimesis and Alterity*, London: Routledge.

Tiles, M. (1984) *Bachelard: Science and Objectivity*, Cambridge: Cambridge University Press.

Tranquille, Father. (1634) *Véritable relation des justes procédures observées au fait de la possession des Ursulines de Loudun, et au procès de Grandier*, Poitiers: I. Thoreau et Veuve A. Mesnier; reprinted in F. Danjou (1838) *Archives curieuses de l'histoire de France*, Paris: Beauvais 2: 5.

Turner, V. (1969) *The Ritual Process: Structure and Anti-Structure*, Ithaca, NY: Cornell University Press.

Turner, V. (1982) *From Ritual to Theatre: The Human Seriousness of Play*, New York: Performing Arts Journal Publications.

Uleman, J. (2005) 'Becoming Aware of the New Unconscious', in R. R. Hassin, J. S. Uleman and J. A. Bargh (eds) *The New Unconscious*, Oxford: Oxford University Press.

Verene, D. P. (1981) *Vico's Science of Imagination*, Ithaca, NY: Cornell University Press.

Verene, D. P. (2002) 'Coincidence, Historical Repetition, and Self-Knowledge: Jung, Vico, and Joyce', *Journal of Analytical Psychology*, 47, 3: 459–478.

Vico, G. (1948) *The New Science of Giambattista Vico (Unabridged Translation of the Third Edition, 1744)*, trans. T. G. Bergin and M. H. Fisch, Ithaca, NY: Cornell University Press.

Walker, D. P. (1981) *Unclean Spirits*, London: Scolar Press.

Webb, E. (1999) 'Eros and the Psychology of World Views', paper presented at Eranos 1997, Ascona; published in German translation in *Eranos Jahrbuch, NF.8*, D. Clemens and T. Schabert (eds) (2001) *Kulturen des Eros*, Munich: Wilhelm Fink, 179–230.

Whalen, P. J., Rauch, S. L., Etcoff, N. L., McInerney, S. C., Lee, M. B. and Jenike, M. A. (1998) 'Masked Presentations of Emotional Facial Expressions Modulate Amygdala Activity without Explicit Knowledge', *Journal of Neuroscience* 18, 1: 411–418; reprinted in G. Claxton (2005) *The Wayward Mind: An Intimate History of the Unconscious*, London: Little, Brown.

Wiener, J. (2004) 'Transference and Countertransference: Contemporary Perspectives', in J. Cambray and L. Carter (eds) *Analytical Psychology: Contemporary Perspectives in Jungian Analysis*, Hove: Brunner-Routledge, 149–175.

Wilkinson, M. (2006) *Coming into Mind: The Mind–Brain Relationship – A Jungian Clinical Perspective*, Hove: Routledge.

Winnicott, D. W. (1951) 'Transitional Objects and Transitional Phenomena', in *Through Paediatrics to Psycho-Analysis*, London: Hogarth Press, 1987, 229–242.

Witztum, E. and Goodman, Y. (1999) 'Narrative Construction of Distress and Therapy: A Model Based on Work with Ultraorthodox Jews', *Transcultural Psychiatry*, 36, 4: 403–436.

Woodman, M. (1980) *The Owl was a Baker's Daughter: Obesity, Anorexia Nervosa and the Repressed Feminine*, Toronto: Inner City Books.

Woodman, M. (1982) *Addiction to Perfection: The Still Unravished Bride*, Toronto: Inner City Books.

World Health Organization (WHO) (1992) *The ICD-10 Classification of Mental and Behavioural Disorders*, Geneva: WHO.

Yankowitz, S. (1974) 'Terminal', in K. Malpede (ed.) (1984) *Three Works by the Open Theater*, New York: Drama Book Specialists.

Zwicky, J. (2003) *Wisdom and Metaphor*, Kentville, Nova Scotia: Gaspereau Press.

Index

Locators in **bold** represent major entries.
Locators in *italics* represent figures/diagrams.
Locators for main headings that have subheadings refer to general aspects of that topic.